GREAT
WOMEN TRAVEL
WRITERS

GREAT WOMEN TRAVEL WRITERS

From *1750* to the Present

Edited by

ALBA AMOIA *and* BETTINA L. KNAPP

continuum

NEW YORK • LONDON

2005

The Continuum International Publishing Group Inc
15 East 26 Street, New York NY 10010

The Continuum International Publishing Group Ltd
The Tower Building, 11 York Road, London SE1 7NX

Printed in the United States of America

Library of Congress Cataloging-in-Publication Data

Great women travel writers from 1750 to the present / edited by Alba Amoia and Bettina L. Knapp.
    p. cm.
   Includes bibliographical references and index.
   ISBN 0-8264-1683-7 (hardcover : alk. paper)
   1. Women travelers.   2. Travelers' writings.   3. Voyages and travels.
 I. Amoia, Alba della Fazia.   II. Knapp, Bettina Liebowitz, 1926–
 G4654.W66 2005
 910.4—dc22   2004026446

The first step [toward wisdom] is to learn to be at home anywhere, and the second is to be at home nowhere.

(Buddhist monk quoted in Jacob Beaver, "Diary," *London Review of Books,* April 3, 2003, p. 35)

Contents

Introduction

Travel is sacred. Travel is a quest. Travel is a passion. Travel is escape. It is a learning process, a distraction, a novelty, a dream fulfilled. It may inspire joy, terror, longing, or bring on fatigue; it may serve to test one's linguistic skills, or to ward off boredom and even depression. There are as many reasons for travel as there are gourmet dishes. Paralleling the unending emotions catalyzed by travel is the insatiable appetite for discovery and exploration.

In the chapters highlighting the lives of the twenty-two women profiled in this book, we and our contributors probe the diaries, correspondences, creative works, and studies left to posterity by a diverse group of frequently heroic women of the eighteenth, nineteenth, and twentieth centuries, in chronological order. Serendipitously, the list begins and concludes with Russian women, Ekaterina Dashkova and Valentina Vladimirovna Tereshkova.

These original essays highlight an international family of courageous—or foolhardy—wanderers, such as Lady Hester Stanhope, Alexandra David-Neel, Isabelle Eberhardt, Karen Blixen, Freya Stark, exulting over tropical landscapes, or snow-covered mountains, suffering through months of physical turmoil and mental anxiety. We focus on their startling experiences, their sorrows, loves, and hatreds, their visceral and cerebral reactions to the perennially altering land- and seascapes that they faced and traversed.

How did the foreign places they lived in or visited shape their lives and their memories? Each chapter broaches travel from an individual point of view, depending on the globe-trotter's penchants and yearnings, and her artistic, religious, philosophical, political, and psychological needs. These are marvelous stories.

Although modernization, standardization, and mechanization have greatly simplified travel in our day, wars, terrorism, and epidemics make voyages risky or even impracticable. But the positive, democratic value intrinsic to travel postulates a need to meet and try to understand other people and places. A page has already been torn out of history by a growing number of female space venturers—perhaps the most exciting women travelers of all. To them we pay special tribute.

ALBA AMOIA
BETTINA L. KNAPP

CHAPTER

1

Princess Ekaterina (Catherine) Romanovna Vorontsova Dashkova

(1743–1810)

> The comparisons which I made [of foreign countries and their
> forms of government] to my own country . . . made me ardently
> desire to travel.
>
> (*The Memoirs of Princess Dashkov*, 27)

The princess who ironically called herself "Catherine the Little"—a conspirator, politician, philologist, linguist, and memori-
alist—kept close company with "Catherine justly called the
Great" (Ekaterina Dashkova, *The Memoirs of Princess Dashkov*, trans. and
ed. Kyril Fitzlyon, 288; page numbers henceforth in parentheses).

Dashkova's energy was unbounded—even into her sixties, after
retirement from public life, according to the description of one of her
contemporaries:

[S]he helps the masons to build walls, she assists with her own hands in
making the roads, she feeds the cows, she composes music, she sings and
plays, she writes for the press, she shells corn, she speaks out in church and
corrects the priest if he is not devout, she speaks out in her little theatre
and steers the performers if they stray from their parts, she is a doctor, an
apothecary, a surgeon, a veterinary, a carpenter, a magistrate, a lawyer; in
short, she hourly practises every type of incongruity; corresponds with her

> brother . . . , with authors, with philosophers . . . with poets, . . . with all
> her relations, and yet appears as if she had time hanging on her hands.
> (Catherine Wilmot, based on quotation in Fitzlyon introduction, 19)

That "Catherine the Little" also traveled extensively is a matter of public
record. But there are sparse physical descriptions in her *Memoirs* of the
lands she visited, for she was far more interested in people:

> I shall abstain from describing [Switzerland], for more skilful pens than
> mine have done so, contenting myself with naming persons I had the privi-
> lege of meeting there. (131)

and again:

> I shall say nothing of the beautiful country through which we travelled
> [down the Rhine on two large boats] or the pleasure that can be derived
> from seeing the landscape of the Rhine. Better pens than mine have
> described it all before. (134)

She brusquely sweeps the reader out of Italy—"I shall pass on at one
swoop to Vienna without a glance at Padua, Vicenza and Verona on the
way" (181)—for "I have so little taste for detailed descriptions of my journeys" (227).

But when she views a place with disfavor, she pauses to provide
descriptions, as, for example, in Poland, on her way to Warsaw. Her children having caught measles in Grodno (then in Poland, now in Belorus-
sia), she was forced to halt her journey and remain in ugly Grodno for five
unbearably long weeks:

> There was no help to be obtained from anywhere in that semi-barbarous
> country, where peasants have none of the Russians' resourcefulness and
> hospitality, and where poverty and filth reign supreme. The roads were
> impassable for anything but their kind of light carts (*brichki*), and my car-
> riages could advance only with the help of thirty Russian cossacks who
> went half a day's journey ahead of me and felled trees in order to widen the
> road through the immense forests. (143)

In Italy, she finds the opportunity to make a thrust against Roman Catholic papal nepotism by describing the seventeenth-century palace built by

Count Vitaliano Borromeo on Isola Bella (the largest and most famous of the Borromean islands):

> The huge edifice, . . . only half finished, would have been too vast a country house even for a Sovereign. It can only be explained or excused by the fact that [the Count] was a nephew of the Pope who, in those remote times, could afford all kinds of prodigal magnificence. (166–67)

By contrast, she is ecstatic about the landscapes of lakes Maggiore and Lugano:

> So enchanted were we with the beauties of nature that we found it hard to leave a place which seemed to us to be a paradise upon earth. Orange and lemon trees grew there in the open like birch and lime trees in Russia, and we saw some of them in flower and others already bearing ripe fruit. (166)

For a woman who wrote that "[a]rchitecture was of all the arts the one I had most taste for" (175) and "nothing interested me as much as architecture, and, therefore, I include it among my pleasures" (220), she provides surprisingly little architectural description of the foreign cities she visited. She preferred to dwell on the people she met—nobility, statesmen, writers, men of letters, and artists. She sought them out to obtain political information for both herself and Catherine the Great.

Ekaterina was born in St. Petersburg into the influential Vorontsov family. She was held at the baptismal font by the then empress of Russia Elisabeth, and her godfather was the Grand Duke (later Emperor Peter III, 1761–1762). Peter would have made the Vorontsov family star shine even brighter had he been able to realize his avowed intention of repudiating his legitimate wife, Catherine, and marrying his mistress, Elisabeth Vorontsova, Ekaterina's sister. Michael Vorontsov, Ekaterina's uncle and de facto adoptive father, with whom she went to live when she was seven years old, was Chancellor under Peter III. It was in her uncle's house, in the winter of 1758–59, that a friendship started between the fifteen-year-old Ekaterina and the Grand Duchess Catherine, who was almost twice her age.

Chancellor Vorontsov's house was furnished in "the best and latest European style and could truly be called princely" (38)—indeed, his furniture had belonged to Madame de Pompadour, who had sold it to Louis

XV, who then presented it to the chancellor in the hope of encouraging his pro-French sympathies (38, Fitzlyon n.1). In this setting, the uncle provided the best masters and the best education for his own daughter and for Ekaterina: instruction in four languages (especially French), good manners, dance, and drawing. "And yet, what was done for the improvement of our hearts and minds? Nothing at all" (24), she writes bitterly. "Ever since I was a child I craved for affection, I wanted the sympathy of those I loved, and when at the age of thirteen I began to suspect that I was receiving neither, I was overcome by a feeling of loneliness" (25). Having lost her own mother when she was two, perhaps Ekaterina saw a mother figure in the Grand Duchess Catherine.

When measles affected the child's eyesight, she sat in deep dejection all day and brooded. But as soon as her illness passed, she began reading avidly and became increasingly interested in politics. Although Bayle, Montesquieu, Voltaire, and Boileau were her favorite authors, she had access to all the books in the library of her aristocratic household. Russian educational theories, based largely on translations from the French of such authors as François Fénelon and Anne-Thérèse de Lambert, emphasized the benefits to girls' morals of reading worthy books (Barker and Gheith, eds., *A History of Women's Writing in Russia*, 41).

At the time of her marriage in 1759 to Prince Mikhail Ivanovich Dashkov (who died four years later, leaving her a widow with two children), she had her "own little library of nine hundred volumes. . . . I acquired the Encyclopedia and Morelli's dictionary and never would the finest piece of jewellery have given me as much pleasure" (27). She was passionately fond of music as well: "My harpsichord and library between them made time fly as if on wings" (32). An outlet for her "relentless curiosity" about foreign lands was her constant questioning of all the foreign ministers, artists, and men of letters who visited her uncle almost daily.

Her travels began only after she had played an important role in the coup d'état that made Catherine sovereign in 1762. John Shuvalov, an influential Russian public figure of the time, wrote to Voltaire that "a woman of nineteen [had] changed the government of the Empire"; the Austrian minister in St. Petersburg informed his foreign office that Princess Dashkova would probably become a member of the new government; and the princess herself was reported to claim first place in the empire after the empress, thereby infuriating Catherine, who denied her former friend's prominence in the coup d'état. Catherine wrote to Stanislaw-August Poniatowski (later king of Poland, 1764–95), imploring him to disabuse Voltaire of any notions he might have of Princess Dashkova's importance (Fitzlyon introduction, 14–15).

By 1768, relations between Catherine the Great and "Catherine the Little," who knew too much about the events of 1762, were beginning to deteriorate. Her position having become untenable, Dashkova applied for permission to travel abroad, but her request was denied. She undertook instead a journey of about three months and 1,300 miles to Kiev and back to St. Petersburg, making detours to see different cities and particularly the German colonies that the empress had established and that were of great interest to her (113). Her topographical and artistic description of Kiev is arresting:

> The many caves hollowed out of the hill on which part of the city is built make it a very curious place. In several such grottoes or recesses can be seen, incredibly well preserved, the bodies of saints who had lived and died there. The Cathedral in the precincts of the Pechory Monastery is remarkable for the ancient mosaics on its walls. There are fresco paintings in one of the churches representing the different Councils held before the separation of the Eastern Church. These frescoes are of extraordinary beauty and must have been painted by great artists. (113)

Returning to St. Petersburg (1769), her relations with the empress were still uncordial, but now at least she was able to obtain the empress's permission to travel abroad. Accompanied by her two children, a male cousin, and a friend, she set out in December 1769 on a highly successful two-year tour through Western Europe, during which she was an object of admiration and curiosity.

The group left for Riga by post-horses, stopped there for a few days, then hired horses to take them to Berlin, where they stayed for two months and where, at the palace of Sans Souci near Potsdam, Dashkova met Frederick II, the queen, and her sister. She considered Frederick "unquestioningly one of the greatest of kings" (117). In Königsberg she called on Countess Keyserling, who prevailed on her to stay for six days; and in Danzig she stayed at the "Hotel de Russie," where she played one of her boyish pranks. The hotel was frequented by all Russians and all really distinguished travellers. Consequently, I was all the more shocked at seeing in the main room two pictures representing two battles lost by the Russian troops, who were shown wounded, dying, or standing on their knees before the victorious Prussian troops. (115)

What did she do about this grievous situation? She ordered oil paints to be brought in—blue, green, red, and white—and with her brush and the aid of the Secretary and the Counsellor of the Russian Legation in Danzig, she "made the troops exchange their uniforms. The Prussians—supposed to be victors in the two battles—became Russians, and the defeated were given Prussian uniforms" (116).

Crossing Westphalia to reach Hanover for a fleeting visit, she notices that "the peasants' horses were of a fine breed, and the land well looked after. That is all I can say about the place" (119). On to Aachen (Aix-la-Chapelle) and then Spa (in the Belgian Ardennes) to take the baths and waters for her rheumatism. At Spa she met a certain Mrs. Hamilton, who became her lifelong friend, and allowed her to bring her linguistic skills to the fore. Dashkova socialized with Monsieur and Madame Necker,

> but only with the English did I live on terms of friendly intimacy. Lord and Lady Sussex came to see us every day, and with the help of French and German I was able in three weeks to understand all I read in English, even Shakespeare. (119)

Armed with such extraordinary linguistic baggage, she resolved to go as far as England. When she arrived in London, Horace Walpole rushed to see her, and "found her 'extraordinarily frank and easy . . . very quick and very animated,' with a pleasing smile and fierce eyes, not ugly for a Tartar, able to talk well on all subjects, to sing sentimental songs in an agreeable voice, and to understand Latin. 'In short . . . a very singular personage'" (Fitzlyon introduction, 15–16). Her visit to England lasted thirteen days—with trips to Bath, Bristol, and Oxford and their environs, and ten days for sightseeing in London.

Then the crossing from Dover to Calais—"not very pleasant . . . with the waves splashing water over us even in our cabins" (121). She made short shrift of Brussels and Antwerp, proceeding to Paris for only seventeen days—during which I wanted to see no one except Diderot. I went round churches and monuments, and visited the studios of famous artists, as well as theatres where I always sat in the gallery among the humblest members of the audience, wearing an old black dress and shawl and a close cap in order to escape all notice. (121)

Diderot was much impressed by the princess, though not by her looks:

By no means pretty, . . . with a high and broad forehead, fat cheeks, rather deep-set eyes neither large nor small, black hair and eyebrows, a flat nose, big mouth, thick lips, bad teeth, thick neck typical of her nation, convex bosom, no waist, quick in her movements, no elegance or distinction whatsoever, very affable; the general effect of her features is one of character; she is serious-minded, has an easy command of our language, does not say all she knows and thinks, but what she does say has the ring of truth about it and she says it simply and definitely. . . . At the present time, December 1770, her age is twenty-seven and she looks like forty (quoted in ibid., 16).

She, in turn,

admired Diderot in all he did, admired him, too, for those outbursts of his caused by his warm-hearted way of feeling and looking at things. His sincerity, his loyalty to his friends, his shrewd and profound mind, and the interest and esteem he invariably showed me, were all traits that won me over for life. . . . This extraordinary man was but little understood. Virtue and truth were the well-springs of every one of his actions, and the general good was his ruling passion and constant pursuit. The very liveliness of his mind sometimes led him into error, but he never ceased being sincere, for he was his own dupe. (124)

Writing toward the end of her life about the letters she had received from Diderot, Dashkova judges that

one of them, especially, deserves to be known because it displays the depth and the acuteness of his genius. It was written at the time of the dissolution of parliaments, and the picture he draws of the feeling which that event had produced in serious and well-intentioned minds, of the motives behind it and of its inevitable consequences, make this letter into an accurate forecast of what has since happened in the French Revolution. (128)

Her morning excursions in Paris lasted from 8:00 A.M. to 3:00 P.M. and ended at Diderot's door. She took him home in her carriage to dine, and often the two would talk until two or three o'clock in the morning (122). They discussed, for example, Russian serfs, and she tried to convert him to the advantages of serfdom, but it is unlikely that they had a meeting of minds on this subject (126, Fitzlyon n. 1).

One day the princess and her group went incognito to Versailles, which she found "anything but fashionable and grand":

> As the public was admitted to view the King sitting at table, we . . . entered with [the crowd] into a room which appeared to me very dirty and very squalid. Louis XV, the Dauphin, the Dauphiness and the Princesses Adelaide and Victoria came in and I saw them take their seats and have a hearty meal. Whenever I passed any comments, as I did, for instance, on noticing Princess Adelaide drink her soup out of a mug, the ladies around me immediately asked questions: 'Do not your King and princesses do the same?' they would say. 'There are no King or Princesses in my country,' I replied. 'Then, Madam, you must be Dutch.' 'Perhaps so.' (126–27)

(During her second visit to France in 1779, however, Dashkova was given to understand that she would do well to go to Versailles, for Queen Marie Antoinette desired to make her acquaintance in the home of Madame de Polignac. The queen talked to Dashkova's children about dancing, adding to her great regret she would soon have to give it up "because . . . in France people are not allowed to dance after reaching the age of twenty-five" [160].)

From Paris, on to Aix-en-Provence, where Dashkova found Mrs. Hamilton, Lady Carlisle, her daughter Lady Oxford, and other English families. Always busy improving her English, she went on excursions with Mrs. Hamilton to Montpellier, Marseilles, Hyères, and along the Royal Canal, then proposed to her a visit to Switzerland via Lyons, at a time when Louis XV provided her some food for political thought:

> Our journey to Lyons is not worth describing. . . . But in Lyons itself we saw all the best products of its factories. . . . At that time . . . most of the population considered it their duty to worship their king [Louis XV], and the thought of guillotining [him] would not have occurred to them in their wildest dreams. (129–30)

From Switzerland she sent a fine picture of a beautiful Greek girl by Angelica Kauffmann to Empress Catherine and writes: "The work of that charming artist and charming woman was not yet known in Russia, and the picture gave Her Majesty great pleasure" (140).

On to Germany, where again her artistic insights come to the fore:

> In Düsseldorf, while admiring the magnificent picture gallery, I could not refrain from pointing out to the Director that he had a beautiful 'St John' by Raphael hung in the embrasure of a window, because he failed to recognise in it the work of that great master who had painted it in his last manner. (134–35)

The great art lover Dashkova stopped in Dresden "for a few days, all of which I spent almost entirely in the beautiful picture gallery admiring and studying the pictures, for which, indeed, a lifetime would not suffice" (137).

She returned to Russia in December 1771, after a two-year absence, and found that relations with the empress had undergone considerable improvement—thanks to Diderot, who had written tactful letters to Catherine emphasizing Dashkova's allegedly friendly remarks about her, and thanks also to Voltaire, who wrote to Catherine describing the princess's visit to his home in Ferney, during which she had spoken of the empress for four hours, which flitted away like four minutes (Fitzlyon introduction, 16). Not only did Catherine receive the princess kindly; she gave Dashkova 70,000 rubles.

For the next four years Princess Dashkova divided her time between the two capitals and her estates: Kirianovo, near St. Petersburg, and her favorite property, Troitskoye, about sixty miles south of Moscow. She became a member of Russia's foremost learned body, the Free Economic Society, wrote articles in various periodicals, chiefly on literary themes, published translations from Hume, and avidly collected books for her library (ibid., 16–17).

In 1775 she again asked authorization to leave Russia on the pretext of wishing to provide an education abroad for her son. She spent the years 1776–79 in Scotland, settling in Edinburgh in one of the apartments of Holyrood House, the ancient palace of the sovereigns, for the duration of her son's classical studies at the university. She writes enthusiastically about Edinburgh University's professors, all of whom were generally esteemed for their intelligence, intellectual distinction and moral qualities. Strangers alike to envy and to the pretentiousness of smaller minds, they lived together in brotherly amity, their mutual love and respect making of them a group of educated and intelligent people . . . whose conversation never failed to be instructive. (147)

From Edinburgh she made trips to the Highlands, took the waters (hydropathic treatment) for her rheumatism at Buxton and Matlock, and bathed in the sea at Scarborough (in Yorkshire, probably the oldest seaside resort in England)—"both the happiest and most peaceful [period of my existence] that has ever fallen to my lot in this world" (147).

Upon the completion of her son's studies (1779), they left for Ireland, landing at Donaghadee. On to Coleraine (in Londonderry) then "the Giant's Causeway, which is indeed well worth a visit" (149)—but without telling us why, nor providing any sort of description of the unusual promontory of columnar basalt extending along the northern coast of County Antrim (Northern Ireland), built, according to locals, by a race of giants as a roadway to Staffa (an uninhabited island of the Inner Hebrides, Scotland), where a similar structure occurs.

Then on to Dublin:

My stay in Dublin even now seems to me like a happy dream which lasted a whole year. . . . Dublin Society was then distinguished by its elegance, its wit and its manners, and enlivened by that frankness which comes naturally to the Irish. (149–50)

They made excursions to see Kilkenny and its castle, Killarney and its beautiful lake, Cork and its fine harbor, and Limerick and the magnificent country around it (150–51).

Leaving Ireland in 1780, they landed at Holyhead in Wales ("[T]here are many most romantic places in Wales" [151]), then on to London, where she was presented at Court, visited all the royal castles and houses, made excursions to Bath and Bristol, and after a farewell visit with the king and queen went to Margate and sailed for Ostend in Belgium; thence to Brussels and Antwerp, continuing into Holland and visiting Rotterdam, Delft, The Hague, Leyden, Haarlem, and Utrecht (151–52). To travel down the canals of Holland, she hired an entire cabin in a *trekschuit*:

Trekschuits are long barges pulled by one or two horses. They contain a small and very clean cabin which can be hired by the well-to-do or the gentry, and a large or common cabin where people pay a modest sum at so much per head. The roof of these two cabins corresponds to the upper deck of a coach in other countries, and a place can be obtained on it at a still lower price. These barges leave at a certain fixed time every day, and their arrival at any place also takes place at regular intervals and at stated times. (152)

On her return to The Hague she again saw the Princess of Orange and supped with her every night during their stay. The Prince of Orange was also present, "though he ordinarily fell asleep at table however early the hour" (153). Then back to Brussels (where she made two fossil and botanical expeditions in the neighboring hills, finding a number of fine fossils and several plants never seen at home).

Only two days could be allotted to Lille, for she was in a hurry to get to Paris, where the Hôtel de la Chine had been rented for her. She again saw her friend Diderot, as well as Monsieur de Malesherbe and his sister, Madame Necker, and a few other old friends who extended the same friendship as during her first stay. She often lunched at Abbé Raynal's; Diderot visited her almost every day. A pupil of D'Alembert coached her son in mathematics and geometry, and Houdon made a large bust of her in bronze. At Madame Necker's, she made the acquaintance of the Bishop of Autun; she had tea with Falconet and his pupil, Mademoiselle Collot; and at the opera and the theater she occupied a box belonging to Marshal de Biron, "a most courteous old nobleman with manners that were traditionally typical of the French Court in former times" (163–64).

Leaving Paris, she traveled to Switzerland by way of Verdun, Metz, Nancy, and Besançon. Reaching Geneva, she received as a gift a portrait of Voltaire by the Swiss painter Jean Huber (165), whose series of pictures representing Voltaire's domestic life was purchased by Catherine II. From Neufchâtel, they went inland to see the interesting villages of La Locelle and La Chaux de Fonds and their romantic environs. "We travelled in local carts, for the roads are a little narrow there" (165). After visiting Geneva and Lausanne once again, they traveled by way of Savoy and Mount Cenis to Turin to begin their Italian tour.

In Turin, Dashkova was "very well received by Their Majesties the King and Queen of Sardinia and all the Royal family" (166), and she was accorded a special visit to the fortifications (citadel and fortress) built by the King of Sardinia at Alessandria, after which she proceeded to Novi (Ligure), Genoa, and Milan and its countryside, with excursions to lakes Maggiore and Lugano, as well as to the Borromean islands.

Parma, Piacenza, and Modena were a matter of days, and although she spent over a week in Florence, she devotes only one sentence to Italy's most famous city of art: "There we spent over a week pleasantly, visiting the famous picture gallery, the churches (also full of the most lovely pictures), the libraries, and the Grand Duke's Cabinet of Natural History" (167). By contrast, her lengthy descriptions of Pisa and Lucca—their history, topography, architecture, government, and the people's violent sports—fill several pages. These are two of the very few long place descriptions in the *Memoirs*.

During the hot months when malaria was rife, she spent her days on the banks of the canal at the Baths of Pisa, "the only place where we could enjoy fresh air, but it was . . . choked up with all kinds of filth" (169). An ecologist *avant la lettre*, she writes:

> The heat and lack of air were stifling, and though at night there was no sun to scorch us, yet it seemed to me as if some malevolent being was busily pumping out with a pneumatic machine all the air there was in Pisa. (169)

From Lucca, she went on to Leghorn, where she admired the quarantine hospital,

> an institution so humanitarian in its purpose and which interested me immensely. I was struck by the order and cleanliness that reigned within it. . . . [S]everal persons there . . . had come from places where an epidemic was suspected. I, therefore, sprinkled my children's handkerchiefs with Marseilles vinegar, and all the time we were in the building made them sniff a mixture of that vinegar and spirits of camphor. . . . (172)

Then, via Siena, to Rome, where Cardinal de Bernis was most attentive, and Pope Pius VI spoke to her in St. Peter's about his idea of forming a museum in the Vatican to solve the problem of conservation of Greek and Roman antiquities; she, in turn, praised his plan for the "noble undertaking" of reclaiming in its entirety the Via Appia passing through the Pontine Marshes (174).

She and her group visited Tivoli twice, then,

> [a]fter thoroughly examining all that was worth seeing in Rome and its
> environs, without omitting the horse-races which appeared to me very
> ridiculous, and the theatre which was somewhat disgusting since men acted
> female roles, we went to Naples . . . (176)

where her house had a charming view of the bay and of Vesuvius opposite.
On the day she ventured to the top of Vesuvius, she was overcome with
fatigue, but having no faith in Neapolitan medical doctors, she called in
"an Englishman who, though not a professional physician . . . very prop-
erly, administered castor oil, thus allowing my bowels to resume their natural function, and saved my life" (179).

Her life having thus been duly saved by an Englishman, she was able
to meet the *italianissimo* Abbé Galiani, friend of the Encyclopedists, as
well as several artists and men of letters. Her encounter with Sir William
Hamilton and his collection of antiquities gives rise to an aphorism on the
subject of human ignorance and mental sloth:

> I envied [Sir Hamilton] only his star-stone ring. This stone, although so
> well described by Pliny, was, because an example of it could not be found,
> long considered as imaginary. . . . Such is men's attitude to things whose
> truth they are too lazy or too ignorant to demonstrate, for the most conve-
> nient and the shortest way of dealing with what one does not understand
> is to deny it. (177)

Also in Naples she stands in admiration of the British sculptress Anne
Seymour Damer, another "strong" woman like the princess herself:

> [I]t was not in her boudoir that her friends found her—rather did they find
> her [in her studio] wrestling with a block of marble, trying to impart to it
> the shape she wanted. (177)

Damer also shared with the princess a love of learning and of languages.

Regarding Dashkova's suggestions for "rescuing from the effects of
time and oblivion" the invaluable treasures found in Herculaneum and
Pompeii and unceremoniously stored in the neighboring royal villa of Por-
tici (subsequently the treasures were transferred to the National Museum
of Naples), she uncannily presents a plan "to be publicised all over

Europe" for returning the treasures to their original places and bringing to life the two dead cities—"all of which could be viewed on payment of so much per head" (178)—precisely the plan that is being developed by some Italian entrepreneurs today.

The return trip to Russia led the group back to Rome, then on to Loretto in Ancona (where the house of the Virgin Mary is supposed to have miraculously arrived). The princess was fortunate enough to see all "the treasure and wardrobe of the Madonna" (180), for some of the treasures were removed to Paris by Napoleon in 1797.

She stopped at Bologna "to admire the masterpieces of that school" (180), made short shrift of Ferrara, then on to Venice, where she received as a gift two Canalettos and bought some old engravings by the earliest masters "in order to have a series showing the gradual development of the art till it finally reached its present degree of perfection" (180). Venice's gondolas "have a somewhat gloomy appearance" (180), but Dashkova has nothing to say on the subjects of the Venetian government and its buildings, in accordance with her principle of leaving description to more skillful pens.

To reach Vienna, a fatiguing journey through the Tyrolese mountains was necessary, but was rewarded by a meeting with Prince Wenzel-Anton Kaunitz-Rietburg, Emperor Joseph's First Minister, to whom, at dinner, she delighted in delivering a long lesson on Peter the Great and his "exaggerated reputation" (185). She disabuses Prince Kaunitz who sees Peter I as "the Creator of Russia":

> Long before Peter I's ancestors had been called to the throne the arts had found a home in Russia, and pictures which are masterpieces of painting and date back to those distant times can still be found in our monasteries. We had historians who left more manuscripts than all the rest of Europe put together. . . . [Peter] would not have destroyed that priceless heritage which was our ancestors' character if he had not valued foreigners so much above Russians. . . . Under Catherine II the area of [Petersburg] has expanded four-fold and official buildings are far more magnificent, and all this has been accomplished without any taxation and without discontent. (183–85)

After Vienna and Prague, a few days were spent at Dresden, where "we visited the wonderful picture gallery several times and found it as inexhaustibly interesting as ever" (186), but Count Heinrich Brühl's gallery of pictures was no longer there, having been bought by Catherine the Great, "who loved and encouraged the arts and obtained for Russia some master-pieces of painting and scultpture such as it never had before" (186–87). On to Berlin, where she was treated with the same kindness as before by the whole royal family. Then the route of Königsberg led through the area that Dashkova calls "Livonia"—that is, the lands on the eastern coast of the Baltic—to Riga (now the capital of Latvia) by way of Memel (today Klaipeda, the chief port of Lithuania), to reach Petersburg in July 1782.

Empress Catherine now invited her to become director of the Academy of Sciences, and Dashkova also became the first president of the Russian Academy, founded at her own suggestion, to set down "rules of grammar and a good dictionary to do away with the absurdity of using foreign words and terms while having our own which were far more vivid" (217).

Upon the empress's death in 1796, Dashkova was deprived of all her offices by Catherine's successor, Paul I. She was sent into exile for over a year in Novgorod Province, where she lived in a peasant's hut in a place

> over sixty degrees latitude north . . . , surrounded by marshes and vast impenetrable forests, which made it impossible to go out even during the brief and late summers. . . . What rendered our situation still more melan-choly was the fact that the freezing over of the marshes had opened up a way across them which shortened the road from Petersburg to Siberia by several miles, so that most of the unfortunate exiles were now driven past my very windows. (271)

Then she was permitted to live on her estate near Moscow (Troit-skoye), until her death in 1810.

In 1786 Catherine the Great had asked Dashkova to accompany her to Finland on the occasion of the empress's meeting with King Gustavus III of Sweden. The meeting between those "two enlightened Sovereigns" gave rise to some interesting reflections recorded in the *Memoirs*. Dash-kova is aware of the false notions that may be gained by travel, and which may warp one's good judgment. She puts us on guard against misconcep-tions that may form in the mind of a "travelled king." Dashkova's words of warning about political distortions are as applicable today as they were in the eighteenth century:

I have very little faith indeed in the sincerity of crowned heads when they have to deal with each other; I think, even, that in spite of all the resources which intelligence, wit and courtesy can afford, they find each other boring after a while, and politics in the end render their daily intercourse both embarrassing and heavy. . . . His Majesty had a great deal of wit and intelligence and was very eloquent, but he also had the prejudices of a king, and, what is worse, of a travelled king—that is to say, he had false notions about everything he had seen abroad. For these illustrious travellers are only shown the most favourable side of things; everything is so arranged that they can see only the deceptive exterior. Another evil attendant on the travels of sovereigns . . . is that neither incense nor adulation is spared to gain them over. When they return home, therefore, they expect adoration from their subjects. . . . This is why I have always been against these illustrious personages travelling abroad. (228)

Alba Amoia

BIBLIOGRAPHY

Barker, Adele Marie, and Jehanne M. Gheith, eds. *A History of Women's Writing in Russia*. Cambridge: Cambridge University Press, 2002, pp. 38–42, 51–54, 320.

Dashkova, Ekaterina Romanovna Vorontsova. *The Memoirs of the Princess Dashkaw Written by Herself* (composed in French [*Mon histoire*, 1804–1805], edited by Mrs. W. Bradford. 2 vols. London, 1840).

———. *The Memoirs of Princess Daskov*. Trans. and ed. Kyril Fitzlyon. London: John Calder, 1958.

———. *Mémoires de la Princesse Daschkoff. Dame d'honneur de Catherine II Impératrice de toutes les Russies* (1805). Ed. and annotated Pascal Pontremoli. Paris: Mercure de France, 1966.

Hyde, H. Montgomery. *The Empress Catherine and Princess Dashkov*. London: Chapman and Hall, Ltd., 1935.

Polovtsov, Aleksandr. *The Favourites of Catherine II*. London: Herbert Jenkins, 1940.

Russischer Biographischer Index. Fiche no. 150, pp. 296–429 (microfilm). In Russian.

2

Friederike Brun

(1765–1835)

> To which people [German or Danish] I actually belong, I really
> don't know; for that reason I am completely lacking an exclu-
> sionary love of country, which has allowed me to keep my eyes
> and heart open to the advantages and the shortcomings of peo-
> ple and countries that I've seen.
>
> (Friederike Brun, *Wahrheit aus Morgenträumen*, 7)

Born in Thuringia, two miles from Gotha, Germany, Friederike
Sophie Christiane Münter was hardly four weeks old when she
became a traveler. Her father, Balthasar Münter, was a learned
cleric who was called to Copenhagen to serve as pastor at the German
church in that city. Ties between Germany and Denmark, strong since the
Reformation, were at their height when the Münters arrived in Copenhagen. Brun's autobiography, *Wahrheit aus Morgenträumen*, portrays the for-
mative influence on her of this intellectually and literarily active milieu of
which the Münters were an important part. The names of distinguished
families—the counts Bernstorff, Reventlow, Schimmelmann, and Stol-
berg—evoke a long-ago era, as do the literary figures of this pre-Romantic
period, especially the influential poet Friedrich Klopstock.

The deep feeling for history that is evident in Brun's writings, especially the sympathy across time for vanished civilizations in Italy, may owe
something to her mother, Magdalena Sophia Ernestine von Wangen-
heim, whose aristocratic Thuringian forebears traced an unbroken line of

descent from the year 1133. Brun speaks of her mother as a remarkable woman, but she describes herself as her father's favorite. As a child she rose early with him, prepared his tea, then sat with him as he played the hymns of the Bach sons or the music of Georg Benda and Johann Adam Hiller. He played even his own hymns, for which he was famous. These early mornings awakened in Friederike the desire to produce similar "holy and sweet-sounding poetry" (*Wahrheit aus Morgenträumen*, 74–75).

As was typical of the era, only two brothers and one sister survived childhood. Friederike herself was a very strong child, a restless girl, if not a tomboy, active "from first cock crow until late in the evening, with irrepressible liveliness" (*Wahrheit aus Morgenträumen*, 143). Her spontaneity included the tendency to speak her thoughts out loud. Her schooling, such as it was, took place at home, while she also enjoyed a great deal of freedom. Gardening, along with reading, was a favorite activity. She created her own idyll in the branches of a willow tree in the garden in which she sat writing poetry that she secreted in a "nest" in the tree. An inclination for solitary pursuits was balanced by intense friendships with a varied circle of people with deep and passionate interests. Both the solitariness and the sociability reflect traits of the late-eighteenth-century literary movement known in German as *Empfindsamkeit* (Sentimentality). It coupled an emphasis on intense inner states and the sharing of these with like-minded souls. She was precocious enough to read at the age of seven the sentimental novels of Samuel Richardson, scenes of which she dramatized with friends, and her later travel accounts are, like the letters in Richardson's novels, addressed to dearly loved, but distant, friends. Besides a fondness for popular German writing in this sentimental vein, at the age of thirteen she began to learn English and soon could read Ossian: "I lived and floated in his chiaroscuro world of spirits and lost myself in the noble, pure feelings that he exhales" (*Wahrheit aus Morgenträumen*, 145).

Her autobiography ends just before her marriage in 1783, at the age of eighteen. Constantin Brun, nineteen years older, was a man of modest background who through exceptional industry had become a phenomenally successful businessman. After their marriage, they traveled to St. Petersburg, where he served as Danish consul; later he became director of the Danish East India Company. During the early years of her marriage,

Brun read widely in the history of art and antiquity and also in modern and classical literature. In 1784 Karl was born, and in 1788 her first daughter, Charlotte. In the winter after Charlotte's birth, Brun became, overnight, exceedingly hard of hearing, a condition from which she suffered the rest of her life, even though she reports in her writing of conversations, of visits to concerts, and of being awakened to the sound of nightingales. In May of 1790 her second daughter, Auguste, was born. That fall Brun, with Karl and Charlotte, accompanied her husband on a business trip to Germany, France, and Switzerland. In slow stages they reached Switzerland at the end of March 1791. In Nyon she met the poet Friedrich Matthisson (1761–1831) and Matthisson's friend, Karl Viktor Bonstetten, from a Bernese patrician family, a man of wide learning and cultivation and a well-traveled friend of Thomas Gray and of Madame de Staël. On her first meeting with Bonstetten, Brun described him in her diary as "a man after my own heart—his tender countenance expresses benevolence, a happy disposition, and a pure, cheerful sensibility" (*Bonstettiana* VI, 349) and he remained the passionate (though probably not sexual) attachment of her life, the man who shared her literary interests and her love for antiquity. Brun's relationship with Matthisson and Bonstetten was an intensely sentimental one that was memorialized in her first volume of poetry. In July 1791 the Bruns returned to Copenhagen, where Friederike's last child, Ida, was born in August 1792.

In the summer of 1795, Brun and her two older children traveled to Germany, where she met Klopstock, Herder, Wieland, Schiller, and, at the spa in Carlsbad, Goethe. With Matthisson and his party, they then headed south, stopping in Switzerland to visit Bonstetten, who spent two and a half weeks traveling with Brun in northern Italy. She and her children continued their journey, arriving in Rome in November. Her husband was supposed to join his family there that winter, but he was prevented from doing so by Napoleon's Lombard campaign. Not until August 1796 were Brun and her children able to leave Italy. They went to Bern, where they remained, in Bonstetten's vicinity, until returning to Copenhagen in August 1797. After the French invasion of Bern, Bonstetten spent the years 1798 until 1801 with the Bruns in Copenhagen.

From 1802 onward, accompanied by one or another of her children, Brun traveled in Italy and Switzerland with periodic returns to Denmark. In Geneva in 1805 she met Madame de Staël, with whom she thereafter maintained a correspondence. By 1810, Constantin Brun, impatient with his wife's travels, ordered her to return to Denmark or risk never seeing her children again. By this time, he was one of the most successful businessmen in Europe, his trade having flourished even during the continental blockade, even after Denmark's reversals during the English bombardment in 1802.

In the years following her return to Denmark, Brun worked on her autobiography, continued to prepare her travel accounts, and published two further volumes of poetry (1812 and 1820). The Bruns' home in Copenhagen or at their country estate, Sophienholm, offered a cultivated setting for intellectuals as well as other cosmopolitans and emerging Danish artists, poets, and writers. Friederike maintained an extensive correspondence, including with Bonstetten until his death in 1832. Until her own death in 1835, one of the major topics of her letters was the inhospitable climate of Denmark, even in spring.

In a letter to Matthisson, dated 1 March 1802, Bonstetten gave a description of Friederike Brun that, from the distance of two centuries, helps to capture her personality: "Our dear Brun has difficulty fitting into the world of Geneva. Her unconstrained character, her perpetually open heart (which indeed doesn't know how to close), suffers under this chilly sky. She is like an orange blossom that has gone astray at the foot of Mont Buet" (*Bonstettiana* IX/I, 146).

The sentimental vein is particularly strong in Brun's first travel accounts, from the 1790s. Viewing the Roman amphitheater in Nîmes, France (February 8, 1791), for instance, she writes: "How mighty was the effect of this widespread human construction. I could never be tired of simply sitting there and feeling" (*Prosaische Schriften* 1, 43). Her reactions to the mountains of Switzerland on the 1791 journey show the influence of Edmund Burke's concepts of the sublime and the beautiful. Evidence of terror and sublimity are everywhere, for instance at Fort d'Ecluse:

> Our path suddenly went downhill; we arrived at the edge of a mountain where we saw, as if it had been brought there by a magician, two colossal mountains before us. Their venerable crowns strained into the empyrean, while their base was sunk in depths that provoked lightheadedness. In height and in form they seem to me to be the primordial progeny of Creation. (*Prosaische Schriften* 1, 161)

Indeed, Switzerland was the setting for some very fine poems in this vein that appeared in her first volume of poetry, which includes a foreword by Matthisson to Bonstetten reminding him of the genesis of the poems in the spring of 1791. These poems were, he writes, "composed in the lap of the Alps, on the shores of Lake Geneva," where the three formed their literary friendship (*Gedichte von Friederike Brun geb. Münter*, vii). The titles give an idea of the sentimental itinerary: for instance, "Die Insel auf dem Bielersee (An Rousseau's Schatten)," "Chamounix beym Sonnenaufgange," and "Der Frühlingsregen am Genfersee." (Brun's "Ich denke Dein" was one of the sources for Goethe's poem "Nähe des Geliebten.") Besides their enthusiastic tone, these poems combine many classical references that are evidence of Brun's wide reading.

She made a pilgrimage on May 18, 1791 to the Isle of Saint-Pierre, following in the footsteps of Jean-Jacques Rousseau. Her account shows a thorough reading of the Fifth Promenade of *Reveries of the Solitary Walker*, in which Rousseau described his idyll on the island in 1765. Brun took the exile at his word when he wrote that he set out to compose a florilegium of the island that would keep him busy the rest of his days:

> With pounding heart I climbed the island, wandering along narrow, overgrown paths under lovely groves of oaks. How everything moved me! This high entwined dome of shadows under which he roamed deep in reflection; this meadow full of flowers in which not the smallest plant was foreign to him; the flocks of birds that twitter chorus-like their undisturbed spring song and that flutter around me as they once did him. . . . I sought the place where he liked to sit, at the tip of the island. (*Prosaische Schriften* 1, 332)

Rousseau, when the lake was not calm for rowing, liked to find a charming and isolated nook where he could dream undisturbed and where the view, he wrote, was limited only by the distant range of blue mountains. After enjoying lunch served in his humble room, Brun, in a nice inversion, refers to the prospect outside the window, hemmed in by the peaks of glaciers: "The view is limited, but vast for the imagination" (335).

On her second journey to Switzerland, beginning in July 1795, this Rousseau-influenced picture was disturbed, especially in Zurich, where she had dear friends and where fierce conflicts raged between partisans and opponents of the French Revolution. She shows the same passion for long walks on high alpine paths, for soaking in the splendor of nature's vistas, whether at daybreak or at sunset, for the grapes that grow on the shores of Lake Lugano, but she now fears for Swiss institutions because of the threat of French tyranny:

> Dear God! the inhabitants of this paradise desire more than they now have? In their abundant good fortune, their bourgeois comfort under the mildest heaven on the most blessed piece of earth, surrounded by the reward of their labor . . . they now strive for distant visions of unconstrained freedom, of universal equality? Insanity! Why not tear down the eternal fortress of the Alps! (*Tagebuch einer Reise durch die östliche, südliche und italienische Schweiz*, 222)

For Brun on her first trip to Italy, as for the previous generation of German and northern European travelers, antiquity was to be encountered through its monuments, a quest in which they were led by the guiding spirit of the father of modern archaeology, Johann Joachim Winckelmann (1717–68). At the same time, Brun's travels, in the years between 1795 and 1810, took place in a period in which they could not but be affected by modern events, particularly contending armies in central Europe and Italy.

The account of her first stay in Italy, *Tagebuch über Rom* (two volumes, covering the period from November 1795 until September 1796), shows her immersion in the life of the ancient world, under the direction of the Danish archaeologist Georg Zoega (1755–1809), her mentor and constant guide. This was a time when there were no guidebooks for ordinary travelers, and there was probably no one more knowledgeable about the city than Zoega. He introduced Brun to Winckelmann's classification of ancient art, but her deeply felt response to artifacts was mediated by her vast knowledge of literature and history. She always sought to bring the object into an immediate connection with her senses and heart. On a visit to the Vatican:

> [S]uddenly Apollo [Belvedere] appeared to us; for me completely, uniquely, and eternally the God of Light. The far-seeing one, he sends his shafts of spirit [*Geist*] from his high thought-filled forehead! It is unnecessary to span his bow in order to hit his target. The mouth is friendly; with mildness the

right hand is opened; the garment rests peacefully on the left arm, which is extended as if to accompany speech. So the Apollo of the Vatican appeared to me: more beautiful, noble, sublime than anything else I saw. Nothing of scorn or anger was apparent. . . . (*Tagebuch über Rom* 1, 33)

Viewing a statue of an embracing Psyche and Amor, she makes associations with other cultural artifacts, with statues of Plato, Socrates, and Homer, all of whom "lead you back into a world . . . suffused with a serene evening light, a world of charming images and the harvest of the most sublime philosophy and poetry, and into the golden age of the human spirit!" (ibid., 38).

Independent accounts give a picture of a very sociable Friederike Brun, who gathered around her many of the German and Danish artists working in Rome, but what we would most like to know about personalities is left to our imagination: "I spent several hours in the evening with Angelika [Kauffmann] who . . . spoke with me about many things" (*Tagebuch über Rom* 1, 19). Likewise there is not much of Rome, the living city, in this first account of Italy. Sometimes the weather peeps through, but less frequently do Italians.

What interests Brun in this year is the evidence of the Roman and Italian past that the soil constantly turns up or is on display in galleries and public places in Rome. At the Villa Borghese, she gives her reasons for preferring sculpture and for her lack of enthusiasm for painting:

[T]he nature of the plastic art, which provides a much more tranquil and harmonious pleasure, and even more . . . the sense of beauty, truth, and simplicity of the Ancients that is so intimately united in this art; the grandeur or the psychological beauty of the subjects that are treated . . . this Genius of antiquity that surrounds and animates an ennobled humanity has so carried me away that in such a dream world of ideas I am completely lacking any appreciation for the magic of the paint brush. (*Tagebuch über Rom* 1, 245–46)

The opposite of this encounter with ancient history is represented by *Briefe aus Rom* (1816), which concerns the events of the years 1808–10. Brun was in Rome during the dramatic standoff between Napoleon and the Vatican in the person of Pius VII. The letters are an exciting contemporary document, from the point of view of an inhabitant of the city who relies on the same rumors as the Roman populace. She reports the expulsion of the cardinals from Rome, the imprisonment of the Swiss soldiers who refuse to pledge loyalty to the French, and, generally, what she refers to as the "shameful daily tale of French tyranny" (*Briefe aus Rom*, 16). She cites the pope's own words to Napoleon's demands: "Call back my exiled cardinals. Free my guards. Liberate my capital from enemy troops—then I can and will respond" (21). The most thrilling sections of the *Briefe* describe the attempts by the French to force Romans to celebrate Carnival and the resistance of the populace, in support of their pope. "People are laughing at the rulers who want to force an entire people to be uninhibitedly crazy" (28). When the Capitol bells rang at noon to announce the opening of the festivities, the entire Corso was "suddenly swept clean of people! . . . . Wanting to convince ourselves of the truth of this Not-Carnival we drove to the Corso, . . . and everywhere we encountered the quiet of a day of penance and prayer!" (30–31). Though a firm Protestant, Brun was intensely moved by the resistance of the people and their pontiff, "my dear pope, who at this time fights not only for the rights of the Catholic Church but for a free profession of faith for all Christians" (43). On Palm Sunday 1809 she went to the Quirinal Palace for the distribution of palms, an occasion that moved her to write two poems, one dedicated to the pope that later found its way to His Holiness through his private secretary.

In *Römisches Leben*, published at the end of her life (1833), Brun returns to the Rome of 1802–03, when she and her daughter Ida, along with Bonstetten, lived at the Villa Malta. Composed from notes written thirty years earlier, it is the summation of a life of great reflection. Also living at the Villa Malta with their five children was Wilhelm von Humboldt, the Prussian representative in Rome, and his wife, Caroline von Humboldt, with whom Friederike formed an intense friendship. She and the Humboldts, along with Bonstetten, were the center of a lively and sociable circle of German and Danish artists and other inhabitants and visitors to the Eternal City, among them the painter Angelika Kauffmann and the sculptors Rudolf Schadow, Bertel Thorvaldsen, and Antonio Canova. Her relationship with Bonstetten was very intense and often frustrating, but this period was apparently a very happy and productive time. Their mornings were generally spent reading and writing. Bonstetten began to plan his account of the last six books of the *Aeneid* by visiting all the places mentioned in Virgil's epic. Afternoons were spent on excursions in Rome or the Campagna.

Römisches Leben shows exactly how Brun got to know Rome from the ground up with her companion Georg Zoega: "My Ida [to whom this portion of the book is addressed], do you remember our charming promenade on the Palatine Hill? It was a mild, Roman day in autumn, more beautiful than those of our cold springs. . . . We began by measuring the situation and circumference of the Roman forum" (*Römisches Leben* 1, 114). If the weather was inclement, excursions took place indoors. "In this case one visits Rome in its big churches, in which the outer air only slowly penetrates the thick walls. . . . Today [November 10, 1802] we visited first the great and beautiful Maria-Maggiore, one of the seven basilicas of Rome" (*Römisches Leben* 1, 63–64). Before describing the architecture, she gives the pagan origin of the basilica, "built on the foundation of a temple dedicated to Juno Lucina, the special protective goddess of pregnant women or those giving birth as well as of early childhood" (64). In the same entry, however, she turns to the present, recording the effects of the French invasions on Italians:

> The misery of the people, even the middle class, increases daily. Every day you see slink past you people who are near death. . . . All prices have doubled in the seven years since the misery began, in 1796, just as I left the city, while all sources of assistance and supply have become exhausted. The cost of even otherwise cheap, nourishment-poor vegetables is so great that broccoli stalks from the garbage are tradable. (*Römisches Leben* 1, 71–72)

Traces of history are still keenly experienced, for instance, the sight of the many grave monuments on the via Ostia:

> The victorious fleets of Rome landed in Ostia. The Scipios, the Aemilii, their heads crowned with laurels, stepped ashore here; the great Romulus came and went this way, renouncing his life while choosing to die a terrible death in glory for the patria. What a teeming life converged on this melancholy body of water, which now only bears memories!" (*Römisches Leben* 1, 90–91)

But the past, especially its less glorious aspects, now serves as a foil for the present age of barbarism. Brun is quite ferocious in her scorn for the

French and their cultural despoliation, especially at the Villa Albani, which she calls "Winckelmann's temple," in reference to the archaeologist's patron, Cardinal Alessandro Albani:

> Nowhere else in Rome have the French been so wanton. The pious Prince Albani had declared himself very courageously against them. . . . They revenged themselves on this shrine of art, on the common property of humankind. It was wrong to take away the magnificent and colossal bust of Pallas, the relief of Antinous, the statues of Leucothea and other major pieces; it was common robbery to remove the bas-reliefs from the walls, the glorious, ancient colossal masks from the beautiful entrance hall; but to mutilate statues that they didn't want or couldn't take away, . . . assiduously and meanly to break off tiny pieces of tenderly executed marble reliefs— these are features of vulgar outrage committed by this most cultivated people on earth (as this nation is known by its flatterers, the demagogues of all nations). (*Römisches Leben* 2, 10–11)

Friederike Brun's in-between status has much to do with the period in which she came of age, and her travel diaries document the fragility of the Western cultural inheritance during this often violent transition from the traditional order of society to the modern age.

(All translations are mine.)   *Elizabeth Powers*

BIBLIOGRAPHY

Brun, Friederike. *Gedichte von Friederike Brun geb. Münter.* Ed. Friedrich Matthisson. Zurich: Orell Gessner Füssli, 1795.

———. *Prosaische Schriften.* 2 vols. Zurich: Orell, Füssli, 1799.

———. *Tagebuch einer Reise durch die östliche, südliche und italienische Schweiz.* Copenhagen: Friedrich Brummer, 1800.

———. *Tagebuch über Rom.* 2 vols. Zurich: Orell, Füssli, 1801.

———. *Briefe aus Rom, geschrieben in den Jahren 1808, 1809, 1810. Über die Verfolgung, Gefangenschaft u. Entführung des Papstes Pius VII* (1816). [Cited here is the edition *Briefe aus Rom*: Supplement to *An Encyclopedia of German Women Writers*, vol. 12. Ed. Brian Keith-Smith and Herman Moens. Lewiston, N.Y.: Edwin Mellen Press, 2000.]

————. *Wahrheit aus Morgenträumen* (1810–24). Available at http://humanities.byu.edu/sophie/Brun/home.htm

————. *Römisches Leben*, in two parts. Leipzig: F. A. Brockhaus, 1833.

Wilhelm, Doris and Peter-Walser, ed. *Bonstettiana: historisch-kritische Ausgabe der Briefkorrespondenzen Karl Viktor von Bonstettens und seines Kreises, 1753–1832.* Vol. VI. Bern: Peter Lang, 1997; Vol. IX/1. Göttingen: Wallenstein Verlag, 2002.

Lady Hester Stanhope

(1776–1839)

> I ride here in men's clothes just as if I was the Pacha's son. . . .
> The people call out, there goes the queen. . . .
>
> (Lady Hester Stanhope, Damascus, September 23, 1812, in
> *The Nun of Lebanon*, ed. Ian Bruce, 154)

B rash, rash, and extravagantly outspoken, the self-willed, strikingly attractive Lady Hester articulated her free-spirited thoughts, then set them down in her literary legacy: a voluminous correspondence composed during her dramatic and dangerous years of travel. It was her way of arming herself against sorrow and coping with joy. Besides her letters to Craufurd Bruce, the father of her lover Michael Bruce, her correspondents included Duke Maximilian; Count Wilsenheim; Prince Pückler Muskau; General Oakes, the governor of Malta; Thomas Coutts, a banker; General Grenville; and many others who shared this traveler's inner world.

Hester's childhood and adolescence were far from charmed. Her mother, the daughter of the Earl of Chatham and favorite sister of Prime Minister William Pitt (1783–1801), died when Hester was four, leaving her and her two younger sisters bereft. Six months later, her bizarre and at times violent father, Charles, third Earl of Stanhope, wrapped in his inventions and antiestablishment eccentricities, remarried. His new wife, interested only in partying, ignored the three little girls already there, and the three boys to whom she gave birth. Whether living on the Stanhope estate in Chevening Manor (Kent) or in their London residence, the six children saw little of their parents. Hester's father was averse to educating his children. Whenever she requested schooling, she was sent to care for the turkeys, which accounts for the countless misspellings and punctuation errors in her correspondence (which, when here quoted, have been left as in the original). Rather than bemoan her fate, she found an outlet in horseback riding and duly became an extraordinary horsewoman.

Life became so unpleasant in Chevening Manor that on one occasion, when her father held a knife to her throat during one of his tantrums, Hester left home. Her sisters took a similar step via marriage. In the spring of 1800 she moved into the home of her beloved grandmother, Lady Chatham, in Somersetshire. It was during this happy period that she learned to break wild horses and began enjoying London society. Although her name was linked to several eligible young men, the nearly six-foot-tall Stanhope preferred to gad about. Upon learning, however, that her father had categorically denied her favorite half brother, Lord Mahon, a college education, she took it upon herself to remedy his plight. Dictated by her inborn altruism and ingenuity, she contrived a meticulous plan, then asked her uncle, Prime Minister William Pitt, to help her arrange her brother's escape from bondage. He agreed. Lord Mahon was enrolled as a student at the University of Erlangen in Germany on March 2, 1801, and Mr. Pitt conveyed his admiration for his niece's brilliant organizational capacities (Marlin Armstrong, *Lady Hester Stanhope*, 18ff). In September of the following year, Lord Mahon returned to England, joining his sister and friends on a tour through France, Italy, and Germany. That they rode alone on mules through the dangerous mountain pass of Mont Cenis revealed Lady Stanhope's bravura.

With the death of her beloved grandmother in 1803, she came to another crossroad in her life: she had lost a friend and had been left homeless. Thanks to the generosity of her bachelor uncle, William Pitt, she was invited to live in his home, where her articulate, energetic, and witty personality captivated those with whom she came into contact. Her large dark blue eyes and unusually white skin dazzled onlookers, while her flair for entertainment at Pitt's home became the talk of London. So well did she meld with Pitt's political colleagues and members of the Cabinet that he allegedly told her she was fit to sit between Augustus and Maecenas (George Paston, *Little Memoirs*, 219). On a later occasion, King George III, pointing to Lady Stanhope, affirmed that "there is not a man in my kingdom who is a better politician, and there is not a woman who better adorns her sex" (ibid., 219).

With the passing of Pitt in 1806, her fulfilling existence came to an end. Not only had he played the role of father figure in her life, but his understanding of her needs had catalyzed those very talents her father had in vain sought to stifle. Pitt's death left her once again homeless, without funds or position, but thanks to her uncle's foresight she received a regular pension. Her brothers Charles and James, under the command of Sir John Moore, with whom her name had been amorously linked, went to Spain to help fend off the French in 1808. Tragically, only James survived.

Although broken in spirit, the nearly thirty-five-year-old Lady Stanhope made plans to leave England. Among others, she hired a personal physician, Dr. Charles Meryon, to oversee her good health during her peregrinations, and in 1810 she sailed to Gibraltar with her brother James, who was scheduled to join his regiment in Cádiz. It was at this point that she met the love of her life, the handsome twenty-year-old, Cambridge-educated Michael Bruce. The two became lovers. She altruistically refused his marriage offer, believing that a woman fourteen years his senior would be detrimental to his career (Armstrong, 43). In full command, Hester and her entourage sailed to Malta to begin her nomadic journey. Never again would she set foot in England.

Her trip to Greece, with its joys, travails, and harrowing adventures, began in August 1810. Aboard were her beloved Bruce, Dr. Meryon, friends, two Greek servants, a janissary (soldier of an elite corps of Turkish troops), and a dragoman (an Arab interpreter), armed with daggers, pistols, and sabers. Zante (one of the Ionian islands), Patras, Corinth, and Athens were on their itinerary. Upon entering the port of Piraeus, they stood bedazzled before the shifting luminosities cast by the sun on the Parthenon, and on the distant olive groves and cornfields. As happenstance would have it, Hester spotted a young man diving into the waters below. It was Lord Byron. They later met in her rooms in Athens. Not surprisingly, the two took an instant dislike to each other.

Adventurous, but also intellectually curious, Hester and her party set sail in October on a Greek *polacca* to Constantinople. The winds were powerful, the waters rough, the crew and servants increasingly belligerent. They

reached the Hellespont, but so inept was the captain that Stanhope and
her friends left the ship and took an alternative route to Constantinople.

Readers learn that she and Michael received a check from her beloved's
father, Craufurd Bruce, and could continue relying on his financial help
during their travels. Her scrupulous accounting procedures, included in
virtually each of her letters to Bruce's father, were impressive for their
honesty. Insightfully and with tongue in cheek, she shared her knowledge
of Turkish mores with Craufurd:

> One of the greatest men here is . . . to show me his Harem himself when
> he arrives from Bagdad where he has been cutting off heads. The Pacha's
> head was shewn in Constantinople for three days it was in a perfect state,
> altho it had traveled so far, the fleshy parts had been extracted & and sub-
> stituted by perfumed cotton; this is a nasty description, but sights like these
> occasion no disgust here, & the poor head was handed about on a silver
> dish as if it had been a Pine Apple. Yet I consider this much more the effect
> of habit, than any natural disposition to barbarity in the Turks, their perfect
> contempt for death makes them regard it in a much less aweful light than
> we do, therefore they have little to overcome but disgust, which unaccom-
> panied by more serious reflections, does not last long. The manners of the
> Turks, I like extremely they have fine understandings which is expressed in
> their countenances, & a natural politeness which the best bred Englishman
> of the present day cd. not imitate with success; they certainly have an air of
> importance, accompanied with a penetrating examining look, as if meaning
> to measuring any one's mind & person at the same time. (from Terapia,
> February 17, 1811, *The Nun of Lebanon*, ed. Ian Bruce, 87)

Given her flair for the dramatic, Stanhope waited for Friday, the Muslim Sabbath, to make her memorable statement concerning women in
Islamic society. The streets were crowded with merchants, water carriers,
and the faithful. All were waiting for Sultan Mahmoud, Commander of
the Faithful, to enter the mosque. Present as well were the great ministers
of the Sublime Porte, the captain pasha, and the grand vizier wearing fur-
covered pelisses. The bridles of their horses were studded with emeralds
and diamonds. The Kislar Aga, guardian of the harem and of a hundred
black and white eunuchs, was also present in full regalia (Joan Haslip,
Lady Hester Stanhope, 96). Amid the crowd, and in complete disregard of
dire warnings, Lady Stanhope sat tall, stately, and unveiled on her horse.

Onlookers stood aghast in hushed silence. Never before had a woman paraded unveiled on the sacred sabbath or at any other time in this city. Hester gloried fearlessly in the pageant-like happenings. That she chose to show herself off so overtly in a country where women were not only kept hidden, but enslaved, thrilled her to the marrow. The native population, awed by her brilliant blue eyes and ultra-white skin, thought her a boy and not a woman at all.

Her aside to Craufurd on Turkish women was incisive:

> The Turkish women I have seen I think very agreable, every gesture is so remarkably just that you can almost understand them without comprehending their language; their dress . . . only varies in the head dress, which change now and then, but continue to dye their hair, paint their eyebrows & black their eyes. (Terapia, February 17, 1811, ibid., 88)

In keeping with custom, but not without restrained glee, she sent Bruce and Lord Sligo out of her rooms when visited by a Turkish lady. Did Stanhope know beforehand that Bruce and their friend, Lord Sligo, had contrived to make peepholes in the ceiling?

> [T]he Lady & a train of females arrived who took off veil upon veil, & robe upon robe, and having fastened & unfastened various parts of their dress, & displayed magnificent bracelets and zones of precious stones, the fair Turkish ladies expressed great surprise that my eyes had not been blackened & produced a little machine out of her pocket requesting she might black them. I agreed and they all began to assist at the operation, appeared so overjoyed when it was done & laughed so loud, that it became infectious, and Lord Sligo burst out [laughing]. The horror that a man's voice created, is not to be described, & and some of the attendants seemed in a rage. (Terapia, February 17, 1811, ibid.)

The harsh winds blowing in on Terapia from the Bosphorus during the winter of 1811 had made Stanhope ill and increasingly restless, to the point of her entertaining the idea of going to France for a tête-à-tête with Napoleon. Forever confident in her ability to help unravel Europe's difficult political situation, she visited the French chargé d'affaires in secret on the Asiatic side of the Bosphorus. To her dismay, she was sighted by English diplomats. Her plans were thwarted. At the end of May, she opted for the sulfur baths of Brusa (today's Bursa) in northwestern Turkey, delighting in them and in the spectacular fields of white irises, flowering orchards, and mulberry groves in the distance. She took to what she erroneously considered the unsophisticated pastoral life of the wandering tribes of Wahhabis, Anazi Arabs, and Bedouins. What she failed to understand was the complex of hatreds and intrigues marking the relationships between them and other ruling groups. In shocked disbelief, she wrote to Craufurd:

> I have just heard of a most dreadful massacre, which took place at Grand Cairo. It appears that the Pasha of that place has long wished to exterminate the Beys. To accomplish this object he had resource to treachery. Under pretence of conferring some great honor on his son he invited them to an entertainment, and when he had got them in a convenient place he ordered them all to be put to the sword. The slaughter continued several days, and I understand that upward of 6000 People have been massacred. (Brusa, March 18, 1811, ibid., 93)

By July she and Bruce had moved to Bebeck, ten miles from Constantinople. Thanks to her largesse and innate elegance, she fared well with the Turks. She even became relatively friendly with the Turkish pasha and his brother, a phenomenal achievement for a woman in a Muslim land. Here are her sympathetic reactions to them:

> Yet the more I see of the Turks the more I admire them, a vulgar Turk I have never yet seen, tho they appear by their savage conduct upon certain occasions to me considered brutes, yet they have a degree of kindness about them which never can fail to please. (to Craufurd Bruce, Bebeck, July 18, 1811, ibid., 111)

She shares her open but firm reactions to harem life in another letter to Craufurd:

> [T]ho admiring the Turks as I do, I can never agree with Lady W. Montague respecting the agreable lives of their women. Some of them the Georgeans in particular, are beautiful, but a Roman and French woman to my mind infinitely more so, their music is abominable, & their dancing by far the most disgusting thing I ever saw. I do not mean this in a prudish

sense, on the contrary perhaps it may be deemed a profligate one, but I have no idea of passions being excited except that which God created for the purpose, a man. Their dinners are served up one dish at a time to the number of fifty or a hundred, and every one takes a pinch or two with their fingers. The civility I have met with is very great, & tho I must own I can never envy these women with all their luxury, yet I must confess they appear the best natured people in the world, remarkably well bred, & possessing very good natural understanding, with great quickness, & much eloquence. (Bebeck, July 28, 1811, ibid., 117)

Lady Stanhope's increasingly large entourage, including members of the diplomatic corps, lived under her dynamic spell—her cumulative intelligence, courage, multiple kindnesses, and lavish lifestyle. Nonetheless, her increasing frustration vis-à-vis her plans to meet with Napoleon troubled Bruce. To relieve her tension, he suggested a change of scene. Egypt and the pyramids, he reasoned, would serve as a good antidote. The prospect of wintering in Egypt delighted Stanhope. Little did she realize what fate had in store for them as they set sail on a Greek ship for Alexandria in October 1811.

The waters were calm when suddenly, without warning, the winds reached gale force, obliging the travelers to take shelter amid a group of small islands nearby. No sooner had the winds subsided, than the ship made for Rhodes. A southerly gale set in two days later on the open sea. After the initial panic, Stanhope wrote to Craufurd "From a miserable Village near the extremity of the Island of Rhodes":

We are all thank God much better in health than one cd. possibly expect after all our hardships, that of being nearly lost in a storm, that of the ship sinking from a leek she sprang, the fear of never reaching land in an overloaded boat, of starvation for a day & a half on a bare rock without even a spring of water, of again leaving that friendly rock in the night from the danger of being washed off (as the wind had changed & the sea came in another direction) to land on an unknown coast to find a habitation either under rocks or trees. Fortunately we succeeded in landing near a mill about three miles from this miserable place where we passed the night. The next day we came here such poor figures, as eyes never beheld half naked & half starved but in good Spirits . . . (early December, 1811, ibid., 127)

In December Lady Stanhope set up household three miles outside Rhodes, remaining there long enough to order new wardrobes for herself and for her companions. At this juncture, she decided to wear men's clothes only: pantaloons, a leather cartridge belt, sword, yellow babooshes, and a many-colored turban. She was delighted with the effect (Haslip, 121).

After a brief bout with fever and shivers, she, Bruce, and friends took an English frigate to Alexandria, arriving there in February 1812. On to Rosetta and Cairo by ferryboat, where she nearly drowned in the Nile. She topped off her tour with a visit to the pyramids—a dangerous affair at the time because of marauding Bedouin tribes. The pasha, Mehemit Ali, gave her and Bruce two French mamelukes to protect and guide them through yet another thrilling experience.

Sailing on the Nile in May 1812, she wrote to Bruce's father about their intent to dazzle the pasha, Mehemit Ali. To this end, she bought a regal Tunisian costume of purple velvet elaborately embroidered with gold, appropriate pantaloons, a colorful turban, a girdle, two cashmere shawls, a pelisse, waistcoat, saber, and saddle. She achieved the wanted effect. So impressed was the pasha with his visitors, that he

> ordered out 4000 cavalry & appointed us to meet him to see them reviewed. He made us ride home with him & gave me one of his own horses & B. a sword. Every body took the tone from him & we have been better treated & more talked of than any people who ever visited Cairo. . . . The Pachas receiving us standing (the greatest Compt. a Turk can pay) the review given on purpose even my being taken for the Pachas son an Arab Chief taking my hand to kiss after his masters all these little circumstances small as they are have made people envious. . . . I am so well disguised by my dress & have so adopted Turkish manners as to be able to enter a Mosck during prayers & depart again unabused. I take off my shoes go up the fountain as they do put on an air of solemnity & respect & attract no attention whatever. (to Craufurd Bruce, May 2, 1812, ibid., 136ff.)

She and her entourage fared less well in Damietta, overwhelmed as they were by fleas, mosquitoes, flies, and foul odors. Understandably, they set sail for Jaffa as rapidly as possible, landing there on May 15, 1812, and continuing on to Jerusalem, she at the head of her caravan of eleven camels and thirteen horses, two mamelukes, and a group of janissaries. To

reach Jerusalem, her caravan had to pass through territories governed by
the Arab sheik Abu Ghosh. Christians had warned her of his thriving
business: levying taxes on those going to Jerusalem. After meeting Lady
Stanhope, however, Abu Ghosh was so impressed by her fine manners
and strong stance that he honored her with a huge feast: among the
dishes, a freshly slaughtered sheep served with mincemeat rolled in vine
leaves, kusas (vegetable marrow) stuffed with rice, boiled chicken, and
other delicacies (Armstrong, 53). Not disinterestedly, Stanhope was lavish
with gifts of money, aware that without these incentives she would neither
gain access to areas forbidden to women nor meet with Muslim dignitaries. En route, she suddenly felt overwhelmed by the prophetic words an
English seer, Samuel Brothers, had spoken to her when she was but a
young girl: she would visit Jerusalem, spend seven years in the desert, after
which she would be declared queen of the Jews, and lead forth a chosen
people (Paston, 226). The first part of the prophecy had already been fulfilled. On this memorable day, she chose to wear a mameluke costume,
consisting of a satin vest, a loose red cloth jacket shaped like a spencer
and trimmed with gold lace, and loose full trousers of the same cloth, over
which she wore a flowing white burnoose, whose folds formed a becoming
drapery to her majestic figure (ibid.). On the road to Ramallah she headed
a procession of eleven laden camels, seven servants, two mamelukes, and
a bodyguard of janissaries that had been provided by the governor of Jaffa
(Haslip, 128). She reveled at the sight of exotic gardens and open fields
studded here and there with storks.

Cognizant of the ways of the world, she wrote to Kengi Ahmet, the
governor of Jerusalem, expressing her desire to be received by him. Forth-
with, she was invited to meet him in a room at the top of his palace overlooking the Great Mosque—believed to have once been Solomon's
Temple. Visits to the Church of the Holy Sepulchre, Bethlehem, Nazareth, Mount Carmel, Haifa, and Acre followed. At Nazareth she was
housed in a Franciscan monastery. On her return through the narrow and
poorly lit streets one evening, her horse stumbled on a stone and fell. She
was pinned beneath it and suffered bruises on her head, collarbone, and
knee. The stoic that she was, she minimized the pain in her letter:

> My horse fell with me . . . & hurt me so much that I cd. hardly turn in my
> bed for a fortnight, but I am well again now, except a slight indisposition

brought on by the imence heat which gives me such a headache I can hardly
see. Sitting quite still with all the doors & windows open the perspiration
runs down people's face like water. . . . (to Craufurd Bruce, Saide, August
2, 1812, ibid., 147)

After only a week's delay, she valiantly continued on by horse or ass. In
July she and her company ascended Mount Lebanon, with its lavish culture of vines, olives, and figs. The spectacular scapes—like sequences of
undulating palettes, their composition intensifying the play of shadings—
dramatized their foray into the unknown.

During her stay in Sidon, she visited the ancient ruined city of Tyre, the
homeland of antiquity's Dido, the founder of Carthage. Unassuageable,
she and her party rode on for four more hours, pitched their tents, and
unloaded their camels. Most meaningful to her was the invitation
extended to her to visit the residence of the powerful Druse emir, Beschir,
at Dayr el Kammar, about a mile and a half from Sidon.

It is my wish that B. sd. get perfectly acquainted with the Druses[,] a people
whose religion is so wrapt in mystery and uncertainty[,] but I have learnt
from the man who knows the most of them of any person existing that they
believe in transmigration. (to Craufurd Bruce, May 2, 1812, ibid., 137)

Stanhope had been long intrigued by the Druse hermetic religious sect,
whose origins were veiled in mystery. Fascinating to her was their dual
form of worship: Druses living in Egypt, Syria, Lebanon, and Safad were
encouraged to practice both their own and the state religion of the land
they inhabited, to avoid discrimination and persecution. Unlike Christians and Muslims, they practiced neither persecution nor proselytism.
Nor did they, like Christians, Jews, and Muslims, relegate nonbelievers to
eternal damnation. They believed in one ineffable, incomprehensible,
God, creator of the first creature, a universal intelligence who became
manifest in the person of Hamza.

Despite the oppressive heat and the fact that 40,000 Arabs were warring with each other, by some magic momentum the indefatigable, restless, and determined Stanhope again triumphed over physical distress.
Once the talk of English salons, time and toil had transformed this
vibrant beauty into a sophisticated and knowledgeable woman, who, with

her beloved Bruce, forged ahead, searching for that ever elusive sense of fulfillment. Nor was she dissuaded from traveling when she learned that the bubonic plague had reached Smyrna. From Damascus, she wrote pridefully to Craufurd:

> I ride here in men's clothes just as if I was the Pacha's son, & tho some-
> times followed by 2000 people to my own door, not a soul insults me, altho
> I wd. not accept the guard the Pacha offered me here, & ride out with my
> own Janissary & a Greek boy only. . . . The people call out, there goes the
> queen. . . . (Damascus, September 23, 1812, ibid., 154)

In another letter to Craufurd, she pooh-poohs those who advised her

> that it was madness to think of coming here unless I put on the dress of an
> oriental female, that I never cd. stir out, that it was so dangerous & that
> the people here were rash fanatics that even Englishmen were obliged to be
> constantly attended by the Pachas people. However here I am, not lodged
> as other people have been in a Christian house, but in that of a Turk, &
> close to the famous Mosque. (Damascus, September 23, 1813, ibid., 154)

While marveling at all she had seen in Damascus, she had but one all-encompassing dream: to go to Palmyra, where the once powerful and strong-willed Zenobia had reigned (266–272 C.E.) as queen of East Asia Minor, Syria, northern Mesopotamia, and Egypt. Zenobia's lack of diplomacy—having referred to her son as emperor—caused her downfall. The Roman emperor, Aurelian, vowing revenge at her slight, conquered Palmyra, seized the queen's gold, put her officers and advisers to death, and took Zenobia hostage back to Rome.

Stanhope's determination to be the first European woman to visit Palmyra beat down the very real hurdles facing her on this trip. When the pasha of Damascus proposed sending his troops to escort her through the desert, to everyone's amazement she declined his offer. Despite his powerful army, she realized that he was not only incapable of dominating the astute desert tribes, but reasoned that at the slightest danger his soldiers would abandon her. With this in mind, she wrote to the Great Emir Mahanna el Fadel, chief of the Anizi tribes (one of the most powerful Bedouin tribes occupying the Syrian desert area), asking to meet with him. Because illness prevented him from calling on her, he sent his son,

Naser, who agreed to protect her on this perilous journey. Although counteradvised by everyone, she put herself under Mahanna's protection, for he, above all other tribal leaders, she believed, understood the far-reaching subtleties of hostile tribal interrelationships. Nor did the spread of the bubonic plague to Acre, Tyre, and Sidon deter her in her plans (to Michael Bruce, March 18, 1813, ibid., 190).

The stalwart English lady, Bruce, and Dr. Meryon set out for Palmyra in pageant array on 20 March 1813. Their caravan was eye-arresting: seventy camels, bodyguards, and Bedouin chieftains on their mares, carrying lances decorated with ostrich feathers and wearing brightly colored keffiyehs drawn over their mouths like visors. A few days later, when Naser and his Bedouins began stealing from Stanhope's servants, she demanded immediate clarification. Either embarrassed or taking umbrage, Naser declared that some mares in the vicinity had been stolen by enemies. With that, he rode off, leaving the travelers alone. The fearless Lady Stanhope bided her time. Upon his return twenty minutes later, she thought his actions to have been a ploy to test her courage. When, after a week, they arrived at their destination, she knew she was fated to be *dàr el Sytt* (queen of the Arabs).

As she stood on the heights of the mountain pass overlooking Palmyra, she was awed and dismayed at the sight of the mutilated but once-superb columns covering a three-mile area of colonnades, monuments, tombs, and temples. In Michael Bruce's words:

> We descended from this height and were led first into the [V]alley of the [T]ombs, and after passing these venerable monuments we entered a colonnade a mile long with two rows of Avenlhien columns on each side. On each column there is a pedestal jutting out of which I suppose statues used to be placed, and above it an inscription in Greek and Palmyrian. Here we found children, boys and girls dressed with great elegance, crowned with myrtle and carrying garlands of flowers in their hands. . . . They began to dance to the accompaniment of their own kind of music. They danced in a circle and were extremely graceful in their movements. Nothing could exceed the beauty of this scene, the magnificence of the arch under which we stood, the picturesque group of old women among the columns, the cavalcade of warriors which followed Miladi Hester, and the imposing grandeur of the ancient ruins. (ibid, 194)

Anxious to see the Valley of the Tombs, Stanhope walked the length of the 4,000-foot colonnade (northwest to southeast), ending at the triumphal arch in a line with the gate of the temple. Dr. Meryon reported from the scene that beautiful girls between the ages of twelve and sixteen stood on the pedestals in graceful postures, their youthful forms showing through a transparent covering. As soon as Stanhope had passed, these youthful forms of beauty jumped down and escorted the great English visitor to the triumphal archway. There they danced round her, and a wreath was held suspended over her head. Thus was Lady Hester Stanhope crowned queen of the Arabs, the first European woman to enter Palmyra. The prophecy had been fulfilled (ibid., 196).

She and her party left Palmyra in April, reaching Hama and Latakia (ancient Laodicea), the site of new explorations, in May. News that Craufurd had been taken seriously ill added to the cooling of passions between the lovers. Craufurd's unwillingness now to further support their lifestyle encouraged Stanhope to suggest that Bruce leave for England and find some worthwhile endeavor in keeping with family tradition. Although he left Latakia in October 1813, and the void in her life was great, they continued writing amorous letters, Stanhope signing hers of June 25, 1814 "The Nun of Lebanon" (ibid., 291).

Adding to her pain was news of the rapidly advancing plague. Surely, her sadness had served to weaken her physically. Raging fever was followed by delirium. Dr. Meryon, also struck down by the plague, was so weak he had to be carried into her room to tend to her. He feared for her life. Her recovery, delayed by an attack of ague, left her greatly fatigued. She moved into a dissaffected and dilapidated Greek convent, Mar Elias, on a lonely hilltop of Mount Lebanon, with a superb view of the sea, and not too distant from Sidon, but which required borrowing large amounts to refurbish. Having fully recovered from her illness, she left for Baalbek with Dr. Meryon. No longer traveling in grand style, and with only a few servants, they pitched their tents in what had been the Temple of the Sun, but was now a dilapidated mosque. On to the famed Cedars of Lebanon in the cold of winter. Upon arriving at the ultra-strict Maronite monastery of Mar Antonius, in which all female creatures, animal or human, were barred entry, Stanhope, now subject to behavioral extremes since her bout with the plague, made a point—to the horror of the monks—of riding her she-ass directly into the hall (Armstrong, 75).

Upon her return to Tripoli, where she was entertained by dignitaries, she moved into Mar Elias (January 1815). Days later, she plunged into a new venture. She had been apprised of a secret copy of an Italian manuscript, written long ago by a Frankish monk living in a Syrian monastery, claiming that vast amounts of buried wealth existed in Ascalon (Palestine). Her mind soared with anticipation. She and Dr. Meryon set out in March to search for this storehouse of riches. Forever indulging in the dramatic, she rode in high style on horseback under a crimson palanquin decorated with six golden balls that glittered in the sun's rays. The digging began. Optimism soared. After fruitless days of searching, nothing but a large, headless, yet superb statue of an armed warrior of the late Roman period was unearthed. Unable to contain her disappointment, and despite the archaeologists' wishes to retain the statue intact, she had it smashed to smithereens. In a letter to the British consul, John Barker (April 20, 1815), she shamefacedly admitted that she had committed the crime, "that it might not be said by ill natured people [that] I came to seek for statues not treasure" (*Nun of Lebanon*, 338).

Outside of a visit to Antioch, most of her days were now spent at Mar Elias, where she busied herself writing to emirs, sheiks, English friends, and relatives. When Dr. Meryon requested to leave her service in 1817, she agreed. He subsequently married, then returned with wife and child only to once again leave Lady Stanhope's service.

Although her behavioral patterns seemed increasingly quixotic—ranging from extreme kindness to cruel rages—her fundamental generosity remained intact. She invited the ostensibly famed General Lousteneau, whom she had met and befriended when he lived on charity in Haifa, to live in her home. His victories over the English in India had brought him fame and fortune, both of which he had lost over the years. When first they met, Hester had been impressed by the accuracy of his prophetic words concerning Bonaparte's fate in 1814: "Madam, at this very moment in which I speak to you, Napoleon has escaped from Elba" (quoted in Haslip, 177). Was it happenstance that had brought General Lousteneau's alleged son, the handsome officer, once in Napoleon's Imperial Guard, to Mar Elias in January 1820? (Haslip, 214). No sooner had she met the handsome young Captain Lousteneau—a beggar as well by this time—than she was struck by his resemblance to Sir John Moore, with whom she had been in love as a young girl and whose untimely death at the battle of Corunna in Spain had caused her great grief. She gave him lodgings. After his untimely death in August 1820, she mourned him.

Increasingly withdrawn from the world stage, she inhabited her own remote domain. Her blurred vision, caused by the continuously glaring sun of the Middle Eastern deserts, made matters worse. When in 1820 volleys of gunfire broke out near Mar Elias, and rebellions against the sultanates became increasingly disruptive, her innate generosity encouraged her to shelter and feed fleeing peasants whose crops had been burned and whose lives were in danger. Still they stole from her.

Discouraged by the turn of events, in 1821 Hester moved to another deserted monastery, Dar Djoun, in the mountains of Lebanon—where eagles and vultures swooped and jackals howled outside her gates (Haslip, 220). There she spent the next eighteen years of her life as a virtual hermit, clothed in a medley of rags. The refurbished ruin took on the contours of a labyrinth. Her mystical trajectories found empathetic company not in diplomats and political figures but rather in dervishes, magicians, wise men, astrologists, craniologists, physiognomists, and occult scientists. Emir Beshyr sent her a mare and a she-ass said to be a lineal descendant of the ass on which Christ had ridden into Jerusalem. In time the mare gave birth to a foal with a natural excrescence on its back in the form of a Turkish saddle. She was convinced that the animal, whose birth was a miracle, was destined to carry the Messiah into Jerusalem (*Nun of Lebanon*, 399).

Now famous for her travels and her religious hold on surrounding tribes, Stanhope's presence elicited many visitors. Among the few favored with an interview was the celebrated French poet, Alphonse de Lamartine. She received him on September 13, 1832, in her bedroom, from which she now rarely budged. He found it so dark, he could barely make out her noble, grave, tender, and majestic features (Alphonse de Lamartine, *Voyage en Orient*, 299). During their conversation he asked her if she ever entertained the idea of visiting England. "No. Never," she replied. "Your Europe is finished. I read the stars. Leave me my desert!" (ibid., 300 ff.). Commenting on Lady Stanhope's reclusivity, her bent for occultism, and her disgust for European religions, he praised her deism, for being a blend of ancient desert mysteries—Islam, Druse mysticism, Christianity, Judaism—and her own brand of astrology and occultism. Together they accounted, he explained, for her extraordinary generosity to the poor. Nor did he believe her mad as others had claimed. Madness was nowhere written in her beautiful and straightforward gaze. Although her conversation frequently changed course, when she focused on mystical matters her words were lucid. She had a prophetic mind (ibid., 306). Solitude, he added, concentrates and fortifies all the faculties of the soul (ibid., 312). Clearly, her genius had kindled the heart of the great Romantic poet.

When Dr. Meryon returned to Dar Djoun in July 1837, he was aghast at Lady Stanhope's poverty, the rapacity of her servants who had stolen nearly everything she possessed, her unpredictable mood swings, and her moments of uninterrupted talking followed by learned discourses on astrology. At times her face took on an expression of cruelty, and she was driven to beating her servants. In sadness, she did not weep. Rather, she howled. Her teeth mostly gone, her grin took on inhuman contours. More and more did she rely on medicine men who believed in bleedings and the drinking of strange concoctions made out of tree bark and other natural elements, which served only to weaken her physically. That she overindulged in Turkish baths aggravated her so-called asthma—in reality, tuberculosis.

She generally remained in her bedroom, resting by day and fully awake by night, smoking her pipe that a servant would refill every fifteen minutes. Unwilling to reveal the increasingly thin contours of her body, the still coquettish Lady Stanhope had taken to wearing large white robes, veiling her chin with a kaffiyeh. For the peasantry in near and distant areas, she had become a holy woman.

Prior to Dr. Meryon's departure for England in August 1838, he saw despair written on her face (*Nun of Lebanon*, 402). Her room and house had been transformed into a conglomerate of dust, dirt, and cobwebs. Creditors hounded her. Her pension had been stopped. When not overly weak, she tended to her correspondence. The once dynamic and gorgeously attractive Lady Hester Stanhope, now a prey to high fevers, was wasting away. She died on June 23, 1839, at the age of sixty-three. News of her passing spread from town to town: the Sytt had died.

Mr. Moore, the British consul at Beirut, and Mr. Thomson, an American missionnary, buried her according to her wishes in the garden of Dar Djoun that she had designed. The vault in the garden of Dar Djoun was opened; the servants took out the bones of Captain Lousteneau, and they were piled at the head. A servant stuck a lighted taper through each of the eye sockets of the Frenchman's skull. In the dead of night, with the terrible heap of bones lit by the tapers, Stanhope's body was laid to rest, and the Union Jack was placed over the plain box (ibid., 406).

When the British consul and the missionary entered her thirty-five-room house, they found it filled with trash, dirt, moth-eaten Arab saddles, old medicines, and sundry other worthless objects. Lady Stanhope had lived on the magic of illusion, and she became a legend.

Bettina L. Knapp

BIBLIOGRAPHY

Armstrong, Marlin. *Lady Hester Stanhope*. London: Gerald Howe, 1927.

Cleveland, Catherine, Duchess of. *The Life and Letters of Lady Hester Stanhope*. London: J. Murray, 1914.

Correspondence of Mr. Thomas Coutts, Lady Hester Stanhope and others (by kind permission of Messrs. Coutts). Dyce-Foster Collection. South Kensington Museum (correspondence between Lady Hester Stanhope and Sir Hildebrand Oakes and others).

Haslip, Joan. *Lady Hester Stanhope, a Biography*. London: Cobden-Sanders, 1934.

Lamartine, Alphonse de. *Voyage en Orient*. Paris: Librairie Nizet, 1992.

Paston, George. *Little Memoirs of the Nineteenth Century*. London: Grant Richards and New York: E. E. Dutton and Co., 1902.

Stanhope, Lady Hester. *Memoirs of the Lady Hester Stanhope, as Related by Herself in Conversations with her Physician; Comprising her Opinions and Anecdotes of some of the Most Remarkable Persons of her Time* (1845). 3 vols. Ed. James Hogg. Salzburg, Austria: Institut für Anglistik und Amerikanistik, Universität Salzburg, 1985.

——. *Travels of Lady Hester Stanhope*. (Narrated by her physician Charles Lewis Meryon) (1846). 3 vols. Ed. James Hogg. Salzburg, Austria: Institut für Anglistik und Amerikanistik, Universität Salzburg, 1983.

——. *The Nun of Lebanon: The Love Affair of Lady Hester Stanhope and Michael Bruce*. Ed. Ian Bruce. London: Collins, 1951.

Strachey, Lytton. *Books and Characters French and English*. London: Chatto & Windus, 1922.

Fredrika Bremer

(1801–1865)

> To travel in foreign countries, which I have done a lot, has
> always worked wonders on me. It revives me and is beneficial
> to me. It encourages me to discover new objectives as I try to
> fulfill my life's mission. . . . I shall again be going away for a
> while to foreign countries and shall return later to work, live—
> and die—in my beloved fatherland where perhaps, before I die,
> I'll see the dawn of [a] more beautiful day.
>
> (Fredrika Bremer, 1856 letter to the editor of *Biografiskt Lexikon*)

Fredrika Bremer was fifty-five years old when she went "away for a while" on a journey that lasted five years (1856–61) and took her to many countries in Europe and in the Middle East. She was born in 1801 in Åbo, a small city in Finland where her grandfather had settled. He was a clever entrepreneur who became a rich and prominent citizen of the little town. Fredrika, however, recalled hardly anything about her birthplace, because her family moved to Sweden when she was only three. When, in 1856, she had already become a renowned novelist not only in Sweden but in Europe as well as in the United States, she wrote to the editor of what was then the Swedish *Who's Who*:

> The first clear memory I have of my childhood is of the cabin of the ship
> that, in the year 1804, brought my parents over to Sweden together with
> their four children. I sat in the cabin impatiently kicking my tiny feet up

against the windowpanes that shut me in. As a consequence I and my siblings, with our nursemaids, were allowed to go on deck and dance around the mast. I consider this to be proof of my lifelong love of freedom. (1856 letter to the editor of *Biografiskt Lexikon*)

Her parents brought up their many children to study and memorize in order to become brilliant conversationalists. Tutors in English, German, and French were hired. The girls were expected to learn all social graces and were subjected to the regimented upbringing of their well-intentioned but authoritarian father, who took the family on a yearlong European tour in horse-drawn covered carriages, but at home forced his daughters to carry on feminine pursuits and wait for marriage.

Her early success as the anonymous author of *The H—Family* (published in Uppsala in 1831) coincided with her father's death, an event that set her free. Her brother was nominally her new legal guardian, but she went to court to win her own majority, promising herself to make women's lives visible in her writings. She hired a tutor, Per Böklin, a philosopher and theologian, who instantly became interested in this unusual pupil and her quest for what the role of women should be in this world. Eventually he fell in love with her, but she withdrew, reluctant to give up her freedom. She fled to Norway, where she spent more than four years intermittently during the 1830s.

In Norway she stayed at the estate "Tomb" owned by her friend Countess Stina Sommerhielm, who graciously let her come and go as she wished. Bremer needed solitude in the morning for her writing, and in the afternoon and evening she read or socialized with friends and acquaintances. In an 1835 letter to her family she described how she found life in Norway healthier and more carefree than in Sweden: there was less class consciousness and more equality between the sexes. She had heard that people way up in the north—north of Trondheim—enjoyed a nobler culture than that in the south where the "Tomb" was located. When she asked why this was so, she was told that people in that cold and dark northern climate, which prevailed for the greater part of the year, had fewer diversions and less entertainment and therefore were intellectually driven to search their inner world: "It is there that they must find what makes life desirable and beautiful." Bremer was skeptical: "The very struggle for bread, for existence alone, must be a heavy task up in the north, which hardly leaves time to pursue a culture of refinement."—"Not at all, to administer food is not a difficult assignment. The big fisheries, their most important commercial business, can easily answer their needs. Their material ones are few. For the most part those inhabitants are well-fed and think of themselves as happy people." Perhaps they are better off, Bremer pondered, than those who live in Paris or in London. She remarked, however, that the Norwegians are somewhat *aigre-doux* (bitter-sweet) when it comes to their relationship with Swedes. But Bremer thought the Norwegians had a right to be *aigre-doux*.

Homes of the New World: Impressions of America (1853–54, Eng. trans. 1854), *England in the Autumn of 1851* (Eng. trans. 1853), and *Life in the Old World* (1860–62, Eng. trans. 1860–65) are the titles of three global works by Bremer that together comprise thirteen volumes and constitute a remarkable travelogue. Her travels remade this novelist into an outstanding journalist. Her journalistic technique may be summed up as follows: stay still in place, focus on what happens to surround you, keeping in mind what you think is missing, and write down what triggers your interest. She started writing her vivid journals after leaving home, illustrating them frequently with drawings and watercolors. She went around with pen and paper, paintbox and sketchbook, sitting down here and there, talking to different people. They were genuinely curious about this tiny person—barely five feet tall—who was world-famous and yet seemed so pleasant and unassuming. She sketched their portraits while she asked them questions about life in that given place, or she drew pictures of its flora and fauna. Then she went home to write her impressions. These finally were collected in her magnum opus, her thirteen volumes of travelogue. The breadth of this work is stunning, and its flavor fresh and spicy with an ample pinch of humor. It is a real tour de force.

Our multifaceted verbal artist began her colorful and engrossing tale in Norway—understandably, since Swedes and Norwegians are siblings, and, as siblings, they habitually compete. Sweden is the big brother, and as big brothers the Swedes sometimes act condescendingly toward their rivals, which, of course, leaves the younger brother fuming. There is a Swedish saying to the effect that what Norwegians like best to hear people talk about is Norway and the Norwegians.

Bremer spent the years 1849–51 in the United States and has told us what it was like to travel using all kinds of transportation means: steam-ships to and from America, riverboats down the Mississippi, stagecoaches on rocky prairie roads to reach Swedish immigrant settlements, the ship on the Ohio River that transported both animals and people and had the passenger deck placed between the hogs and the poultry decks, a rickety train out to Concord, Massachusetts, to see Ralph Waldo Emerson, and so forth. Of course, she most often went by horse and buggy, but when, at the age of almost sixty, she arrived in Jaffa, her destination being Jerusalem, she was told that the only way she could get there was on horseback. That she had never done before. Dauntless, she mounted, and rode for two days over the plains and up through the mountains along steep ravines and over high peaks until she reached the holy city. "It seems that I was born to sit on horseback," she wrote then.

Her travelogue is chockful of surprising details, sharp-eyed observations, ironic commentaries, comic episodes, philosophical discourses, historical studies, and here and there a sermon. This richness puts us on a labyrinthine path into the searching mind and generous heart of Fredrika Bremer. In Philadelphia, for example, she spent time with Quaker families and was deeply moved by their spirit, yet she had a hard time keeping awake during their services. Her first impression of Chicago? The ugliest city she had ever encountered! In New Orleans, she commented that the white women used much too much white face powder. In Cuba, the crescent moon floated like a boat instead of standing straight up as in Sweden, and during the sugarcane harvest she heard the whips of the slavedrivers whining outside her window late into the night. In Washington, she was present in the Senate when the message arrived that President Taylor was dying and was not expected to survive the day. Bremer had been in the White House for tea just a few days earlier. She was present when the new president, Millard Fillmore, was installed. She had gone every day to the Senate to hear the debate on the "compromise bill." Should the new state of California become a free or a slave state, or would the compromise win (meaning that California would become a free state, but in recompense the free states would have to return to their owners those slaves who had escaped from the slave states)? Bremer waited and waited for the debate to end and the voting to begin, but in the end she was overcome by the heat and humidity—despite four daily cold baths—which forced her out of Washington. She left town together with Dorothea Dix, the lobbyist for special treatment of the mentally ill. Before they reached Baltimore, Dix had told Bremer the entire fascinating story of her life.

In New England, and especially around Boston, Bremer met many humanists and scientists, legislators, and preachers whose names we recognize from streets and avenues in Boston and Cambridge. She met feminists and abolitionists, artists, actors, and authors, and stayed a few days with Robert and Maria Lowell. Henry Wadsworth Longfellow gave a dinner in her honor. She spoke at length in her heavily accented English with Nathaniel Hawthorne, who later admitted he had understood not a word—but when the two saw each other again in Rome, Italy, he was beguiled by her friendly personality. And, of course, Bremer could not think of New England without the genius of Ralph Waldo Emerson, who had reviewed her books and who received her so graciously at his home in Concord, Massachusetts.

In her book about America she included four letters reflecting on her many encounters and adventures. These letters are addressed to the Danish Queen Caroline Amalie, whom she befriended on her stopover in Denmark on her way to America; to the Danish theologian Hans Lassen Martensen, whose magnum opus in systematic theology Bremer had read in galley stage in his home; to the Danish professor of physics Hans Christian Örsted, who had invited her to listen to his lectures; and to her mentor and old friend Per Böklin. In these letters she theorized about the United States' role in history and its meaning for the future of democracy, about what influence women would have in shaping a new society, and what would happen to the Negro after the "doomsday of a civil war" that she perceived was approaching.

Back in England in the fall of 1851, she wrote a series of articles sketching a grim portrait of British social conditions for the Swedish evening paper *Aftonbladet*. By now she had learned how to incorporate skillfully her wonderings, her observations, and her conclusions. She focused on the gap between rich and poor, wretched poverty and unscrupulous affluence, dirty streets and houses with broken windows on the one hand and, on the other, colossal sums of money that the Crown spent to house its horses and dogs. Her social conscience sought relief. She sensed a change for the better and saw a ray of hope in the involvement of the socialist unions. Her experiences had converted her to a Social Democrat of Christian persuasion. She, together with Florence Nightingale and Harriet Beecher Stowe, were the first women invited to speak at the first International Socialist Congress in Brussels, Belgium, in 1857.

Why did Fredrika Bremer travel so prodigiously, exiling herself from her native country for years on end? Why did she write so extensively about what she saw, heard, tasted, smelled, and touched? She was a novelist of the Romantic school, like the Brontë sisters. Why, then, did she not sit at home—she was well off and could live comfortably—and concentrate on her writing? Her ambition had never been to execute an all-encompassing Baedeker guide. The answer is fairly simple. She had early on become painfully aware what a terrible handicap it was to be a woman. Accordingly, she decided to find out whether it really was in God's design for women to be subordinate to men. She knew that only through study could her question be answered: study like a man, but think as a woman. With her mentor, Per Böklin, she had delved into philosophy. The Hegelian philosophy of history was predominant at the time, and Bremer happily adopted its view that world history was in constant development toward a higher goal. Women, she believed, finally would be recognized for what they are and be seen as the equals of men.

When she heard that changes in this direction were beginning to take place in the United States, she felt compelled to witness the development and its ramifications with her own eyes. Early on she had come to the conclusion that men think and feel and express themselves differently from women, so she warned Böklin not to change a single word in the manuscripts of her *Homes of the New World: Impressions of America*. Women must speak their thoughts and feelings as they see fit. To achieve her end, she lent her senses, her thoughts and imagination to her sisters around the world, thus helping them to form a woman's perspective on life. In addition, she was convinced that it was equally important for men to learn to understand women's way of conceptualizing the world, women's habits of thinking and feeling. Foremost in her mind was an emphasis on all women's aspiration to peace. That women could make peace, cause it, and effect it, was, for Bremer, an axiom. Her faith in women's desire for peace compelled her to write an appeal, published on the first page of the *London Times* at the height of the Crimean War, in which she called on all women in the world to unite for peace.

What Bremer had seen, and the arguments that she had heard in America about the Negro and about the abolition of slavery—that the Negro is incapable of logical reasoning, that the Negro has a genius for music and dance but has no understanding of government and needs a strong hand to lead him—was by analogy what finally made her into an outspoken feminist. In the novel *Hertha* (1856), which she wrote after her return home from England, her heroine, Hertha, is a feminist who is fiercely fighting patriarchy in the person of her father, who really is an ogre. Hertha's goal is to abolish the whole unfair, patriarchal system and let equal rights be the law of the land. Women should have the right to vote and to pursue any profession that they choose—but to say so overtly was rather risky in 1856. Hers was an attack against the ruling conservative establishment. Therefore, she fled Sweden as soon as the book was ready and before the reviewers had time to express their opinions. She knew they would be less than favorable, and she was right.

Life in the Old World contains pages from Bremer's diary during the five years she spent traveling from Sweden to Switzerland, then over the Alps down to Rome. Religious and ethical issues surface now and again. The individuals she searched out to visit and to interview or with whom to correspond were often leaders of social and religious movements. In Switzerland she examined the Free Church disestablished from the state, which had intrigued her as a model for the church of the future, but she found it too patriarchal and conventional, lacking in energy of the spirit. Therefore she went on to Italy to familiarize herself with the Catholic culture, the Mother Church of all Christian denominations. For a week she stayed in a nunnery, following its routine, but was bothered by the Mother Superior, who sought desperately to convert her. Bremer also had an interview with the mighty pope, Pius IX, who was "much more polite to me than I was to him," she wrote. In Rome she composed her last novel, *Father and Daughter* (1860). The theme is reconciliation between a headstrong daughter and her loving father, who in the end lives in the charming home with its flourishing garden that the daughter has created. This novel turned Hertha inside out: patriarchy was replaced by matriarchy. *Hertha* is Bremer's strongest statement for the feminist cause; *Father and Daughter* is a much weaker sister. But these two novels assured Bremer's place as Sweden's foremost feminist, the mother of the Swedish women's movement.

On this, her last journey, she felt herself to be more and more of a "pilgrim." She was now looking for the sources of civilization in order to be able to discern the future. She had been unhappy when her ship was denied entry into Egypt due to a cholera epidemic, but she sailed on to

Palestine—to that land where the crucial events of world history had occurred and she could walk from place to place contemplating and meditating on the life and death and resurrection of Jesus Christ, her Lord and Savior.

Bremer was rather perplexed by the chaos, noise, and commotion that greeted her, and the ruckus in the Holy Sepulchre. She disliked the pictures, the singing, the ceremonies, the competition in and around churches and mosques, with monks, priests, and mullahs, and throngs of people everywhere. At first she was repelled by this Oriental culture, but, as always, after having given herself time to reflect, Bremer became more tolerant. Later, in Constantinople, she wrote a commendation of Hagia Sofia's unadorned magnificence, from which we can surmise that she had the tumultuous memory of the "kitsch" in the Church of the Holy Sepulchre in mind.

It might be easier to recite the countries in Europe that were *not* visited by Bremer than to enumerate all those she saw. Apart from her two minutely detailed volumes on *Two Years in Switzerland and Italy* (1861), one country in particular must be mentioned: Greece, the cradle of Western civilization. Together with friends she studied its history and the great classical authors. She lived in Athens for two years; and when it became too hot in the summers, the king and the queen lent her their yacht to sail around the islands. Bremer was intensely interested in all she saw, and she made it quite clear to the royal couple that she was not satisfied with the country's slow progress toward equality. She even quarreled with the queen over the education of women.

When Bremer returned to Sweden from Greece, she was sixty-one years old and had still four more years to live. At first, her life was very busy with correspondence to and from people whom she had encountered; then there were her manuscripts to edit, and many, many solicitations for money, for articles and poems. She had numerous friends, and her keen interest in Swedish politics made her social life stimulating and varied. She applauded the new liberal government, and she in turn was applauded. After a few years, however, she began to withdraw. Her eyesight was failing, and she had to hire a student to read for her. Like Mohandas Gandhi, she took up spinning, practicing every day. As she had preannounced in her letter to the editor of the Swedish *Who's Who*, she had now finished her "life's mission," and she was grateful that she could die in her "beloved fatherland," where she had been able to see a new dawn rising. She died at Årsta, near Stockholm, in 1865.

Brita Stendahl

BIBLIOGRAPHY

Bremer, Fredrika. *The H—Family* (1831). New York: Harper, 1844.

————. *England in the Autumn of 1851; or Sketches of a Tour of England.* Trans. L. A. H. Boulogne: Merridew, 1853.

————. *Homes of the New World: Impressions of America* (1853–54). 2 vols. New York: Harper, 1854.

————. *Hertha* (1856). New York: G. P. Putnam, 1856.

————. *Life in the Old World* (1860–62). 3 vols. Philadelphia: T. B. Petersen, 1860–65.

————. *Father and Daughter: A Portraiture from Life.* Trans. Mary Howitt. Philadelphia: T. B. Petersen, 1860 [?].

————. *Two Years in Switzerland and Italy.* 2 vols. Trans. Mary Howitt. London: Hurst and Blackett, 1861.

Stendahl, Brita K. *The Education of a Self-made Woman: Fredrika Bremer, 1801–1865.* Lewiston, N.Y.: Edwin Mellen Press, 1994.

CHAPTER

5

Princess Cristina Trivulzio di Belgiojoso
(1808–1871)

I shall rest at night at the foot of a tree where I staked my tent.
By day I shall cross hill and vale on an excellent horse.
(Princess Cristina Trivulzio di Belgiojoso,
Souvenirs dans l'exil, trans. Brombert, 200)

The princess brandishing an Italian flag, marching into Milan at the head of a battalion of volunteers in defiance of Austrian occupation, is the same Princess Trivulzio di Belgiojoso who had held sway in a Parisian salon, would cross uncharted deserts and inhospitable mountains on horseback in the Middle East—and wrote voluminously.

An intellectual and a revolutionary, she moved between Milan and Paris—wherever a literary salon or a barricade was to be found (Giuliana Morandini, *La voce che è in lei*, 61). She was one of the few important women figures of the Italian Risorgimento and of Italian and French political and cultural life in the nineteenth century, the translator into French of Giambattista Vico's *Scienza nuova*, and the author of travel writings and of at least a dozen volumes on Italian history and politics.

Dynamic, volatile, untiringly involved in political plots, and often calumnied, Trivulzio was an ardent patriot, an active conspirator against Austria, and "a thorn in Metternich's diplomatic side." She staunchly upheld Italy's right to become a nation and passionately advocated a constitutional monarchy with a free press, education for women and the lower classes, and the right of nationals to travel freely (Beth Archer Brombert, *Cristina*, 5–6). Humane and generous, capable of abnegation and sacrifice, and aware of social inequities, she had an innate sense of tenderness, charity, and compassion toward the poor, the humble, and the suffering. In her grandiose conception of things, she gave of herself and of her possessions, both to help the needy and to emancipate and resurrect Italy. She embraced socialist ideas, understanding that political problems are compounded by social problems, and that freedom would be a sorry thing indeed if it did not elevate people morally at the same time as it brought material improvement (Luigi Severgnini, *La Principessa di Belgiojoso*, 52). Her social ideas were based on Saint Simonianism and Fourierism, and the idea of the phalanstery in which the group's every need, including food, would be satisfied, work would be done freely, according to individual aptitudes—an idea that she would energetically apply on her property in Ciaq-Mag-Oglou in Turkey (see below).

Born in Milan to the wealthy aristocratic Trivulzio family, Cristina was brought up in the Lombard liberal tradition but was a misfit in her society because of her personal choices and her conspiratorial tendencies. An unidentified French phrenologist had concluded that she was strong-willed, vain, self-possessed and gregarious, masculine and bellicose, like a Bradamant (the "Virgin Knight" warrior-heroine in Ariosto's *Orlando Furioso*), a Joan of Arc, or a Catherine Sforza, and wrote that as a child she must have had a passion for reading tales of chivalry. Refuting the phrenologist's deductions, she asserts that she had always been horrified by the spilling of blood and that until her marriage she had never read novels other than those of Maria Edgeworth (1767–1849, an English author of innocuous novels, most dealing with Irish life). To the phrenologist's presumption that she was happy and vivacious in her childhood and was now subject to fits of melancholy, she replies:

> The opposite is true. I was a morose child, serious, introverted, quiet. I do not know how I acquired the even and cheerful disposition that I now enjoy. . . . You say I was vain and liked to look at myself in the mirror. It's only very recently that I suspect I might be beautiful; . . . in my childhood I thought I was positively ugly, and I still think I was an ugly child. Often

I was punished because I preferred to wear old dresses rather than new
ones, which I used to put on backwards rather than look into a mirror.
(quoted in Aldobrandino Malvezzi, *Cristina di Belgiojoso*, vol. 1, p. 47)

Might there be a link between her aversion to looking into mirrors and
her later manly comportment? The French philosopher and political figure Victor Cousin described her as of female sex but masculine in character (Severgnini, introduction, *Ricordi dell'esilio*, 11). Her anticonformism
roused criticism even among the French avant-garde. Considered anaph-
rodisiac by her contemporaries (though her name is linked sentimentally
and sexually with the French historian François Auguste Mignet and with
George Sand [Brombert, 6]), she was nonetheless feminine and seductive.
Despite her love for Mignet, she set an example for the emancipation of
women, rejecting ties and vowing to lead a life that could not be the usual
one. She yearned for the freedom of a "gypsy," having had enough of
ideological, social, and marital disappointments (Morandini, 62).

As a feminist, she strongly denounced the condition of women, protested against injustices, sought equality of the sexes, and expressed her
social concerns with ethical rigor. She saw woman not as inferior but as
"tenacious, persevering, and unyielding in her convictions" (quoted in
Severgnini, 251). The first to offer the West a description of harem life on
the basis of personal experience, she wrote that if a Turk treats a woman
as though she were deprived of reasoning power, it is because *she* does
nothing to better her condition *(Vita intima e vita nomade in Oriente*, 113).

Trivulzio was trained in drawing and design, music and singing; she
read in French and English, and wrote prolifically in Italian. A skilled
horsewoman and passionate mountain climber, she knew her way along
the paths and slopes of the mountains reflected in Lake Como. At sixteen
she married, against the will of her parents and of Milanese aristocracy,
the dissolute Prince Emilio di Belgiojoso, eight years her elder—probably
because they had similar patriotic ideals (he had an established reputation
as a Carbonaro). It was a marriage of impulse for her, of convenience for
him (Brombert, 22). A rake and a squanderer, Belgiojoso eventually
infected his already sickly wife with syphilis. In fact, she suffered physically her entire life from convulsions, fainting spells, palpitations, headaches, nausea, visceral pain, and thoracic discomfort, but she cured her
own wounds and fevers, and always retained her mental equilibrium and
direction of purpose (Brombert, 22, 121).

The couple separated by mutual consent after four years of marriage—a separation that sealed her destiny. The disenchanted princess henceforth would study, travel, and write. She had found the intellectual freedom she needed, and her spirit of independence soared. During her "bookworm" period, besides undergoing the influence of Chateaubriand's *Itinéraire de Paris à Jérusalem* (1811) which combines travel, aestheticism, and religiosity, she became knowledgeable in medicine, economics, and agronomy. When doctors were unavailable, her acquired knowledge of diseases and pharmacology allowed her to help those around her, as well as herself. During her later travels in Turkey she discovered a tobacco-like leaf, *tombeky*, that, used in a narghile, relieved her neuralgia more effectively than any Western medication (Brombert, 31).

Having disseminated Risorgimento ideas throughout Italy, she was under surveillance by Austrian police spies and in 1830 was forced to flee to France, where the July 1830 revolution had reawakened the hopes of Italian exiles abroad. As a political propagandist, she went to Marseilles, spending several months collaborating with Italian insurrectionary committees. She then went to Toulon and Lyons to contact the most important expatriates, but ultimately decided that, as the guiding spirit of Italian exiles in France, she would be more useful in Paris. Meanwhile, the Austrian government had sequestered her possessions in Italy and frozen her assets, so the princess herself was now a political refugee, precipitated from a life of splendor to a state of absolute isolation—without even a maid! Her anguish and distress mounted in Paris:

> Rich heiress, brought up in the traditions of Milanese aristocracy, I knew absolutely nothing about the realities of life. Never had I touched money and I could not imagine what a five franc piece represented. On the other hand, I did not hestitate to classify an ancient coin according to its value. . . . I could paint, sing, play the piano, but did not know how to hem a handkerchief, cook a boiled egg, or even order a meal. The task of ordering and paying for my household had always been entrusted to a servant. . . . But . . . for a few weeks, I prepared my modest meals with my own white hands. (*Souvenirs dans l'exil*, trans. Brombert, 115)

Her initial difficulties ended when to her rescue came Madame de Récamier, the Duchess de Broglie, and the "Hero of Two Worlds," the

Marquis de Lafayette, whose assiduous visits she received in her kitchen, and who helped her to cook in her modest fifth-floor mansarde at 7 rue Neuve-St. Honoré (now rue Vignon) within sight of the Madeleine. Refusing to borrow money, she was reduced to giving drawing and painting lessons, but a career in journalism began with the publication in *Le Constitutionnel* of her articles on Italian politics (Brombert, 93). Not only did she further defend the Italian revolution in a series of articles in the *Revue des Deux Mondes*; she had the courage to address the French Chamber of Deputies on the subject of the ills afflicting Italy, calling for the help of France for the triumph of liberty and the defeat of foreign tyranny—and she was soundly applauded (Severgnini, 51).

Having regained possession of her revenues (though her estate remained sequestered until 1838), she opened a scintillating salon that dominated the mundane intellectual scene and became a point of reference for exiles as well as for Liszt, Lamartine, Hugo, Balzac, Dumas fils, Sand, Merimée, Vigny, Tocqueville, Cousin, Rossini, Bellini, Chopin, Meyerbeer, Delacroix, Ampère, and others who gravitated toward her. She herself frequented the numerous salons in the Paris of citizen-king Louis Philippe, where she reached the apex of popularity and notoriety. Among those who celebrated her smile and her beauty were Heinrich Heine, who would immortalize her in his *Florentine Nights*, and Alfred de Musset, who felt one could get lost in her big black eyes and never again find one's way (Severgnini, 35) and who, for nine years, refused to believe he could not seduce her (Brombert, 6).

After ten years in exile in France, she was permitted to reenter Italy in 1840. Returning to the ancient estate of the Trivulzios at Locate near Milan, she developed an experimental social project for farmers inspired by Saint-Simon and Fourier. After the failure of the 1848 revolution in Lombardy, she went to Rome, where the Republic was struggling for survival, and at the behest of Giuseppe Mazzini served as general director of Roman hospitals and head of a committee to help the wounded. Intrepid under the bombings during the French siege, she quickly organized ambulance services, with Margaret Fuller working at her side, and gained the admiration of William Wetmore Story and Henry James (Brombert, 67). She personally wrote and issued a manifesto exhorting the women of Rome to go to the pilgrims' hospice in order to manufacture cartridges. When the short-lived Roman Republic fell and French troops entered the city in July 1849, she fled to Rome's port at Civitavecchia, boarded the ship *Mentor* going to Malta—"no Shangri-La" (Brombert, 196)—and thus began her Eastern peregrinations—to Malta, Greece, and Constantinople—as recorded in *Souvenirs dans l'exil* (1850; *Ricordi dell'esilio*, 1978). She describes and analyzes her adventures pungently and provocatively, with an attentive and knowing eye, searching for truths not found in the works of storytellers and travelers.

At first she writes humoristically of her own ignorance in thinking that the capital of Malta bore the same name as the island and learning with great surprise that the capital city is Valletta. This offers her an opportunity to display her knowledge of the fact that the city takes its name from its founder, "the great master La Valette" [Jean Parisot de la Valette (1494–1568), Grand Master of the Order of the Knights of Malta, who defended the island against the Turks led by Soliman II in the siege of 1565, and founded the city of La Valletta]. But then she gives vent to her antipathetic feelings toward the city's drab, monotonous streets and buildings, the arid, parched countryside, and the small stature of the "dissolute" people with their yellow, bilious complexion, round flat faces, big wide mouths, short flat noses, bulging lifeless eyes, low narrow foreheads, wooly hair, guttural, nasal speech, and "ferocious ignorance" (*Ricordi dell'esilio*, 31). The island of Malta, filled with refugees (including hypocritical Jesuits driven from Naples about whom she is quick to ironize), offers "much to arouse not only horror but disgust" (ibid., 29–30). But it is only rarely that Trivulzio's princessly fastidiousness shows through in the East. As far as Malta is concerned, however, the only thing "beautiful, good and excellent" is the sun ("Apollo"), and she can "understand all those lovely ladies who allowed themselves to be ensnared by Apollo" (ibid., 31).

She offers some humoristic linguistic considerations connected with the origins and development of the Maltese language, then turns to political matters connected with the granting of a "shadow of a constitution" by the English government. The highlight of her visit in Malta, however, is the spectacle aboard a Moroccan ship anchored in the harbor carrying to Mecca Muslim pilgrims, including Moors, Arabs, Maltese, Tartars, Malaysians, soldiers, sailors, holy men, merchants, intellectuals, musicians, courtesans, and slaves in variegated costume. She seems thoroughly to relish her first taste of the Orient, but she leaves Malta as soon as she receives enough money to do so, and reaches Athens after having been quarantined on the island of Aegina (in the Saronic Gulf of Greece) because of the spreading cholera epidemic.

In Athens, she stayed several months fraternizing with her compatriots who had taken refuge there, and visiting the city and its historic surroundings. "For me until now, Greece had been no more than two points in the past and nothing in the present. Ancient Greece was the homeland of all cultured people at a time when culture was not in common currency," she writes in *Souvenirs dans l'exil* (trans. Brombert, 197). More than by the beauty of Greece's ancient monuments, she was struck by the squalor and neglect of the forsaken people. She saw their society as so deprived of civility that each victim of a robbery was obliged to steal in order to survive, and she marveled at the benevolence with which Greeks treat their thieves (Severgnini, introduction, *Ricordi dell'esilio*, 89). She was also appalled by the armed turbaned figures that foreign ministers employed to eliminate their adversaries: they "seem to spy on passersby, showing their teeth like real bulldogs" (*Ricordi dell'esilio*, 143); thus, for her own self-protection, she carefully avoided the Austrian embassy, "not wishing to offer Baron von Sturmer," she writes whimsically, "the occasion to immortalize me in a patriotic song, or some other honor of this sort" (ibid., 144).

Hoping to fare better in Turkey—"perhaps the Turkish government will be more 'christian'" is her ironic remark (quoted in Brombert, 197)—she wrote to request financial help from a U.S. representative in Rome, who commented sadly on the fact that "the lady . . . who represents and defends certain principles is obliged to flee from Christianity to a pagan country in search of security and tolerance" (quoted in Severgnini, 187).

Leaving Athens at the end of spring 1850, she set sail on the French ship *Telemachus* for Constantinople. Her descriptions during the voyage abound with charming images: "The sea is so smooth," she writes, "that one feels like putting on a pair of skates and gliding over its surface" (*Ricordi dell'esilio*, 147). The port city of Smyrna (Izmir) in the distance, set out in the shape of an amphitheater, appears to her as though rising out of the sea, its elegant minarets resembling the crowns of aquatic plants. Surely she has reached the fabulous land of Arabian tales! When she steps ashore, however, and sees the city up close, she is consternated at the sight of the "dark and filthy streets, crammed with a raucous and coarse population" (*Ricordi dell'esilio*, 148). (In her later work *Asie Mineure et Syrie, souvenirs de voyage* [1858; *Vita intima e vita nomade in oriente,* 1993], she will contrast Greek villages that "sadden and do not attract" because they are founded with only practical considerations in mind, while Turkish villages do "enchant and attract" because the Muslim, having an innate taste for natural beauty, sets his village in the shade of beautiful trees, in the midst of green fields, or on the banks of clear streams. Unfortunately, however, both Greek and Turkish houses, seen up close, are all equally ugly, dark, and uninhabitable [*Vita intima*, 78–79].) In Turkey, for example, in the city of Cerkes (ancient Antoniopolis), she will ask her reader to

> [i]magine scattered shacks made of wood and mud and falling to pieces.
> . . . The spaces between the houses have become garbage receptacles. Half-
> wild dogs, jackals, and birds of prey function as street cleaners. . . . There
> are cities in inland Asia Minor in which people have to cross the streets . . .
> [on] stilts. . . . Add to this the fact that a person of medium stature risks
> bumping into the protruding roofs of the houses if he strays the slightest
> bit away from the center of the street. That's a faithful description of
> Cerkes and of all the cities of Asia Minor. (ibid., 41)

In the Jewish quarter of Smyrna she enters a café that she compares to some lowly tavern on the outskirts of Paris, and where she gives a demonstration of her agility in crossing her legs and sitting on her heels, duly impressing her audience. Her feat, she writes tongue-in-cheek, gains her an invitation to visit the harem of a rich financier. Here she sees "girls and women whose splendorous beauty is beyond description" (*Ricordi dell'esilio*, 149), and she artistically and literarily brings into play contrasts of gold (blond) and lignite (black): the colors Ariosto uses to depict Alcina (Carnal Pleasure personified in *Orlando Furioso*) are gold (the curls of her long blond hair), pink (of her cheeks), and ivory (her forehead), while all the beauty of the women in Smyrna undulates in "soft waves, black and shiny like lignite" (ibid.). As for the European ideal of the full-breasted woman, Trivulzio notes here the "imperfection" of Turkish women's breasts, which she attributes to their mode of dressing and to their obesity (ibid., 150). But her interest in Oriental women would go much further than their anatomy and external appearances.

Leaving Smyrna, the next spectacle to meet her eyes was the "magnificent view of Constantinople and the banks of the Bosphorus" (ibid., 159).

She felt she might regain her strength amid the natural and artistic beauties of Constantinople, after three years of intense emotion and struggle.
But life in Turkey would offer its challenges: whenever she settled in new
lodgings, she had to choose a room with a northern exposure "so as not
to disturb the microscopic creatures that generally prefer to settle in rooms
with a southern exposure" (*Vita intima*, 126). Since the owners of her
Turkish lodging were not familiar with candles, they provided light for
her by burning resinous wood—lots of light but much more smoke. She
feels she deserves a Legion of Honor for bravery as she lies on a couch
between two windows in search of a breeze, surprised to see this princess
wearing only a cotton shift under a muslin robe, legs and feet bare, and
surrounded by handkerchiefs "to mop the sweat that streams down my
face and shoulders" (*Souvenirs dans l'exil*, 35, trans. Brombert, 200). Coffee
"not only is served without sugar, but inevitably half of the cup is filled
with dregs" (*Vita intima*, 140–41). And in a Turkish cemetery, she is dis-
concerted by the people picnicking on the grass, playing music, and dancing—while stray dogs extract human bones and flesh from broken caskets
in open graves (*Ricordi dell'esilio*, 162).

As for the ablutions that the Turks repeat several times a day, she is
hygienically daunted by their use of small dirty basins of water (*Vita
intima*, 141). Nor can she adapt easily to the Oriental usage of not mixing
solids and liquids as she consumes their copious meals, including:

> pilaf . . . , nothing less than a whole roasted kid or lamb [stuffed with raisins
> or rice], served with a soup made with lemon juice, which Europeans find
> unpalatable. The rest of the meal is composed of fifteen or twenty hors
> d'oeuvres: meatballs, every type of vegetable cooked in water and oil, zuc-
> chini with garlic in a sauce of clotted sour milk, tiny balls of rice or ground
> oats wrapped in uncooked vine leaves, pumpkin puree, sweets and jams
> served together with all the rest; dried, candied, and fresh fruits . . . ; honey,
> oatmeal cooked in milk and honey. . . . At the end of the meal . . . a large
> cup filled with *sherbett*, that is, water and syrup, is presented, around which
> wooden spoons are laid out; each guest in turn dips into the *sherbett* and
> brings the spoon to the mouth as many times as desired. *(Vita intima*, 70)

These gigantic meals satisfy hearty appetites but not the delicacy of the
princess's palate.

Contemplating the skyline of towers, minarets, and fortresses along the Golden Horn, she observes that "Paris and London are obviously the work of man, whereas Constantinople and its numerous suburbs seem to to have blossomed from the bowels of the earth like the trees of the forest" (*Ricordi dell'esilio*, 160). But her "critical spirit" intrudes, and she is surprised to find herself comparing the inner city to

> the dirtiest [Italian] village. . . . Black houses of rotting wood lined up along muddy streets . . . bazaars that they make such a din about are nothing but ugly sheds with their floors floundering in the mud, and they are plunged in darkness; the black, sticky walls are covered with cobwebs. (ibid., 160–61)

In the bazaars—"real museum[s] of knickknacks and trinkets, . . . perfumes"—her sight grows dim in the face of so many displays of percale prints, Persian and Indian cloth, and the eternal obligatory souvenirs to take back to Western women: perhaps some Turkish slippers with their upturned toes that are "impossible to wear"?; or perhaps she can send her friend a musk-deer bladder that produces the same immediate temporary somnolence that she experiences during Father Coeur's preachings in the church of St. Roch in Paris? (ibid., 161).

She retreated into the silence of a rented Turkish-style country home in a little village on the banks of the Bosphorus. How different from European living is her lifestyle there! And how advantageous it is to live in the East when one is exiled and has little money!

> To work, chat, or dream, one snuggles into a corner of a divan with one's legs tucked under. If sleep overcomes you, you stretch out your legs, lean back, close your eyes and you are asleep. Are you hungry? You clap your hands and are brought a platter of sliced roasted meats, garlic, raw onions, soured milk, an infusion of boiled grapes . . . . You place the platter on your knees . . . [and after being brought] an egg cup of coffee, you smoke through a carafe of water. This simplification of life delights me. What madness, I told myself, is the life of Europeans who claim they cannot do without a room for dining, another for chatting, for sleeping, etc., which require a multitude of furnishings. (*Souvenirs dans l'exil*, 35, trans. Brombert, 199–200)

As for the Eastern view of money, she is disabused of her Western standards when a harem woman requests some of the princess's used underwear; Trivulzio throws her instead a few piastres that are rejected: "I really thought, as a true Westerner, that money could substitute for buying and selling" (*Vita intima*, 95).

Focusing on the place of Christian Armenians in Turkish Muslim society, she first offers some historical background, beginning in the eighteenth century, of the Armenian people. They experienced religious persecution, but their merchants played an important role in the economy of the Ottoman Empire. Now she sees them as "people that have lost their nationality and at the same time are vile, greedy, crafty and cunning" (*Ricordi dell'esilio*, 163). She condemns their religious hypocrisy, but explains that their underlying fears and humiliations have caused them to renounce their faith in order to save their lives—and here she makes sharp analogies with the "cowards of Paris" blinded by fear after the February Revolution, whose comportment was not much different from that of the Armenians (ibid., 164–65). Little could Trivulzio know—and how horrified she would have been—that, from 1894 on, a plan for Armenian extermination was pursued under Ottoman sultan Abd Al-Hamud, culminating in the massacre of about 600,000 Armenians in 1915.

She meets swirling and howling dervishes, whose mystical rituals and hypnotic trances leave her skeptical about their capacity to reach heaven. She had always imagined a dervish to be a sort of Muslim beggar monk, a sort of holy man endowed with supernatural secrets; she discovers that nothing is further from the truth. Thanks to a few meaningless accoutrements, "every Muslim can transform himself instantly into a dervish" in order to gain "the veneration of the faithful"(44–45). He begs in order to earn a living during his travels, but easily becomes a thief if citizens are not generous. She concludes that the true dervish is a do-nothing and an imposter, who sometimes becomes a brigand when circumstances permit (46).

If the dervishes offered nothing new under the sun, on the banks of a small river at the far end of the Golden Horn she had occasion to see "many novelties" (*Ricordi dell'esilio*, 172): the harem of a wealthy Muslim slowly being drawn to the location in open *arabas* (wheeled carriages) draped in red woolen cloth embroidered with gold and silver, as though it were a religious procession. The heads of the oxen drawing the *arabas* were covered with tassels and ribbons of colored wool "resembling a Louis XIV wig" (ibid., 171); in front and behind walked black eunuchs bearing sabers and cudgels. At the side of the procession gravely walked the pashas with their retinues. The musicians played and the gypsies sang, predicting good luck, while the pathetic Turk, lying on a Smyrna rug carried by a slave, smoked his pipe in a sort of ecstasy; his eyes half-closed, watching the surrounding spectacle through a pink veil of opium fumes.

Trivulzio is mesmerized by the "sad and bizarre" sight of the pretty young women in the open carriages

> whose faces are uncovered . . . [and whose] physiognomy bears the imprint of malice and coquetry without the slightest trace of candor or naturalness. . . . Their big black eyes sparkle with gaiety, malice, and something very feminine. . . . Their childlike cheeks are vividly colored. . . . Their laughing mouths show little pearly teeth, and dimples abound on those charming faces. Some of them have their hair knotted at the top of the head; others intertwine it with precious stones and let it flow down their shoulders. Laminated pink gauze pants peep out from beneath layers of velvet mousseline and satin skirts, topped by layers of bodices and sleeves. (ibid., 171–72)

She is always amazed by women's costumes in the East: a Turkoman woman, for example, wears "an infinite quantity of turbans piled one upon the other . . . that rise to inaccessible heights . . . [and] scarves rolled spirally six or seven times to form a tower as high as that of the goddess Cybele" (*Vita intima*, 119). She also describes the sort of cape (*ferragiah*) that covers the entire figure of the woman, allowing her to preserve her incognito, "so that any infidelity on her part is not risky" (ibid., 113). Trivulzio almost seems to be suggesting that the veiled anonymity of Muslim women allows them to enjoy the same license as that of Venetian ladies under their dominoes.

Analyzing the harem as a mechanism of confinement and oppression of the woman—and not only in Turkish society—Trivulzio offers long descriptions of the various types of harems: those of the wealthy, those of the middle class, and those of the poor; those in the provinces and those in the cities. She is happy to note that polygamy is a greater stain among the rich than the poor, and that as one works up to the bourgeoisie and the higher spheres, vice intensifies. She praises the peasant couple she observes in the countryside: he loves his wife as a father and as a lover, and she is free—not a prisoner within the walls of his harem. "The life of of the Turkish peasant couple resembles that of the Christian peasant," she writes, "and, I say regretfully, the former could serve as a model for the latter" (ibid., 101). But at the same time she points out that the Turk who has never left his province is profoundly ignorant; he knows only the pleasures of the senses and repose, which he prolongs and varies as much as he can through use of opium, hashish, alcohol, and tobacco, even as the wealthy, noble Turk of Constantinople who has frequented European society "hide[s] a horrible skeleton" under his silks and brocades (ibid., 108–9).

Montesquieu's *Lettres persanes* spring to mind as one reads Trivulzio's *Vita intima e vita nomade in Oriente*, a combination of autobiography, narrative, and politics. By the device of the European woman visiting Asia Minor and Syria, she is able to shift her viewpoint and reveal the unreasonableness of some European conventions and refinements. On the one hand, she delights in narrating how the Arabs see "Frankistan" (Europe) as a land of enchantment and refinement. On the other hand, she debunks the conventional image of the Eastern harem in the Western mind as an artificial paradise, a fantasy of the *Thousand and One Nights*, a mysterious retreat filled with marvels of luxury, art, magnificence, and voluptuousness. Far from it! The harem is "a [filthy] place of darkness and confusion, infected, . . . full of smoke . . . and foul air" (33). She liquidates the traditional topos of the harem as a temple for male sexuality, and observes the monotony of existence of "these women who [having gone to sleep fully dressed] rise in the morning with their frills, frippery and finery of the preceding day all crushed and crumpled" (105). She shudders at their ugly makeup and dress, their complete lack of maternal duty (nor do their offspring consider their mothers anything more than servants), their faces that express at one and the same time stupidity, coarse sensuality, hypocrisy, and hardness. "I think that in no other place there can be found creatures more debased than Turkish women of the middle class; their faces reveal their debasement" (106).

Throughout her travels, she stresses that our beliefs are habits, but the truth is something relative and local. She makes comparisons between women in Oriental societies and those in Italian and French societies; for example, she treats the question of social attitudes toward the sterile woman, but puts her in the Orient, where "the sterile woman [is] scorned, despised and rejected, and . . . must grovel in the mud. The lowliest female slave, so long as she's pregnant, is authorized to trample on her who has produced no offspring" (*Vita intima*, 120–21). She notes that the same cures used for the barrenness of cows and mares were used for women in Turkey. Her analysis of the role of Turkish women beyond the childbearing age is insightful: they may be old and ugly, but they are useful to men for their intrigues and expediencies; while in the West, women, to attract men, exercise the art of flattering their vanity, and men are easily beguiled (*Ricordi dell'esilio*, 166). In the Levant a woman must please physically; otherwise, "even if she's the Queen of Sheba" (ibid.), no one would heed her, for vanity has no part in amorous relationships, whereas in the West vanity is indispensable.

> Asiatics, in their manner toward women, lack what we call deference, delicacy, and reserve; they are not respectful . . . . But their spontaneous homage seems more flattering than that of the very refined Lovelaces of Paris and London. Here they address themselves directly to beauty. Nothing is less ethereal, true, but nothing is more real. (*Souvenirs dans l'exil*, 34, trans. Brombert, 200)

Trivulzio traveled in Asia Minor for five years (1850–55), crossing the territories of the Kurds and the Turcomans, and on through Syria to reach Palestine. Except for a few intrepid missionaries and Lady Hester Stanhope, Europeans rarely ventured into these lands at that time (Brombert, 207). Expecting to find inspiration in the untouched beauties of nature, Trivulzio set out in search of "superb countrysides where one finds no trace of human work" (*Souvenirs dans l'exil*, trans. Brombert, 200).

She had purchased at a low price from an influential Turk in Constantinople a vast terrain in Asia Minor and decided she would form a colony on the property. Setting out for the region of Angora (ancient Ancyra, today's Ankara) with her entourage, including a small escort of horsemen, she rode "only seven or eight hours a day" without much effort, and found dangers along the way "more imaginary than real." Privations were quite bearable, but she does admit that when she thought about possibilities of lack of food and shelter, sudden snows or hurricanes, or serious sickness, despite herself she felt "a sort of weakness combined with anguish, which one must carefully avoid, because it would be the end of the traveler who succumbs" (*Vita intima*, 57). Sometimes she questioned her own temerity and obstinacy, and sometimes confessed her fears, but always onward did she go.

The group reached the fertile, picturesque valley of Ciaq-Mag-Oglou, with its river and wooded hills, six hours from Saffran Bolo in Anatolia. On the land furrowed for so many centuries by the soldiers of Mithridates, Pompey, and Tamerlane, she muses, not a single area has escaped a tragic and bloody history, as well as deceit and betrayal under the Turkish sultans. A watermill, a sawmill, and a dilapidated house awaited her on her newly acquired property. In short order she made the old house livable and began planting and constructing and furnishing the barns. Settling down for a life of privation, and firmly rejecting the entreaties of her friends to return to Paris, she was determined to survive by dint of her own ingenuity. Setting up a model farm, she hired workers (mostly Italian exiles), purchased cattle and livestock to provide meat and milk, a flock of sheep, poultry, and horses for transport. Wheat and rice would be grown, with Trivulzio herself supervising the planting and the harvesting. Her little community worked with enthusiasm. She cared for sick local Turks, who believed in her marvelous powers of healing; she sold embroideries at the local market; she began outlining a novel and two plays that would later be published; and she wrote stories on Turkish life and legends that appeared in the *Revue des Deux Mondes* and the New York *Tribune*. Thus, twice did the princess have to eke out a living with her own talents—in Paris and in Ciaq-Mag-Oglou.

She left Anatolia in January 1852 to enter into "the nomad's life" (*Vita intima*, 23). On horseback with her escort, she was bound for Jerusalem. On the way to Saffran Bolo, she was stopped by a throng of sick and crippled people, who assaulted her with requests to be examined and cured. Her experience with her own maladies and with the Roman ambulances were of great help in this respect. The two weeks she spent in Angora in the Galatian territory in February 1852 were plagued with violent headaches caused by exhalations from stoves and burning coal; nonetheless, she admired the famous Angora goats' silky hair, graceful movements, and quick running speed, as well as their ability to rout the most menacing dogs or huge Angora cats covered with thick down "quite like that of swans" (ibid., 49). In fact, she describes a whole menagerie in the region: the gentle buffalo, jackals, panthers, leopards, wild boars, sheep attached to scaffolding to support the heavy weight of their tails, greyhounds with curled drooping ears, and the robust horses of the Turcomans of Cappadocia (ibid., 50), noting with interest that no Turk or Arab would ever mistreat an animal. (Trivulzio does not hesitate, however, to note cases of maltreatment of women.) Rather, they converse with their animals in a language consisting of words and intonations that are not understood by humans but very well by the beasts: "There would be an extraordinary dictionary to compose," she writes, "not of the language spoken by animals but of the language they understand" (ibid., 52). Trivulzio is highly sensitive to sounds, both of language and of musical instruments, of cowbells and birds (ibid., 98–99). The whole subject of language interests her, including the language of horses:

> It seems as though our European horses are mute compared to the Arab horse that has an entire language that lends itself to the most varied nuances. . . . Our horses [proceeding along the Lebanese coast] ingenuously expressed their impressions of the beautiful nature surrounding them. (ibid., 97)

She offers many romantic descriptions of untouched nature in the area of the Mediterranean, but each scene includes living creatures. For example, when she caught her first glimpse of the Mediterranean on the trip to Jerusalem, after describing the fish in the calm and limpid waters, and the smooth sandy beach, she closely identifies herself with the horses dipping their hooves into the foam of the waves, pawing the ground, breathing in the air through their vermilion nostrils, shaking their long manes, and quivering with pleasure under the caresses of the wind and the sea (ibid.).

Her group descends into Turcoman territory, passing through Kirsehir, a name not even on their maps, but she finds the town, surrounded by monumental tombs, worthy of her attention. She gives a detailed description of one of the most majestic tombs, with its inscriptions "in Arabic or Turcoman" (ibid., 63–64). Her strangeness to the locals is matched by her own surprise at their way of dressing and wearing their hair. The women touch her all over, laugh, then run away as though they had carried out an act of unequaled audacity (ibid., 61). Onward through mud to Caesarea (today's Eregli), where the ornate costumes, traditions, and roof-terrace festivities of the Armenian population are described in rich detail (ibid., 67–68). Here Trivulzio pauses to describe and comment on the national dance of the Ottoman Empire, the belly dance, which she finds graceless and indecent (ibid., 69).

On to Medem, after which she rode horseback for five days on the tracks of Rome's ancient roads through the magnificent but deserted Taurus Mountains, giving proof of her sangfroid and adaptive spirit: she suffered unbearable cold, slept in a tent, and constantly risked brigand attacks. She pursued her dangerous way through the territory of Giaur-Daghda (mountains of Giaur, Turkish name of the Amanus massif), reached Adana, close to the sea, where she found the influence of Western civilization more conspicuous, then proceeded toward Antioch and Latakia, via Alexandretta, which she cannot wait to leave because of its tumbledown houses and miserable bazaar. By contrast, she is enchanted and would like to stay on in Antioch (the ancient capital of Syria), with its cascades of Daphne (Harbiye). Contemplating here the fallen columns of a ruined temple, possibly dedicated to Venus, Trivulzio remarks on the fragility of monuments, bringing to the reader's mind Shelley's famous poem "Ozymandias." Similarly, in Latakia, she preferred the beauties of nature—orange, olive, and fig groves, and the solitary palm trees, to Vespasian's Arch of Triumph—"*rovine insignificanti*" (insignificant ruins) (*Vita intima*, 145–6); and in Sūr (ancient Tyre) she will exclaim "Where are its ruins? Surely the sea has swallowed up the whole capital of King Hiram" (ibid., 172). And later, as she stands on the spot where the trumpets of Gideon's army had blared, she wonders what remains of Jericho.

All along her way, as she braves the scorching midday sun and the polar nights, she offers her readers nice poetic images: of "a very hot sun shining on us, while the icy ground grinds under our steps" (*Vita intima*, 42); of losing herself in "a labyrinth of laurel, daphne and myrtle" (ibid., 127); and, after heavy rainstorms, of "numerous rainbows slinging themselves from one mountain to the other, like bridges being built by the spirits of the air" (ibid., 137). Likewise, she associates in her mind painters who might best capture the aspect and features of the men she meets along her way: no one better than Alexandre Gabriel Decamps (1803–60), the French painter who traveled in Asia Minor and reproduced Oriental life and scenery with a bold fidelity to nature, to paint the Anatolian horsemen in his green turban and rich cape of white wool woven with gold and silver; or Salvator Rosa (1615–73), to portray the handsome faces and bearing of the bandits of the Giaur-Daghda massif (ibid., 85).

Following the Mediterranean coast to Beirut, she passes near the ancient city of Byblos, whose fortifications were built by the Crusaders, and today is called Jubayl (*Vita intima*, 164); en route she meets an English missionary couple, offering an occasion to satirize about Syria's invasion by naive English and American missionaries "whose candor and good faith are surely more remarkable than their intuition and intelligence" because, she goes on to explain, the Orientals use conversion as a source of income—those who convert three or four times can indeed become wealthy and earn a sort of "pension" as well (ibid., 165–66).

Upon reaching Beirut, summed up as "the least Asiatic of the cities of Asia; the most European of the cities of the Orient" (*Vita intima*, 167), she scans the horizon in search of the cedar forests of which the Holy Scriptures speak. In vain. The cedars had been relegated to a tiny area of Lebanon (even tinier today). Even though Trivulzio writes that one should read the pages of the Old Testament under the Eastern sky, where the story of old Job is renewed each day, and where biblical Semitic types have preserved their physiognomy intact and not undergone the metamorphoses common to other peoples, she warns her readers not to bring along in their mind's eye vivid images from the sacred texts when visiting biblical lands. Her own tendency is to anticipate with her imagination the aspect of a famous place, then to remain cold in the face of reality. (Nazareth and other sites in the Holy Land will disappoint her because she did not find her own mental images of scenes from the Scriptures.) She is honest enough to confess that when she was on the famous plain of Marathon in Attica, rather than feeling moved by the memory of Themistocles, the only thing she found worthy of note was that it was extremely hot that day (ibid., 178), thereby demonstrating that she wrote not as a travel writer but as a recorder of her personal reactions. She was looking for things other than sites and monuments. Hers was a search for truth, a social inquiry. She gave almost exclusive attention to the human environment—to people, understood psychologically and emotionally as individuals as well as a collectivity—and she sought to solve problems that might better the lot of the poor and the oppressed. If she sometimes dwells romantically on landscapes in her travel writing, she never fails to consider them as a natural condition—the physical limit of the people who inhabit them (Giorgio Cusatelli, preface, *Vita intima*, 15).

From Beirut she proceeded to Sayda (ancient Sidon), then Sūr, reaching Jerusalem in the spring of 1852, before Easter celebrations. It was her first look at the city, but she experienced a déjà vu—"all the fascination of a return" (*Vita intima*, 183). Contemplating the "grand spectacle" of Jerusalem, she was filled with a sense of well-being and deep joy, a feeling that remained with her during her entire sojourn. Of value are her studies of the effects of rival religions and cultures in the area. Although she tends to reject as superstition many expressions of Islam, she observes with respect manifestations of Judaism (e.g. prayer at the Wailing Wall) and scarcely conceals her emotional involvement in the Christian message of the Holy Land. But in the space of a single day she may pass from marvel and admiration to horror mixed with pity and disgust: during her visit to the leprosarium, it was not the disease that horrified her (she succeeds admirably in her objective detailed description of the deformities and mutilations of the lepers), but rather the grotesqueness of the intimacies between a totally disfigured leper girl sitting on the lap of a man without human form.

As for the river Jordan's banks, waters, and woods, they particularly aroused her and she hoped to retain their images forever. "The Jordan is not only a great historical river, it's a marvelous river that magically transforms the nature surrounding it" (ibid., 198). When her group went to the banks, they had planned to break their journey at the magnificent Greek convent of Saint Saba before high noon, but a group of Englishmen had stopped there just before them and gotten drunk. The monks became embroiled and had shut the doors to all foreigners. "In Europe, anyone who shuts his door in the face of a stranger is a boor, an ill-mannered lout and nothing more; in the Orient, it's a scourge, a disaster, perhaps even murderous" (*Asie Mineure et Syrie, souvenirs de voyage*, 236–37), she writes, for she and her group were without water and could have died of heat and thirst. She questions: "Was the sight of the Jordan then of such great importance to me?" and answers her own rhetorical question rhetorically: "It seemed to me I'd be the happiest person in the world if only I could find myself at a hundred leagues from the Jordan" (ibid., 238–39). Should they turn back? She wanted to weep, but they stayed. One of her Arab escorts left the group and after two hours brought back some milk curds; she succeeded in getting the monks to pass water over the convent's fortifications and not fire at them if they took shelter in the shade beneath the convent's old ruined tower. After resting, they set out again after midnight so as to reach the banks of the Jordan before the sun was too high in the sky. She stood on the heights overlooking fleecy clouds that brought certain images of the Scriptures to her mind, and the Dead Sea shone in the distance like a dark jewel. She perceived a green ribbon meandering through the dry sands; beyond, the blue mountains of the Moab—"un beau tableau" (ibid., 240). Finally reaching the banks of the Jordan, she reclined with a book in her hand and a hookah at her side: "It's the remembrance of such hours that makes European life seem so lackluster and tedious for the voyager who has traveled up and down Asia," she writes (ibid., 243). Her body was tired but well, her spirit calm, lofty, and satisfied.

After a month in Jerusalem, the time arrived for her return voyage, during which she revisited Aleppo, then, leaving the Mediterranean at Adana, turned inland and reached her hermitage after eleven months of peripeteia (Severgnini, 205). During her absence from Ciaq-Mag-Oglou, the farming activity had gone into deficit; undaunted, she rolled up her sleeves and found other ways to earn some income by writing for European and American magazines. She learned that the attempted coup engineered by Mazzini from England on February 6, 1853, to set off a new insurrection against Austria had failed. The Austrian government once again confiscated the possessions of wealthy exiles, and for the third time Trivulzio was deprived of a means of livelihood (Brombert, 210). She worked with her hands, sewing, embroidering, then taking her handicrafts to markets in neighboring towns. Struggling to remain on her farm, she sent more "Asiatic" short stories for publication in the *Revue des Deux Mondes*, and sold her sheeps' wool, some goats and cows, to string along. Even during her pilgrimage to Jerusalem her Parisian friends had tried to call her back to Europe, but her only answer was that the government of the French traitor and tyrant was totally repugnant to her (Severgnini, 209). But after eight years of exile, in July 1855 she set sail for Marseilles, arriving in Paris in November 1855 to live at 28 rue du Montparnasse.

In early 1856 she returned to Italy, having been granted repossession of her property, and for the following three years continued to spend half her time in Paris, working assiduously at her writing, now uninterrupted by political activity. Between 1856 and 1858, in addition to starting work on a 500-page history of the House of Savoy, *Histoire de la Maison de Savoie*, she continued to publish her stories and books on Turkey. She died in Milan July 5, 1871, at the age of sixty-three, after having proved her worth as a writer, political activist, journalist, performer of remarkable humanitarian deeds, and venturesome traveler.

How deeply and how sensibly she "thought things over" is eminently revealed in the last chapter of *Vita intima e vita nomade in Oriente*, in which she takes a final look at Islam, evaluating the good and the bad, and questioning the fate of the theocratic Ottoman Empire. Her analysis shows insight, a real grasp of political history, and foresight. Deeming the social structure of the Turkey she saw to be "truly monstrous" (*Vita intima*, 112), she called for reform—as Mustafa Kemal Atatürk was to do in the 1920s, when he declared Turkey a secular republic, abolished the caliphate and the dervish sects, fought illiteracy, and gained the unswerving support of the people, including the peasants whom Trivulzio had always championed.

(All translations are mine, unless otherwise noted.)   *Alba Amoia*

BIBLIOGRAPHY

Brombert, Beth Archer. *Cristina: Portraits of a Princess*. London: Hamish Hamilton, 1978.

Malvezzi, Aldobrandino. *Cristina di Belgiojoso*. 3 vols. Milan: Treves, 1936–37. Vol. 1: *Le prime armi* (1808–32); Vol. 2: *La Seduttrice* (1833–42); Vol. 3: *Pensiero ed azione* (1843–71).

Morandini, Giuliana. *La voce che è in lei. Antologia della narrativa femminile italiana tra '800 e '900*. Milan: Bompiani, 1980, pp. 61–76, 389.

Russell, Rinaldina. "Cristina Trivulzio Barbiano di Belgioioso." In *Multicultural Writers from Antiquity to 1945*. Ed. Alba Amoia and Bettina L. Knapp. Westport, Conn.: Greenwood Press, 2002, pp. 417–20.

Severgnini, Luigi. *La Principessa di Belgiojoso. Vita e opere*. Milan: Edizioni Virgilio, 1972.

Trivulzio di Belgiojoso, Cristina. "Le donne romane sono invitate a recarsi all'Ospizio dei Pellegrini per fabbricarvi delle cartuccie." Rome: 1849 [?].

———. *Souvenirs dans l'exil*, originally published in Paris in *Le National*, September 5, October 12, 1850; Milan: Istituto Editoriale Italiano, 1946. [*Ricordi dell'esilio*. Ed. and trans. Luigi Severgnini. Cinisello Balsamo (Milan): Edizioni Paoline, 1978.]

———. *Asie Mineure et Syrie, souvenirs de voyage*, par Mme la Princesse de Belgiojoso (originally published serially as *La vie intime et la vie nomade en Orient* in *Revue des deux Mondes*, 1855). Paris: M. Lévy Frères, 1858. 2nd ed. Paris:

Lévy, 1861. [*Vita intima e vita nomade in Oriente*. Trans. Olimpia Antoninetti. Preface Giorgio Cusatelli. Como and Pavia: Ibis, 1993.]

———. "Emina," *Revue des deux Mondes*, February 1, 15, 1856.

———. "Un prince kurde," *Revue des deux Mondes*, March 15, April 1, 1856.

———. "Les deux femmes d'Ismaïl-Bey," *Revue des deux Mondes*, July 1, 15, 1856.

———. "Le Pacha de l'ancien régime," in *Revue des deux Mondes*, September 15, 1856.

———. *Emina*, récits turco-asiatiques par Mme la Princesse Christine Trivulce de Belgiojoso. 2 vols. Paris and Leipzig: M. Gerhard, 1856.

———. "Un paysan turc," in *Revue des deux Mondes*, November 1, 15, December 1, 1857.

———. "Un principe curdo, racconto turco-asiatico"—"Emina." Milan: Redaelli, 1857.

———. *Scènes de la vie turque*. Paris: M. Lévy Frères, 1858 (contains "Emina," "Un prince kurde," and "Les deux femmes d'Ismaïl-Bey").

———. "Zobeïdeh," *Revue des deux Mondes*, April 1, 15, 1858.

CHAPTER

6

Fanny Lewald

(1811–1889)

I recognize as well, as clearly as anyone, what is repellent [about
Rome]. I take no pleasure in all the decrepit houses wherever
one looks; and I am also not happy doing without our clean
steps, our good stoves, and a hundred other conveniences. . . .
And yet I don't know how I will learn to do without Rome,
and I am certain that no day will pass that I won't think back
with delight and longing on this ancient, coarse, and so unique
Rome.

> (Fanny Lewald, in Adolf Stahr and Fanny Lewald,
> *Ein Winter in Rom*, 152)

On the death of her dearly loved father in 1846, Fanny Lewald was
in Naples, and the letter from Königsberg informing her of this
event took nearly three weeks to reach her. In 1881, when she
made her last journey to Italy, the train tracks that covered Europe were
transforming travel into mass tourism, while news, good and bad alike,
traveled with equal rapidity by telegraph. Besides experiencing such material changes in daily life, Fanny Lewald came of age when traditional
political and social arrangements were being transformed. She was an
advocate of change, even radical change, and her writings reflect the tensions between her own progressive ideas and the claims of history and
tradition.

She was born Fanny Mathilde Auguste Marcus in Königsberg, a Prussian city of 50,000 and an important trade center on the Baltic between

Poland and Russia. The uneasy relation between progress and conservatism in the nineteenth century was prefigured in her family: on her father's side, the assimilating efforts of educated Jews who identified with the liberal ideals of the European Enlightenment; on her mother's, the traditional but increasingly uncomfortable heritage of Orthodox Jewry. In the Marcus home (the family name was later changed to Lewald) there was no observance of Jewish ritual; instead, the paternoster before meals and a magnificently decorated tree at Christmas. Fanny's knowledge of religion—Protestantism and Judaism—came from neighbors, childhood friends, and school. The dinner table in the Marcus home was often full of visitors, from her father's business contacts with Poland and Russia. Fanny's home environment also prefigured the socially and politically liberal milieu in which she would be so much at home in her foreign travels.

In connection with her career as a travel writer, some of Lewald's early memories have emblematic character. She describes in her autobiography going to school at the age of six, in 1817, as a journey:

> My father himself took me by the hand to escort me to school. My mother accompanied us to the door, and the nanny . . . put a piece of candy in my hand. I had an uneasy feeling, as if I were going on a trip to a place where something unpleasant would happen to me. (*The Education of Fanny Lewald: An Autobiography*, trans. Hanna Ballin Lewis, 33)

In the event, the experience was quite different. Besides the stimulating method of teaching and the knowledge she gained there, school offered "a preparation for a life in the world of strangers" (42). Presaging the many *Reisebriefe* (travel letters) she would write when she began to support herself, the homework assignments consisted of "two long German essays every week, sometimes in the form of letters . . ." (ibid., 41).

Fanny's schooling ended when she was thirteen, and she was encouraged to pursue more feminine activities. A few weeks after her fourteenth birthday, her parents' last child was born, and, for a while, she was charged with taking over the household. Thus, while she was acutely self-conscious of her lack of education, which she made up for in her later travels, her self-sufficiency, and her readiness to earn her own living were mastered early in Königsberg.

Her emancipation as a writer, however, was a slow one, in part due to family restrictions. Though there were no money worries, a middle-class girl "belonged to her home" (184) until she married, and it was considered unseemly for a young woman to be seen on the street by herself, even to take a daily walk. On a visit to Breslau in the winter of 1832–33, when she was twenty-one, Lewald met and fell in love with her cousin Heinrich Simon, a jurist who would play a leading role in the parliamentary debates in Frankfurt in 1848. On her return to Königsberg, she continued to nurse this infatuation, and in 1836 she turned down an arranged marriage, saying she would marry only for love. Despite a household regimen that her autobiography portrays as stultifying, she wrote letters of local events to her uncle August Lewald that were published in his periodical *Europa*, under the byline "our correspondent in Königsberg." Still, she says that she did not admit to herself she had a talent for writing (ch. 18). In 1840, however, when a letter describing the festivities surrounding the visit of King Friedrich Wilhelm IV to Königsberg also appeared in *Europa*, August Lewald encouraged her to become a writer (ch. 22).

At the age of thirty and with her father's permission, providing she did so anonymously, Lewald commenced her writing career, which she depicts as one of Jane Austen-like work habits. If it was her month to keep house, she could only write in brief moments. Her first two novels, *Clementine* and *Jenny* (both published in 1843) treat, as do Jane Austen's, the problems of marriage, but, unlike Austen, they suggest the problematic nature of marriage for the middle-class woman.

Wishing for an independent writing life, she moved to Berlin in 1844. Though living in modest circumstances, she discovered what freedom and independence allowed her, and she also experienced the afterlife of the Berlin salon era, meeting Henriette Herz and Sara Levy and hearing recitals by Mendelssohn and his sister Fanny. She began work on a third novel and saved for a yearlong trip to Italy.

In 1845, at the age of thirty-four, she arrived in Rome, where her status as an unmarried woman of small means was offset by the reputation she had acquired from two novels. (She had by now abandoned literary anonymity.) With letters of recommendation from home, she was received into the circle of German expatriates that included Ottilie von Goethe and Adele Schopenhauer and a number of artists then working in Rome. Her weekly letters to her father in Königsberg served as a basis for *Italienisches Bilderbuch* (1847), the account of her year in Italy. A second account of that year, *Römisches Tagebuch 1845–46* (written in 1866 but not published until

1927), tells of the personal emancipation she experienced in Rome, of her unconventional circle of friends, of her art education, and of her love affair with the married scholar and writer Adolf Stahr. It also accounts for the beginnings of her serious working life after her father's death. When she returned to Berlin in 1846, it was with the intention of never seeing Stahr again and with the burden of supporting herself and her younger siblings, for whom she and her oldest brother were responsible.

The next four decades were filled with the writing of novels, stories, and travel accounts, which often appeared first in newspapers and journals aimed at the new audience of middle-class women. In the 1860s she took a more public posture in the growing women's movement with essays on the situation of working-class women as well as that of middle-class women who, like herself, were denied equal educational opportunities and thus the free use of their talents. Fanny Lewald was her own best example of the high standards she felt women could achieve if they had the opportunity. She and the divorced Stahr married in 1855, after which they settled in Berlin. Their modest apartment revived the salons of an earlier day, bringing together on Monday evenings the literary and political figures who came through Berlin in the years before and after unification. Stahr died in 1876. Lewald continued to write, traveled in northern Europe, and also made two additional trips to Italy, in 1877 and 1880. She died in 1889 in Berlin.

When Fanny Lewald went to Italy in 1845, she was following in a long tradition of German writers and artists who, longing for a radically different climate and culture, had made the journey before her. Two writers she particularly admired were Goethe, whose *Italian Journey* (1816–28) she knew well, and the poet August von Platen (1796–1835). Their veneration for the past cultures of antiquity and the Renaissance shaped Lewald's ideals of harmony and beauty, but she was also influenced by the tradition of *littérature engagée* by writers such as Heinrich Heine and Ludwig Börne, indeed of myriads of European writers of liberal tendencies. Thus, while she never descends in her writing to what she referred to as the *"Unsittlichkeiten"* (indecencies) that were the stock in trade of socially progressive writers and the popular press, her accounts of foreign places are concerned with the themes of change, progress, and decadence.

In *Italienisches Bilderbuch* we accompany her as she advances in slow stages through Italy, beginning at the end of August 1845 in Milan, where she attends a ballet on the Faust theme. Witnessing the changes Faust undergoes on the Milanese stage, she offers an interesting comparison with her own countrymen: "The thought that a person could be unhappy because he could not grasp the universe in its totality . . . is foreign to Italians" (*Italienisches Bilderbuch*, e-biblio). She progresses through Genoa ("queen of cities, with the sparkling, life-gushing magic of its beauty," ibid.) and Florence ("the Florentines are, like the Germans, not only active, but industrious, i.e., diligent with deliberation," ibid.) before reaching Rome on October 11. She seems to lead readers by the hand, serving as a well-informed cicerone who points out the differences between Catholic worship and the cold Protestant services of Germany, or observing that the Italian poor show none of the subservience of their German counterparts. She notes what are distinctive features, for instance, the absence of villages in Italy, which is even more pronounced by the time she reaches the island of Ischia, off the coast of Naples: "Wherever in Italy several families have settled, a little town—paese—is founded, which has its market in the center, its church, its cloister, and, here on the sea, its harbor, the marina. A cafe, the pharmacy, a few shops, the doctor and a chiropodist are never absent" (ibid.). A set designer would have no difficulty reconstructing many of the streets of Italian cities or the island of Ischia circa 1845 from her descriptions.

Though it is clear from this work how much she loved Italy, as a person who so firmly believed in the necessity—and inevitability—of social and moral progress, Italy was an enormous challenge for Lewald. Counterbalancing evocative descriptions of everyday life, of historical markers, of the physiognomy of land and people, are strong judgments concerning social and political conditions. In Florence she is of the opinion that people would not turn to crime were it not for "the insufficiency of institutions" (ibid.). While admiring some earlier cultural or artistic splendor, she posed the question: How had a country that had once been so advanced regressed into what she considered intellectual darkness? Thus, even the ruins of Rome's republican or imperial splendor were a reflection of a contemporary society that was decadent and moribund: "In Italy the spirit [*der Geist*] and with it the life of society have been placed in chains. Society is like one of those splendid but uninhabited palaces whose dust-covered paintings and furniture, despite the wealth they represent, are so sad and superannuated" (ibid.). Her strongest criticism is for the Catholic hierarchy: "Men seeking work buy bread and onions and lie down to sleep under God's free sky at the portals of cathedrals, while well-fed clerics go home after their sumptuous evening meal and carefully close the doors of the church behind which are stored gold and silver altar utensils—their dead treasures" (ibid.). But Christianity as such also troubled her. Like Goethe, she deplored paintings portraying the gruesome torture of martyrs, while the doctrine of original sin undermined the very notion of earthly progress. "We are," she insisted in Florence, "children of light created for happiness!" (ibid.).

Though she missed the founding of the short-lived revolutionary Roman republic in 1848 (witnessed and reported on by another expatriate writer, Margaret Fuller), Lewald was in Paris during that year of revolutions. *Erinnerungen aus dem Jahre 1848* (1850), written originally as letters to Stahr and others, is important for its vivid firsthand observations. The Paris portion, from March 12 to March 27, begins with a description of the circumstances of travel (uncomfortable, but a princely midday meal was to be obtained in the dining room of the Amiens train station) and the receipt of her baggage at the Paris railway station (large, though not as grand as expected). The city shows much evidence of revolution:

> The paving stones are laid loosely at the street corners. . . . Wrecked bread wagons and overturned buses show where the most important barricades were. . . . The guardhouse—the Château d'eau—in which the guards were burned to death—lies in smoke-blackened ruins. . . . On the boulevards, the trees are felled, the pipes and columns of the fountains are torn down. At the Tuileries, tattered white curtains flutter from the paneless windows. (*A Year of Revolutions: Fanny Lewald's Recollections of 1848*, trans. Hanna Ballin Lewis, 41)

Of the difficulty of getting around Paris,

> the [bus] detours had the advantage of showing a large part of the city. . . . Yesterday we saw four thousand Swiss who wanted to wish the Republic good luck moving into the city hall. They wore red armbands marked with a white cross. Then, followed by a large crowd, they carried the bust of Freedom, a gift from a sculptor, up to the roof. (ibid., 54–55)

Skeptical about "what you are told about attacks by proletarians," she reports of her own experience, on the way to visit a certain Princess G., at having, "to cross the procession of workers twice . . . and although I was in a light-colored formal dress, no one bothered me. On the contrary, they made way very good naturedly" (ibid., 69). Besides attending a charity ball at the Opéra (where the restrooms are attractive), she also attended a meeting of the Central Club of the Republicans on March 16, recording the substance of the evening's debate. In Paris, where the promise and possibility of revolution seemed imminent, she believed that "[w]e are living in a time which seems to break strongly with its past; the battle will be prolonged if the break is only partial, if all the debris of the collapse is not removed" (81).

The failure to found a constitutional government in Germany in 1848 and the continuing political disunity there serve as a palimpsest for *England und Schottland: Reisetagebuch*, recording five months of observations of England and Scotland in 1850 (in two volumes of 500 pages each). With thoroughness she ranges from the Tower, the equestrian monuments, the Crown Jewels, and Parliament to the everyday face of city and country. For instance, the entry for May 26–27 includes Sunday Observances; The Parks; Ladies' Outdoor Dress; The Large Number of Household Servants; Omnibuses; Constables. In that entry she observes of London row houses: "The architecture has something decidedly socialistic about it in that the individual disappears within the total impression. Entire streets and squares consist of houses all two windows wide, all built in the same style" (*England und Schottland: Reisetagebuch*, 24). Lewald was thorough, relying on her own observations and what she learned from others. The emphasis on particulars may owe much to her keenly felt lack of formal education. In her descriptions of houses, for instance, she was informing not only her readers but also herself of very different political and social conditions: "most have two entrances" (ibid., 114), thus underlining the private and public character of the English; as for home interiors, "the fireplace is usually in the center of the main wall" (ibid., 115), making the room conducive to sociability, while the bedroom is "the most attractive region of an English household" (ibid., 118), generally larger than "by us." Moreover, the married couple generally sleeps in the same bed. Along with this indication of intimate arrangements, the reader learns of the size and comfort of the pillows.

Her return to Rome with Stahr, twenty-one years after they fell in love there, is remarkable for her ability to see past the present, past her own prejudices, and to penetrate to the enduring historical character of Italy. This allows her an appreciation for that which her intellect cannot approve. The joint record of their stay, *Ein Winter in Rom* (1869), takes account of all of the contradictory tendencies that Italy represented for her. Her letter on the subject of St. Peter's, dated "Rome, January 1867," is an exemplary essay in appreciation, reflecting on its sublime subject and on the process of appreciation and judgment itself. It begins with a general observation concerning the beauty, magnificence, and grandeur of the basilica, all of which seem to overwhelm the exercise of unaffected religious piety.

> In St. Peter's you can't escape the feeling that God's representative holds court here, and it is surprising, even astonishing . . . to see a person on his knees praying before one of the chapels or at a confessional pouring out his heart into the ears of a priest. (*Ein Winter in Rom*, 188)

She discusses the history of the building, mentions that forty-three popes took part in its construction, and lists painters and sculptors who worked here. She even gives the measurements of the floor space and includes this useful information about the year-round even temperature maintained in the enclosed space: "Thanks to its massive and partly double walls . . . St. Peter's is almost the only church or public building in Rome that the sick can visit without worry at any season or time of day" (ibid., 189).

But Lewald's gift is to weave detail into a larger historical tapestry. The sepulchres of the popes are naturally imposing monuments in their own right, but here they are subordinated to the whole, just as the life and careers of the popes themselves are a part of the large organism called the Roman Catholic Church. Moreover, not only is St. Peter's a representation of the body religious, but the "history of the human race and of our human abilities, desires, and exertions for the past eighteen centuries can be deciphered in its walls" (ibid., 190):

> Therein lies something that moves us powerfully, that forces us to exert all our faculties when confronting it and to apply large standards to it, even when we are unable to reconcile the results with our own understanding.

Whoever thinks of his own needs, his own feelings when he is here; whoever is not transported beyond himself and the present by his astonished
wonder at its perfected totality, by its unsurpassed ennobling beauty; whoever is not able to step back into the past and to look into the future—that
person lacks the historical sense with which alone one can understand and
appreciate Rome. (ibid., 190)

More than any other place, Rome gives material evidence of the achievements of the human spirit, but it also constantly reminds us of the decay
of all human endeavors, whether it be the ruins of ancient Rome or the
often decrepit state of the houses of the modern city.

Again, we return to the themes of change and progress and decay.
After Stahr's death, Lewald returned to Italy in 1877, a journey recounted
in *Reisebriefe aus Deutschland, Italien und Frankreich (1877–1878)* (1880).
Besides containing a nearly 100-page account of Italy's progress toward
unification in 1871, it tells of large changes and small ones in daily life.
Lewald describes the mourning in Rome at the death of Victor Emman-
uel in January 1878 and, the following month, of Pius IX, and speaks of
the hopes prompted by the elevation of Leo XIII as pontiff. Equally interesting to her, however, are improvements in human life and habitation
that show the creative hand of man, from bridges and roads in the Swiss
Alps to hospitals and luxury stores.

It was Italy in particular that encapsulated, in the recurring natural
cycle of life of a warm and bountiful land, this theme of human endeavor
and decay. Ultimately, the issue of change had powerful personal reso-
nance for Fanny Lewald. As Goethe had learned, Italy offered conditions
for personal growth, for freedom, which, as she says of herself, "I required
to the highest degree" (*Römisches Tagebuch*, 44). Her first stop in Italy in
1845 was Milan, where she began her instruction in art history. In Rome
she experienced an unaccustomed freedom among the German expatriate
community and felt a new youth not dependent on the "German bourgeois calendar." And though at thirty-four she felt the time for passion
was past, she fell in love. Thus, despite her criticism for conditions that
seemed to inhibit emancipation for Italians, Italy remained talismanic. As
she conceded when she and Stahr returned to the city in which they had
fallen in love two decades earlier: "One is surrounded by puzzles here"
(*Ein Winter in Rom*, 112).

(All translations are mine, unless otherwise noted.)   *Elizabeth Powers*

BIBLIOGRAPHY

Lewald, Fanny. *Italienisches Bilderbuch.* 2 vols. Berlin: A. Duncker, 1847. (Available at www.gutenberg2000.de/lewald/italbild)

—————. *Erinnerungen aus dem Jahre 1848* (1850), written originally as letters to various correspondents. Abridged and ed. Dietrich Schaefer. Frankfurt: Insel, 1969. [*A Year of Revolutions: Fanny Lewald's Recollections of 1848.* Trans. and ed. Hanna Ballin Lewis. Providence, R.I.: Berghan Books, 1997.]

—————. *Meine Lebensgeschichte, 1861–62.* [*The Education of Fanny Lewald: An Autobiography.* Trans. and ed. Hanna Ballin Lewis. Albany: State University of New York Press, 1992.]

—————. *England und Schottland: Reisetagebuch.* 2 vols. Berlin: Otto Janke, 1864 [2nd ed.].

—————. *Römisches Tagebuch 1845–46* (1866). Ed. Heinrich Spiero. Leipzig: Klinkhardt and Biermann, 1927.

—————. *Reisebriefe aus Deutschland, Italien und Frankreich (1877–1878).* Berlin: Otto Janke, 1880.

Stahr, Adolf, and Fanny Lewald. *Ein Winter in Rom.* Berlin: J. Guttentag, 1869.

CHAPTER 7

Belle Marsh Poate

(1847–1896)

We have gone half way [from Yokohama to Morioka] in a
wretched little Japanese steamer, and the remainder, 200 miles,
by jinrikisha where we could ride, and walked the rest of the
way. . . . We reached Morioka . . . after a very wearying journey
through rain, wind and bitter cold, and were very thankful for
shelter and the tiny charcoal fire. . . . I am sitting on the floor,
my feet covered with a very *smelly* futon. But the sun is shining
once more, and that is cheering.

(Belle Marsh Poate, in Richard Poate Stebbins, *The Japan
Experience*, 120, 195; page numbers throughout refer to this work)

My missionary grandmother, Belle Marsh Poate, would not have
been pleased to learn that a ninety-year-old grandson of hers
had taken it upon himself to publicize some of her intimate
correspondence for an audience of whose nature—indeed, of whose very
existence—she could have no conception. She would not even have been
sure that there would be a twentieth century, much less a twenty-first,
since she regarded the Second Coming of Christ and the end of the world
as events that might very well occur in her own lifetime. Yet in spite of
some of the limitations characteristic of her era, she was a woman lacking
neither in intelligence nor in a sense of fun when, in 1876, she surrendered
local ties and comforts to sail as a Presbyterian mission worker in Japan, a
country then immersed in the process of modernization and Westerniza-
tion known as the Meiji era. Traces of the "culture shock" Belle Marsh

experienced on her immersion in this novel and highly disconcerting environment are preserved in a packet of letters written to her close friend, Mrs. Martha (Mattie) Means of Akron, Ohio, and to Mattie's young sons, Walter and Willie.

Born in Truro, Nova Scotia, Belle was one of the youngest in a family of thirteen children whose ancestry went back to Puritan times in Massachusetts. Most likely because of the early death of one or both parents, she and some of her younger brothers and sisters were brought up by friends or relatives in the United States. In due course she graduated from Lake Erie Female Seminary (now Lake Erie College) in Painesville, Ohio. Subsequently she is said to have taught primary school in Ashtabula, Ohio, supervising two classrooms with the aid of a mirror in the doorway. She enrolled as a Presbyterian missionary assistant in the fall of 1876 and embarked for Japan, where she taught classes and assisted with the music in the Presbyterian mission schools of Yokohama (at that time the Protestant missionary capital of Japan).

When she marrried the Englishman Thomas Pratt Poate in 1879, she surrendered her Presbyterian ties and joined her husband in Baptist missionary service first in Yokohama, later in the northern town of Morioka, a place with few amenities and with the reputation, according to Mr. Poate, of "the unhealthiest city in the Empire" (187). His more sensitive wife described its beauty in a passage typical of her writing style:

Morioka is built in a perfectly level valley, completely surrounded by hills rising one above the other. The highest peak is six or eight thousand feet. The streams run in every direction, and the scenery is so beautiful, it seems to make up for lack of society. Our house stands in the midst of rice fields, and the odors of spring will be overpowering, but now in their covering of pure white snow they are very beautiful. (198)

In a dozen arduous years of missionary service, the Poates made a modest number of converts and also became the parents of five children—two boys and three girls. They returned to the United States in 1892, but Belle Marsh Poate, sapped of strength and in poor health, died less than four years later at the early age of forty-eight, at Sherman, New York.

Even the train journey westward from Ohio to San Francisco was venturesome enough in 1876, when transcontinental rail travel was in its infancy and security considerations would prevent the nature-loving young school teacher from positioning herself between cars for a better view of the Rocky Mountains. As for the trans-Pacific voyage to the Japanese port of Yokohama, her "nervous dread of the dreadful sea" (22) continues to reverberate in the letter to "Folks at Home" that embodies the first impressions of Marsh's new milieu.

YOKOHAMA, October 31st, 1876. . . . I have at last arrived at my destination, with the painful journey done. . . . The ships anchor a mile or so out in the harbor, and are reached from shore by little *sampans*, managed by screaming, nearly-naked coolies. . . . When we were safely in the harbor, they told us we had been through a cyclone, and within a few degrees of the point where we must have gone down. . . .

I haven't got over the effects of my journey yet. . . .

Friday, November 2nd. . . . We ride in "Ginrickis," to be sure, and can go anywhere in the city for five cents, that is one of the *cheap* things. (22–23)

Elsewhere, and with characteristic humor, Marsh will have more to say about *ginricki* or *jinrikisha* transportation:

When two jinrikisha men get to fighting, they bang their "rikshas" together, and then run. This does very well when there is no one in them, but it is not pleasant for two people not at all interested in the battle to be knocked together that way.

. . . Oh, dear, how they yelled and danced! It would have been funny if it were not so sad to see men so angry. Besides, I was a little frightened. . . . (43)

. . . Today, coming home from school, it began to *pour* . . . so I called for a jinrikisha. Two came tearing up, and I got into the first. The other man tried to make me take his, and said there was something dreadful the matter with mine. I didn't understand what it was, but . . . wasn't afraid. He then tried to knock the jinrikisha over with me in it. There was no help within call, but I scolded away at them and finally got off without being tumbled in the mud. (53–54)

Another idiosyncrasy that strikes her in the new society is the fact that men, rather than women, perform the domestic chores in her settlement house. In the letter to "Folks at Home" she writes that her "room is cared for by a *man*. . . . Men do the work here" (23). Later she writes, "I get my washing done perfectly lovely for two cents a piece. A woman . . . has charge of the establishment, though men do all the work" (28). She observes that the woman assigned to her as housekeeper has a "dull intellect," "can't learn to make a bed" (though she "understood my heart" [65]), and that the "girls do not understand English very well . . . but many of the boys speak and write very well" (37). She is pessimistic about the girls, so set in their ways, so "utterly incapable of thinking for themselves. . . . I don't think the Japanese women of this generation, as a rule, will amount to a row of pins. Of course there are exceptions . . . but the moment we try to make them stand alone, they flop down like rubber balls with all the air let out" (59).

The inaugural letter to "Folks at Home" continues, revealing our traveler coping with the vagaries of the Japanese language:

. . . Only two of the girls understand English at all, and they not very well, but I manage to make myself understood by pantomime.

I have learned a few Japanese phrases, and as soon as I learn a word I use it. I make ridiculous blunders, but they are too polite, or afraid, to laugh. Today I tried to tell a girl in Japanese to bring me her book. She hesitated, got up and came slowly towards me, without her book. At noon I said at the table [that] either that child didn't understand her own language or I had made a mistake, and repeated what I said. They laughed heartily and told me the word I used for book meant "Half of yourself." No wonder the poor child looked bewildered.

The difference of a long or short vowel sound makes such a difference in the meaning. Yesterday I asked one of the girls to put a little *phrophet* [?] in the stove. The difference between their words for phrophet [?] and wood being a different sound of *a*. The dear girl did what I wanted her to, and then, modestly bringing me a stick, told me the right word. (24)

Nine-year-old Willie Means is the recipient of the next letter from Yokohama, which offers bits of local color as well as a first allusion to the earthquakes that will disturb Marsh's peace of mind throughout her life in Japan.

> November 17 [1876]. Dear Willie, It is your turn to have a letter this time, and I have a good deal to tell. . . .
> First I'll tell you about my schoolhouse. It is a little square build-ing covered with tiles, and the fence is made of bamboo sticks, standing up straight and held together by wires. The room has two walls; the inner one consists of glass doors, the outer of boards. Both can be slid aside so we are all out of doors. The houses and stores are all the same; the stores have the front always open, only native houses have the doors of white paper instead of glass. (25)

Marsh has not only a keen eye for architecture, but also a sense of seis-mic effects on buildings. Her description of a new building going up in Yokohama is well worth reading:

> In the first place, they put the frame all up. The timbers slip into each other, and were tied with ropes. Then they took it down again, after seeing that it was all going to fit well. Now, they are crossing bamboo withes in and out in squares like a checkerboard to make the outer walls, which will be covered with tiles. If they should put up a house as they do in America, it would soon be shaken down. (36)

The letter to Willie Means continues:

> The first thing you would stumble over [on entering her school-house] would be the pile of shoes on the doorstep. Such odd looking shoes: a piece of wood set up on two other pieces, after the fashion of the foundation of a blockhouse, and they go clump-clumping along the streets making a great clatter, and looking as if walking on little stilts. The shoes are fastened on by means of a strap passing

between the great toe and the others. Those who wear stockings have them made of white or black cloth, shaped like a baby sock, with a *thumb* for the great toe. (25)

She has more to say on the subject of footwear in a later letter (July 26, 1879) to Willie:

> [T]hey make straw sandals here, they use them a good deal in warm weather, and around the yard, but they use the high wooden shoes on the street, *usually*. They always leave them at the door, and when we go to Japanese houses we take off our shoes. . . . I have often wondered how they could select their own shoes from a pile just alike, and get into them so quickly.
>
> The wooden shoes are very clumsy. I don't see how they can walk and run on them, but they do. Last year when we went on a tramp up the mountains my feet got so tired that I got a pair of straw shoes or *zoori* (you must call both o's, *zo-o-ri*), but the strap goes between the toes, and [as] I had no *thumb* for the great toe in my stocking, I couldn't keep them on very well, but they were very easy to walk in. (67)

Continuing her 1876 letter to Willie:

> Boys and girls wear a skirt fastened close around them and opened in front, lapping a little. This with an upper garment with very flapping sleeves is all they ever wear. Such a thing as a hat is never seen on either man or woman. Some of the coolies (poor class of men) wear *very* tight fitting pants close to the skin, with socks made on them. They look much more comfortable in this cold weather.
>
> When the little folks come to school, they come up to my desk and get onto their knees, bowing their faces to the floor. If one comes to ask a question, she bows very low, with her little hands crossed. And it is very funny to see men talk to each other, they keep up a series of low bows all the time.
>
> Saturday A.M., November 18th. Just here [?] we felt the first earthquake since I came to Japan. They said it was a slight one, we would probably have another before long, though the house rocked back

and forth, and I quaked all night. They have them very often here, and some day, I presume [?], this little island will disappear.

Though the houses are injured by the rocking and are always leaking, the winds do more injury than the earthquakes, for they have typhoons, cyclones and all sorts of dreadful things. (25–26)

One of Marsh's most imagistic descriptions of a typhoon is contained in a letter to Mattie Means dated September 23, 1884:

We knew there was a typhoon on the way. . . . It came at last, and such a storm has not been known for many years, the old people say. For hours we sat in total darkness (all the windows had to be shut, and we thought it unsafe to have a lamp), listening to the roar of the storm and the sea. . . .

The next day was clear and hot. The sea, that seemed like some wild monster the night before, was like glass. . . . One thousand houses in Tokyo are reported destroyed, and upwards of fifty people lost their lives in Yokohama. One ship was sunk in the harbor, and the loss at sea must have been fearful. (170)

The 1876 letter to Willie Means offers still more description of the Japanese way of life:

I went to visit a Japanese family a while ago. It was evening, so the paper doors were closed, and instead of knocking we stood outside and called. Such a funny little house, only one room covered with pretty clean matting. (My schoolroom, I forgot to tell you, had padded floors and straw matting.) Not a bit of furniture except a little box of ashes in one corner with a few coals in the middle. This is all the stove the Japs have; they call it a Hibachi (fire box).

People sit on their heels and sleep on a mat. They act very uncomfortable when perched upon a chair. (25–26)

In the later (July 26, 1879) letter to her young addressee, Marsh tells him that

[e]verybody in the country is busy with silkworms. All the best part of the houses are filled with cocoons, and the women are hard at

work pulling out the fine, strong silk thread. They don't let the butterfly come out when they make silk, but throw the cocoons into hot water, then they take out the grub, and the cocoon pulls all out into thread.

We raised a lot of worms just for fun. But we didn't expect to make silk, so we let the pretty butterflies come out and lay their eggs for next year. If you have any mulberry trees, I will send some eggs in a letter and tell you how to raise them. But they won't eat anything else. (67–68)

Marsh's first Christmas in Japan is the subject of one of her most fascinating letters, written to Mattie Means in installments as the festive season continued.

> *Gama no, Ni shia ku Ni ju go Ban*
> December 28th, 1876.

Dear Sister Mattie,

Don't be frightened, I am only visiting here [at the residence of the head of the Yokohama Presbyterian mission], and you will not have to put all that lingo on your letters. Such dreadful names as they have here, but it is surprising how soon one becomes accustomed to them and learns to rattle them off, not like a native exactly, for I don't think it possible for a foreigner to speak *just* like a native.

. . . You want to know all about our Christmas doings. . . . I asked the older boys to help me trim the chapel. So they got evergreens from the country, and I bought red berries and white camelias from a peddler, and we went down on Wednesday to work.

The boys behaved like angels. Such boys at home would set me half crazy with their noise and questions, but they all sat down on their heels and watched me make the wreaths. Then one after another [they] would pick up the greens with a nod and go to work. . . . They have so much taste, all they needed was a hint here and there. The evergreens and vines are *so beautiful*, and the neat little chapel was charming.

. . . [T]here is something very gentle and winning about this people. We know they are deceitful, . . . but they are very pleasant to deal with. I had scarcely time to want anything before it was handed me. They didn't seem to watch me at all, but before my string was gone, more was laid in my lap; and everything was done so deferentially, just as if they liked me, and were glad to work for me.

And nearly every one of the large boys had something on the tree for me. A cunning little picture all framed, a turtle in a pretty little Japanese box, one of the kind that acts like life. And the prettiest of all was a Chinese snowdrop just ready to bloom in a sweet little china pot. They are *beautiful* things, and the gift seemed such a delicate one to come from boys in a heathen country.

One of my scholars gave me a very handsome writing desk, of the Japanese lacquer work. And such *loads* of oranges. How I would like to send you a cargo. Pretty bamboo baskets of oranges and green vines, large boxes holding a half bushel or so. And eggs by the load. It was so unexpected, and made me very happy to be so kindly remembered.

Friday, January 5. . . . On New Year's Day we didn't want to receive calls, so [we took a] cunning pony and trap and [went] to ride.

The horses here are such odd, shaggy little creatures. . . . There are always horse servants, or Bettoes, as they are called, to run by the horses' side. They run so easily, and will travel quite as fast and as far as the ponies. The turnouts are all so tiny it seems like riding in a little dogcart.

We had such a *splendid* ride, away out in the country to Mississippi Bay [named for one of the vessels in Commodore Matthew Perry's flotilla in 1853–54]. We visited two Buddhist temples and three shrines. The Betto ran so easily, we thought it would be fun to play Betto. So we wanted him to get in and let us run by the ponies' side. Miss G. [Frances Gulick, Presbyterian mission assistant in Tokyo] tried her Japanese. "*Betto*," she said, with appropriate gestures, "*Dāōzo* get in here and drive. *Watakshidomo* walk." *Dāōzo* is "please," *Watakshidomo* "we," and that was all the Japanese we could find fitted to the occasion, but he smiled serenely, bowed very gracefully, and did what we wished. Fancy using such a word as *Watakshidomo* every time you wanted to say I. . . .

Another dreadful earthquake day before yesterday. It rocked the house so, the doors won't shut. But I'm not nearly as much afraid as at first. I always keep my wrapper on the bed, and my shoes by the side, so I can run outdoors if the house threatens to shake down in the night. And other people do the same. But the first horror is wearing off. . . .

[Enclosure to Walter and Willie Means]: . . . They are always trying to teach me new words. They pick up things and say "*Ko'ra wa*" so and so. *Ko'ra wa* means "this is." And they are more polite than some little boys in America, for they never laugh at mistakes.

How wide your eyes would open if you could look into our school on Sunday afternoon. That is for the poor children. Almost everyone has a baby slipped in under the back of his coat. You can only see the little heads rolling about. Some of them are covered with sores, and nearly all are so ragged and dirty, it makes my heart ache to look at them. They like to get close up to me, and gaze into my face with such wondering looks. Poor little things. . . . (30–34)

The arrival of spring made possible an initial foray into the Japanese countryside, where preaching the gospel combined agreeably with enjoyment of the landscape and the many Buddhist temples.

To Walter Means, ATAME [now Atami], April 16 [1877].
. . . We started on Thursday morning early for our long, long journey of fifty miles! The first day we had jinrikishas, with one man to pull and one to push. It was a very hard ride over rough roads, and I was so tired when we stopped overnight I feared I should not be able to go on.

The next day our road lay over the mountains and we must try *Ka'goes.* The word *Ka'go* means basket, and if you could take a large bushel basket, cut two sides down, pass a pole through the handles, and fix a board over the top to shade it, you would have quite a *Kago.* One is obliged to double up in a way that seems impossible at first sight, but by getting out now and then to get our feet wakened, we got on nicely. . . .

I don't believe any circus procession ever attracted more attention than we did in our journey. People dropped their work, and calling to their friends, rushed out to stare at the strange creatures. When we stopped to rest or eat our lunch, they crowded round till we could scarcely breathe. And here, if I go out of doors, I am followed by a gaping crowd. I am more stupid than usual, and can't think of more than a sentence or two to say to them. . . .

On our first day's journey, we stopped at the largest Buddhist temple in Japan, at Fujisawa. The old priests were very kind, taking us all through the temple and grounds. The latter were too beautiful to describe. In this temple is a god that they believe can heal the sick. An extremely ugly image painted red, with great glaring eyes, and the poor people, many of whom had come from a long distance, would pass their hands over it, and then over their own poor diseased bodies. It was a very pitiful sight.

The priests took us through the suite of rooms that the Mikado occupies when he stops there. They were very clean and fresh, but I think our President would consider them rather bare. There was no furniture, except the straw matting on the floor, but the walls were covered with really beautiful paintings, each representing a season. The winter room I liked best. Here snow-laden branches trailed along two sides, while here and there old Fujiyama's snow-crowned head reared itself, right out of the air, apparently.

The second day we were in the country, and it was so delightful to breathe the fresh air, smell the cherry blossoms, and be away from the dreadful, dirty, noisy old canal. Sometimes our way was literally strewn with camelias, which grow wild in great abundance. Then the road ran through groves of the beautiful bamboo. They are so wonderfully beautiful, the foliage is light and feathery, and the long slender trunks are a bright beautiful green. The orange trees are not as beautiful as our apple. They are low and spready. . . .

There are such multitudes of temples all through the country, they are always on a hill, with long flights of stone steps leading up to them. I have quite a passion for visiting them, some are very, very old, but few are at all recent, and the grounds so charming.

This is the first I have seen of the country of Japan, and I wish I could paint for you the terraced mountainsides, with the numerous little rills of clear water, and the many-tinted valleys, and on every side the grand old sea.

But I had almost forgotten to tell you anything of the great wonder of Atame. Atame is a contraction of *"Atsu name,"* hot sea; and at certain hours, six times a day, an immense jet of boiling water is thrown a great height into the air, with a great roar and steam. A stone kettle boils all the time. You could boil your eggs at any moment in the bubbling seething cauldron [?]. (40–41)

Later that summer, Marsh and Miss Kate M. Youngman, a senior Presbyterian missionary in Tokyo, ventured into the countryside with some of their schoolgirls for a stay of several weeks at a place called Okigawa, where they rented space in a Buddhist temple as dwelling and base of operations. The interest of Marsh's letters lies primarily in her vivid descriptions of Japanese behavior as it affected two lone women, their pupils and the Japanese preacher who accompanied them.

To Mattie Means [OKIGAWA, Summer 1877]. . . . It is too hot for us to do anything, and the sides of our house are always filled with people, keeping out what little air there is. We have no way of shutting ourselves in, storm or shine we have only the roof over our heads.

We have a thunderstorm every afternoon, and I say, "I can't stand this, I am going home," but we can't afford to pay for our temple and not use it. We had two awful nights, when Miss Y and I were busy all night to keep from blowing away. And yet I am surprised at myself to see how fearless I am. . . .

Yesterday we were invited to visit the great man of the town, but there was to be a funeral here, and I . . . stayed to see it, while the rest all went to the feast. It was certainly the *jolliest* funeral I ever saw. About four o'clock they came marching in front of the temple, carrying the body in a little house about two feet square, looking like a very pretty dog kennel. Some of these are very pretty, the windows filled with red and white silk, but this was a poor funeral. The house was carried on bamboo rods, on the shoulders of four men, and the mourners were dressed in white.

They marched round and round a few times singing a dirge, while the enormous temple bell was rung and the priests clashed their cymbals altogether making a horrid noise. Then the body was placed on a bench. A table with a candle, a box of incense, a dish of food, and two dishes of raisins was placed before it, and then the priests, in a voice very much like a whining dog, told the departed how to find the way to paradise, to cross this river, climb that hill, etc.

Meanwhile the mourners laughed and talked all the time, and seemed much more interested in me than [in] the funeral. I went to the grave, a deep *round* hole. And amid laughter and rude jokes, the body was lowered in a "Saki" [Japanese wine] barrel. And then each of the mourners threw three shovelfuls of earth into the grave. After it was filled, they placed the food on it, and a board bearing the "new name" of the deceased. For they give them another name, and worship them after death.

Then they . . . had a grand feast in the priest's house; they were at it still when we went to sleep, and the temple was full of the "Saki" smell. (46–47)

To Walter Means, OKIGAWA, August 14, 1887. . . . We were wakened in the middle of the night by a great rumpus in the priest's room, which is separated from ours by the usual paper sliding doors. Presently there was a strong smell of Japanese cooking, and then a great shouting, drumbeating, etc., out of doors.

We called to the priest (a clever little fellow who lives here alone, and seems glad enough to have our company) to know what was up, and received the answer that seems to a Japanese sufficient for every contingency. "*Skoshi Yo Arimas Kara*" (on account of a little business). Well, we said, what were those outdoor persons doing, and were informed they had "Yo" also.

This was very satisfactory, but we found the next morning that the spirits in the "bad place" were all liberated on that day, and that was the particular "Yo" referred to. . . .

We are going home next week, for we are all getting tired out, and starvation stares us in the face. We can get very little besides rice, and the rains have made the water so bad that we can scarcely eat that, only to keep alive. Then it is *very* damp, as it is everywhere in summer, and with so much singing, improper food, etc. I have a horrible throat, and none of us are well. (47–49)

To Mattie Means [OKIGAWA, August 1877]. . . . Miss Youngman has been lovely to me all the time. She isn't well at all just now.

Sleeping out of doors and eating rice cooked in horrid water is telling on both of us. . . .

   Continuation, from Yokohama, August 26. Home again, after
adventures enough to fill a book. If I take the time to tell you of our
trip home, I will have none to write duty letters. . . . We [were] a
whole day and night on a little boat, about big enough to lay down
two mattresses, and a roof so low we couldn't get on our knees without bumping our heads. Thirteen of us.

   . . . I . . . am afraid to work much while it is so hot. They are
trying to persuade me to go to the mountains for a week, for I have
perspired all the flesh off. . . .

   It is *dreadfully* hot, and my bureau drawers smell so horridly,
everything is mildewed, but the heat won't be likely to last more
than a month or six weeks more. (50–51)

By 1878–79, Belle Marsh Poate seemed almost desperately overworked
and overwrought, tempted at times to give up entirely, yet unwilling to
accept defeat. She suffered moments of weariness and disillusionment
with both American and Japanese associates. She contracted fevers from
sleeping in the unsanitary surroundings of the Japanese villages. Malaria,
from this time on, would be the bane of her existence as well as that of
her husband and children. Like all her contemporaries, she attributes the
disease not to a mosquito-borne parasite but to poisonous influences in
the atmosphere:

   . . . Think of the amount of poison we breathe in this country. By
constantly dosing with quinine and iron we are able to keep up, . . .
but it has its effect on us all. We soon lose all sprightliness and ani-
mation. I think my *mind* is more affected by it than my body, though
I have had my breakdown. (115)

   To Mattie Means, YOKOHAMA, August 21 [1879]. . . . The summer is dragging its slow length along. We will be so thankful when
cooler weather puts an end to the cholera. It is still raging all over
the island. Has broken out again in Kobe, where it had become
much better. The cremation fires are burning night and day, and
they say a constantly increasing pile of coffins lie all around. The
air is burdened with the horrible smell, and at Dr. Hepburn's [a

Protestant medical missionary] they have to close doors and windows and lie with a handkerchief saturated with cologne in order to sleep at night.

The people so rebelled against restrictions that they have been removed, and we fear it will spread terribly in consequence, but hope for the best. . . . They are in a terrible state of excitement, and some expect an insurrection. I hope there will be nothing of the kind, but we know the higher class of people hate the foreigners, and, if they dared, would drive us out today.

The priests, too, are using their influence against us, and they may conclude their gods are angry with them for receiving us, and [that] this is the sign of their displeasure. I don't think we could rely upon any of them for help. Nobody in Japan has done more for them than Dr. [Duane B.] Simmons [a Yokohama physician and former medical missionary], or has been kinder to his servants, but . . . [t]hey are *thoroughly treacherous.*

. . . [T]he common people believe that Dr. Simmons pays a large sum to the Government, and then he carries people off to the cholera hospital, where he kills them and takes their *galls*, which he sells to the foreigners—and it is the use of these galls that makes the foreigners so much stronger in body than the Japs. Isn't it absurd? And so pitiful. Dr. S. has worked for them nearly twenty years—one of the best friends they ever had.

. . . Have been suffering with malaria a *long* time. I took quinine in the early summer, till I was afraid to use any more. Nearly a month ago I was taken with a very severe pain in my stomach, and at *just* two o'clock every night woke up with a terrible palpitation of the heart and a sinking away feeling.

I grew thoroughly alarmed, never thought of malaria taking that form, and feared my end was near. I was afraid to sleep alone lest I should be found dead, and as Dr. Hepburn was gone, and the other doctors so busy with cholera patients, I could get no medical attendance. At last, after Dr. S's life had been threatened, I found him at home in the evening, and he thought from its occurring at the same hour that it must be malaria, told me to try quinine, which I did, and found *immediate* relief. As long as I take twelve grains of

quinine a day, I get on beautifully, but if I neglect to take it, the
pain comes on.

He has given me arsenic now, as such quantities of quinine are
dangerous. To tell the truth I don't like the idea of taking arsenic,
but the only way we can live in this horrid climate is by drugging
ourselves. (69–70)

Marsh in later years had less occasion for wide-eyed comment on the
Japanese scene and her reactions to it. Her contribution as a travel writer
reached its culmination in 1881, when, having accompanied Mr. Poate and
other mission personnel on one of his evangelical missions in the north,
she returned from Sendai to Yokohama on one of the "wretched little Japanese steamer[s]" (120).

SENDAI, November 14th 1881.
. . . We have already stayed much longer than we expected, and
are waiting for a steamer to take us home. These Japanese steamers
are such uncertain things, I get fairly exasperated. We can never
believe a word they tell us. There is always sure to be a steamer
"tomorrow," and we wait week after week with everything packed,
only to be put off to more tomorrows. . . .

After waiting in Sendai nearly a month, word came at last that a
steamer had left Y[okohama]. . . . In all these harbors, the ships
anchor some miles out in the bay, and are reached by small boats.
To reach this one we had to go twenty miles from the mainland, and
twenty-five miles from Sendai.

We started about two P.M. with only one boatman. No other
could be found. The wind was against us, of course, it always is. It
was bitter cold, and we had no warm clothing, not even flannel
underclothes. The boatman lost his way among the islands of which
there are 800. Night came on, very dark, the water came up over the
boat, nearly choking one of the Bible women. It looked very much
like staying out of doors all night, for a little while. But at last we
saw a light in the darkness, and a little after nine came in sight of
the hotel belonging to the Steamship Company, built on a little
rocky island. No steamer, but we found shelter from the cold and
something to eat.

They brought a few coals in the fire box to warm our fingers. My feet were frosted, and didn't they hurt for a few days! Our supper consisted of rice, served in a wooden tub with a wooden spoon, some fish soup, with various queer tasting vegetables in it, and a slice of some kind of custard with a very strange flavor. That is the usual Japanese bill of fare. Sometimes there are a few slices of raw fish. We each have a little table about three inches high and as big as a small napkin set before us, and we sit on the floor with our feet under us.

The next day we climbed to the top of the rock and watched in vain for a ship. . . .

We were prisoners on that island for nine days. . . .

At last a steamer came and we . . . got on board, but instead of [going] directly to Y[okohama], they took us nearly to the North Pole, stopping three times to load with rice and fish. We were eight days on board. I was too sick to do much. . . . I am not very well and feel no ambition, but presume a little good food will get me all right. . . . (123–26)

Shortly before her return to the United States in 1892, Belle Marsh Poate wrote from Morioka to her friend Mattie Means: "We have lived so entirely among this people that I shall feel afraid of my own" (224). Her natural timidity did not, however, prevent her from successfully introducing her husband and children to an American life as strange to them as Japan had been to her.

Richard Poate Stebbins

BIBLIOGRAPHY

Marsh Poate, Belle. *Letters*. In Richard Poate Stebbins, *The Japan Experience: The Missionary Letters of Belle Marsh Poate and Thomas Pratt Poate, 1876–1892*. American University Studies, Series 9, History, Vol. 110. New York: Peter Lang, 1992.

Selected passages are here made available with the kind permission of the publishers and of the Schlesinger Library on the History of Women in America, where Belle Marsh Poate's quoted letters are preserved at its site in Cambridge, Massachusetts.

Pandita Ramabai

(1858–1922)

The day for sailing from the Golden Gate [of] San Francisco
[for] Bombay arrived. I felt as if I were going to a strange country and to a strange people. Everything seemed quite dark.

(Pandita Ramabai through Her Own Words, 319)

P andita Ramabai's life and work today seem to take the form of a
spiritual, intellectual, and cultural journey written in the language
and metaphor of a lifetime travelogue. To read it, one must return
to the events and vicissitudes that preceded Ramabai's birth. Her father,
Anant Shastri, had been a wealthy high-caste member of Indian society.
When he married his second wife, Ramabai's mother, who was much
younger than he, he decided he would teach her the Sanskrit language
and texts, thus defying the current tradition that deemed women to be
untrustworthy and unworthy of any intellectual occupation. In the midst
of general social disapproval, and after having defied the religious authorities by demonstrating that many sacred texts actually consider women
capable of learning Sanskrit Puranic literature, Anant Shastri went with
his wife to live in a simple home in the Gungamul forest in southern
India. There Ramabai, among other children, was born in 1858.

The couple earned their living by teaching at the residential school, and
they ate the produce of Anant Shastri's rice fields and orchards. But his
generosity toward the many pilgrims who visited him during those years
led the whole family into poverty. Finally they were obliged to take up a

life of pilgrimage throughout India—the outset of Ramabai's lifelong journey. Along with her brothers and sisters, she was educated by her parents during their roamings, according to the strict principles of their religion. She was taught the Sanskrit language, Sanskrit Puranic literature, and modern Sanskrit poetry. The family traveled from one sacred place to another; to earn a living, they often read the Puranas. (Puranikas were those public readers of the Puranas who were considered popular preachers among the Hindus.) But when Ramabai's father could no longer endure such an existence, his children, having learned no other way to survive in the "outer" world, found themselves unable to make ends meet. Meanwhile, famine had begun to spread throughout the land. Of the entire family, only Ramabai and her brother survived starvation. This was, perhaps, the start of her journey.

> My brother and I survived, and wandered about, still visiting sacred places. . . . We had fulfilled all the conditions laid down in the sacred books. . . . We still continued to keep caste rules, worshipped gods and studied sacred literature. . . . But our faith in our religion had grown cold, we were not quite so strict with regard to obtaining secular education and finding some means of earning an honest livelihood. (*A Testimony of Our Inexhaustible Treasure* (1907), in *Pandita Ramabai through Her Own Words*, 300)

She and her brother settled in Calcutta in 1878. They were already acquainted with Brahmanic society, and in Calcutta came into contact with Hindu reformers as well as with Christians. The Bible was the first "Western" text through which Ramabai began to explore Western culture. It would thrust her first toward Europe and then toward the United States. In Calcutta, under the guidance of learned pandits, she studied Hindu sacred texts more deeply, focusing specifically on the condition of women as described in the Dharma Shastras, in which she found "contradictory statements about almost everything" (ibid., 302). She began to wonder about the life and destiny of lower castes, particularly low-caste women. During this period she came to be known as "Pandita" (learned woman) Ramabai, and was regarded as a brilliant, nonconformist scholar.

After her brother's death due to cholera, Ramabai married a Bengali lawyer; a daughter, Manoramabai, was born to the couple. Living in

Kochar, Assam, she continued to study Hindu texts but also delved further into Christian readings. Her husband was quite familiar with Christian teachings, but even though he knew Ramabai's doubts about the Hindu religion and was aware that she was looking for a "new faith," he refrained from encouraging her to consult a Christian scholar or to attend any church. Thus she turned toward the Brahmo Samaj, which was less orthodox than strict Hinduism.

When, in 1882, her husband, too, died of cholera, Ramabai was left a young widow with no resources and a child to rear. Her situation, like that of all Hindu widows, was desperate. She decided to go to Poona (Maharashtra) to join the social reform circle of the Prarthana Samaj; there she found help and began studying English. In this sociocultural environment, religious and social issues (especially the condition of Hindu women) were discussed in a critical way. Ramabai turned again to the New Testament and pondered the necessity of learning in order to achieve independence. A spiritual journey preceded her "physical" one from East to West: she left for England with her daughter in 1883 to look for "the other half of the world," in search of knowledge and freedom. In one of her first writings, she declared that a "person becomes great not because of his grey hair, kinship or wealth. Only he who is greater in learning is great" (*Stri Dharma Niti* (trans. 1882), in *Pandita Ramabai through Her Own Words*, 59). Ramabai wanted—not only for herself but for all Indian women—the freedom that derives from knowledge. Freedom had to develop first in her and their minds; it would lead to physical freedom and to a free interpretation of both Eastern and Western worlds. That freedom would, in the end, lead her back home. She would return to Bombay in 1889, armed with her conviction that "human existence without knowledge must be considered inferior to animal existence" (*Stri Dharma Niti*, ibid., 65).

Having arrived in England in 1883, she lived in the community of the Wantage Sisters in Berkshire, where she received mainly Christian spiritual teaching. She gained new points of view and began a detailed analysis of the differences between Hinduism and Christianity. But she also wanted to study medicine—that was the primary goal of her journey to the West. In her search for independence, she saw in Christian/Western society the only social and cultural environment where a woman, and a widow, could live autonomously and honorably. In England, comparing the life of a woman in India to that of a woman in the Western world (albeit her many cultural and social restrictions), she began working actively to improve the condition of the former. Writing a letter in 1883 ("The Cry of Indian Women") to Sir Bartle Frere, former governor of the Bombay Presidency, she foregrounded the idea of founding a home for Indian women who were victims of their own society and culture (i.e., widows who were expected to commit suicide after the death of their husbands or would find themselves completely abandoned by all, young girls who were forced into marriage, ill-treated women, etc.).

After the suicide of a dear friend, Anandibai Bhagat, who had converted to Christianity on her deathbed, Ramabai, suffering depression, also converted at the end of September 1883. She and her daughter were baptized as members of the Anglican Church. Meanwhile Ramabai's deafness prevented her from continuing medical studies, so she chose instead to teach Sanskrit in the Cheltenham Ladies' College, while she studied English, natural science, and mathematics.

Three years later, in 1886, she was invited to the United States by Dr. Rachel Bodley, Dean of the Woman's Medical College of Pennsylvania (where the first Indian woman doctor, a distant relative of Ramabai, was graduating). There Ramabai discovered another new social and cultural environment. On behalf of Indian women, she spent two and a half years (from March 1886 to October 1888) traveling from coast to coast, comparing the United States to her native country. She studied the American educational system, and the different positions held by women in American society; she made speeches and worked to raise funds to build a home for high-caste Hindu widows in India. The Ramabai Association was created in 1887 in Boston, whose purported goal was to establish a nonsectarian educational institution in India that would welcome mainly child-widows, give them shelter and the necessary education and means to become independent women.

Returning now to the East, Ramabai and her daughter sailed from San Francisco for India via Japan and China in 1888. In March of that year Ramabai opened the Sharada Sadan (Home of Learning), a widows' home at Chowpatty, which was almost immediately supported by the reformers of the Bombay Presidency. The home was transferred to Poona in 1890; but in 1891 the institution, notwithstanding its nonsectarian principles and mainly humanitarian purposes, was strongly attacked on charges of religious proselytism. Several members of the advisory board resigned, and many girls were withdrawn from the institution, but Ramabai in the end was exonerated.

After having experienced both Eastern and Western worlds and cultures, she had returned home, even though there everything seemed "quite dark," to create an important network of supporting institutions in favor of Indian women and their cultural emancipation. A terrible famine having struck the Central Provinces and the Gujarat in 1896, she gave shelter and help to many of the victims in the huts on land of her own in the village of Kedgaon near Poona. There she created a new institution, the Mukti Sadan (Home of Salvation), which later became the Mukti Mission. She then obtained again the support of the reconstituted American Ramabai Association to create other structures, where she welcomed sexually abused women (at the Kripa Sadan, or Home of Mercy) as well as blind or aged women who received help, shelter, and education.

Her daughter and assistant Manoramabai died in 1921. Ramabai died in 1922, after having completed the Maharati translation of the Bible, which was printed in Kedgaon by the girls whom she herself had trained in her house.

Living in a colonized environment, where the Western world was represented mainly by the British, Ramabai had frequently wondered about the secret of their power over the East. As early as 1882 she wrote:

> Upon consideration, it will indeed appear that it is on the strength of a very powerful incantation that the Europeans accomplish all difficult tasks with only a little effort and thus achieve the progress of their community. What is that incantation? It is nothing but the incessant effort of every person in their community. . . . This quality exists in all of them, from prince to pauper, which is why their power is so strong. (*Stri Dharma Niti*, ibid., 41)

An implicit self-questioning, and perhaps a criticism, of the Indian system of castes and of the condition of Indian women is already perceivable in these words. Therefore, her travel in the West had to start in the very country—England—from which the European community came. During the period she spent in the "core" of the British Empire, Ramabai realized that she was considered as part of an enormous, confused, magmatic cultural "whole" to which Western cultures, and especially the Anglo-Saxon one, relegated the rest of the world:

> Some English have such comprehensive classifications of the human race— they have been known to bring under the same category the skin-clad, flat-headed inhabitant of the North American continent, and the descendant of the ancient Aryan race of Central Asia. Some have even a more comprehensive mind still, and embrace under one term "native" inhabitants of India, America, Africa, Australia, and all the islands of the Pacific. One evil result of this confusion is, that the stories related of one race are often supposed to be true of another. (*Indian Religion* (1886), in *Pandita Ramabai through Her Own Words*, 119)

Here Ramabai expresses a quiet but acute critique of one of the main— and widespread—cultural attitudes of the time, Orientalism, and from the point of view of a "native." In this perspective, a systemic functional linguistic analysis of some details of her writing, based on M. A. K. Halliday's *An Introduction to Functional Grammar* (London: Arnold, 1994), can be revealing, especially if focused on the grammatical notion of Subject that is fundamental to Western grammatical tradition. Subject is a label indicating the three main functions a word can assume: the doer of an action; that on which something is being predicated; that of being the concern of a message. During the second half of the nineteenth century, renewed interest in grammatical studies and theories led to a more detailed analysis of these three main functions, which were seen as determining, respectively, the psychological subject, the grammatical subject, and the logical subject of a clause. When describing the point of view of the "Western world," Ramabai uses "Some English" and "Some" as logical, grammatical, and psychological subjects; the term "some" has, in the first instance, a nonspecific deictic (pointing out, demonstrative) function for "English" and adds a sense of indefinite comprehensiveness to the specific noun of a people and a nation (which, in this context of situation, also symbolizes Western culture as a whole). Ironically, this gives us just that kind of "comprehensiveness" that Ramabai implicitly criticizes in this passage. It is as if she were directing against the English that same lack of regard toward cultural differences that they show toward the Eastern world.

This becomes even more relevant in the second instance of the word, where "English" is elided and "Some," as a nonselective plural pronoun, stands alone. By means of these three functions of the coextensive subjects "Some English" and "Some," Ramabai enacts a sort of reverse "Orientalism"—an "Occidentalism," as it were. All Western cultures and peoples are seen as being a whole, judging another whole according to a set of erroneous collective prejudices. Ramabai puts her readers in the same position that they have put her and her culture. Traveling in England and in the United States, she became an observer of the Orientalist generalized and generalizing cultural attitude, which tends to erase particular Eastern cultural identities and ideologically takes possession of them, incorporating them into a Western global (and essentially colonial) vision of the world.

As an Eastern traveler in the West, Ramabai was able to see herself and her country both as a "subject" and as an "object," through the eyes of an observer and yet still an observed "item" of a "Western East." She also speaks for plurality and mutual understanding, like a traveler experiencing plurality herself. In this perspective, she may be collocated among multiculturalist writers. Distancing herself from both "poles," she takes the position of a traveler between cultures, a sort of "bridging writer" who experiences both "strains of thought" and who seems willing to explain to both "hemispheres" the reasons for their cultural attitudes and the misunderstandings that can derive from them:

> I can quite understand, now that I have become accustomed to Western thought, how repulsive are some of the sacred symbols of Hindu mythology. I can, however, assure Christians that to the pure-minded these are mere abstractions. . . . I desire that the races, whom God has in His providence placed in such intimate relations with one another, should understand one another better. (*Indian Religion*, ibid., 120–21)

Interestingly, in this paragraph the "I," referring to Ramabai herself as speaker, is the logical, grammatical, and psychological subject in all the main clauses, thus taking on a further important value: it positions the writer as representative of a whole Eastern culture (and, in general, of all

"misregarded" Eastern cultures), whose self-proclaimed task is to mediate
the understanding of that culture to her audience, the Western mind,
from "colonial" England to "democratic" America.

While traveling and speaking throughout the United States, Ramabai
wrote two major texts: *The High-Caste Hindu Woman* (1887), written in
English for a Western public, and *United Stateschi Lokasthiti ani Pravasavritta* (*Religious Denominations and Charities in the USA*, published in
India in 1889), written in Maharati for an Indian public. "Democratic"
America, the "middle" mooring between "colonial" England and "colonized" India, was therefore also the country where Ramabai, comparing
the three different cultures and societies she knew, could really work at
clarifying the differences among them.

The areas of comparison stressed in *The High-Caste Hindu Woman*
(and in *Religious Denominations and Charities in the USA* as well) are, of
course, the condition of women (in this case, Indian women) and religion.
Through a cross-analysis of Christianity and Hinduism, Ramabai can
actually explain to Western readers the reasons for the many cultural misunderstandings of the Eastern world. To Indian readers, she can show
the cultural, social, and political differences between "old" traditional
England and "new" democratic America, and compare them with India.

The strict link between religion and society is immediately stated at the
very beginning of *The High-Caste Hindu Woman*, in the "prefatory
remarks" in which Ramabai writes: "In order to understand the life of a
Hindu woman, it is necessary for the foreign reader to know something
of the religion and the social customs of the Hindu nation" (*The High-
Caste Hindu Woman*, 1). No introductory descriptions, no acknowledg-
ments, no autobiographical notes. A systemic functional linguistic analysis
of the very first line of the book reveals a prepositional phrase functioning
as "circumstance of Cause: Purpose," through which Ramabai immediately states what her cultural purpose is. She explains the cultural roots
of the socioreligious institutions of Hindu castes: "Without doubt, 'caste'
originated in the economical division of labour. . . . [A]lthough 'caste' is
confessedly an outgrowth of social order, it has now become the first great
article of the Hindu creed all over India" (ibid., 6, 9).

What follows is the description of the basic life stages of a Hindu
woman: "Childhood," youth or "Married Life," and "Widowhood" or old
age. Ramabai writes extensively about the joint family system and about

the degree of freedom a young Indian girl enjoys until the day of her marriage. This day in particular symbolizes in her words a perpetual ban, the end of physical and intellectual "travel" and, therefore, of accumulation of knowledge: "The women's court is situated at the back of the house, where darkness reigns perpetually. There the child-bride is brought to be forever confined" (*The High-Caste Hindu Woman*, 44).

The condition of women is a good field for Ramabai to make comparisons between East and West, thus showing the knowledge of the two "worlds" that she acquired as a traveler, and implicitly restating the necessity of acknowledging and studying cultural differences in order to achieve real mutual understanding. She writes, for example:

> In Europe and America women do choose their husbands, but it is considered a shame for a woman to be the first to request marriage, and both men and women will be shocked equally at such an occurrence; but in India, women had equal freedom with men, in this case at least. A woman might, without being put to shame, and without shocking the other party, come forward and select her own husband. (ibid., 30–31)

Also in this case, a linguistic analysis of some aspects of her writing, performed in a systemic functional perspective, can help us to catch the implicit irony with which Ramabai, the open-minded traveler between East and West, addresses "civilized" (but at the same time colonial) Western society (cf. Paul Bayley and Donna R. Miller, Introduction, in *Texts and Contexts of the American Dream*, 1993). The first clause starts with a prepositional phrase functioning as Circumstance of Location/Space, which signals that all that follows pertains to the "Western part" of the world, as Western culture itself sees it. This is the first term of the comparison. The second term is introduced by the clause starting with "but," an adversative conjunctive that precedes another prepositional phrase functioning again as circumstance of Location/Space, which presents the whole statement as pertaining to the "Eastern part" of the world. This linguistic organization shows Ramabai as a traveler who well knows the importance of carefully taking cultural and social differences into account. Here she narrows the geographical and cultural space of her specifically contrasting assertions to "Europe and America" versus "India," in what would otherwise appear to be perhaps an overly "neat" division of the world, but that here has its rationale.

The clauses introduced by the prepositional phrases "in Europe and America" and "in India" foreground both the geographical and the cultural "poles" of Ramabai's comparison; however, while the reader would expect at this point Ramabai's praise of the Western woman's condition, since the author's primary aim is here to underline the miserable condition of the high-caste Hindu woman, the conjunctive "but" sets up a contrast that unexpectedly is all in favor of the East. The "typical" reality of these two spatial and cultural locations is therefore overturned and the reader is thus invited to reconsider his or her vision of what is the taken-for-granted Western representation of the world.

Religious Denominations and Charities in the USA is a sort of "full-circle" book written and published after Ramabai's return to "her" East. Technically, this may be her only real "travelogue"—a text that tells people at home about people and places abroad. In this text, as elsewhere, the main bases of comparison among English, American, and Indian culture and society are religion and the condition of women. Writing about religion, Ramabai also compares the fundamental political (and sociocultural) differences between "colonial" England and "democratic" America. The English monarchy and the Church of England are presented as two aspects of the same political institution:

> In England the denomination known as the Church of England is integrated with the power of monarchy. The King or Queen of England must belong to this denomination, and all the subjects of that country must bear the expenses of its bishops, etc. The Government extracts a heavy tax from them, whether or not they belong to that denomination. . . . This practice of extracting forced obeisance, in a progressive country like England, is very strange indeed. (*Religious Denominations and Charities in the USA*, in *Pandita Ramabai through Her Own Words*, 181)

America, by contrast, is praised for not linking its many religious denominations to the possession of land and goods, but is criticized for the barbaric practice of slavery, also defined as "strange" by Ramabai:

> Here [in America] there is very little land attached to churches. . . . Another strange thing was that, while this country was engaged in the slave trade, these [church] people did not feel ashamed to accept money from the sale of slaves, and spend it on church expenditure and on good deeds

like evangelization. They were firmly convinced that God had created the
Black people of Africa, like cattle, for their own wilful use. (ibid., 184)

And this is the point where, most ironically, she introduces an implicit
critique of a certain Western sense of superiority:

> In our own country, the three [upper] castes including the Brahmans also
> believed that the people of the Shudra caste were created by God only to
> serve them, and that such service was their only means of salvation. People
> in a state of barbarity always hold such evil beliefs. (ibid.)

Ramabai goes on to criticize Indians for their willingness to imitate the
West in its worst vices, like drinking, smoking, atheism, and the like. Her
point is also a good introduction to the discussion of the condition of
women—who, in the West, actively fight against those typically "male"
vices ("Woman's Crusade," in ibid., 235 ff.). It is interesting that to introduce this subject and the part of the book in which she most extensively
describes Western women's battles and victories, she refers to ancient
Indian religious and mythological traditions:

> As a child, I took great delight in listening to marvellous tales, just as other
> children do. . . . Seven years ago, I had not the slightest inkling that I would
> really be able to witness goddesses like Sita, endowed with the strength,
> comparable to that of Haihayarjuna, to block the force of a great river, and
> able to slay invincible demons like Ravana with their hundred or thousand
> heads. But, happily, in the course of time I was able to witness such won-
> derful things and now have the opportunity to present at least a brief
> account of them to my countrymen and women. (ibid., 195)

She then goes on to make a list of all the main American religious denominations and expresses herself in favor of women preachers. As she has
quoted an Indian myth to introduce her subject, she then makes a sort of
second introduction to the condition of women by creating a "myth"
drawn from her own experience, based on a metaphor inspired by the
landscape of Colorado:

> There is a State called Colorado in the western part of the United States,
> in which a solid, stony, immoveable range of mountains known as the

Rockies has spread across the land since time immemorial. It seems impossible to break through it in order to cut a trail and go across. How would a river, [which is] almost a tiny stream, possess the strength to penetrate the mountains? But behold the marvel! The Arkansas river started quietly to make a way through the Rocky mountains. The sea, the lake and the rivers of the plains must have felt a sad surprise at its unshakeable resolve, and the sky-high range of the Rockies must have pitied it. The smaller mountains must have deplored and condemned it for this risky venture. But the Arkansas river ignored them all. . . . With persistent effort and strong resolve it defeated even the Rocky mountain. The tiny Arkansas clashed against that impenetrable, unbreakable stone range and carved out a way for itself right through the Rocky mountains! Bravo Arkansas! And bravo American women! Even though weak like this rivulet, lacking the support of scriptures, money, popular opinion or religious tradition, and relying only on the strength of persistent effort and resolve, they . . . cut a trail for themselves. I say once again, bravo American women! (ibid., 202–3)

What Ramabai is here proposing to her Indian public is a new myth, which is intended not to replace the old ones but to interpret modern times and new perspectives. She is showing Indian society the necessity of acknowledging and accepting important changes in the condition of Hindu women, in a period of important cultural and political exchanges with the West. She actually indicates the main areas in which such changes are most urgent—areas in which American women have already started their "escalation": education (up to university degrees), employment (permitted to them and on an equal-salary basis), legal rights (the same for women and men in all domains), and the creation of national organizations and women's clubs to support the woman's "crusade" for her emancipation.

Not at random, therefore, in introducing these points, Ramabai uses another parallel between traditional Hindu mythology and the new American mythology she has created out of her travels:

Initially, the Civil War caused untold misery, poverty and suffering; however, they were immediately followed by great good, just as the deadly poison was followed by nectar and the precious gem [when the legendary ocean was churned by gods and demons, according to the Hindu mythology]. (ibid., 223)

What Ramabai creates in this text is an exemplary mythology for the future, the fruit of her journey from the West back to "her" East as narrated in *A Testimony of Our Inexhaustible Treasure* (1907). She seems to have finally reached the real aim of her long journey: knowledge of a complex world of cultures—and freedom, not only for herself but for all women who wished to follow in her footsteps.

Arianna Maiorani

BIBLIOGRAPHY

Bayley, Paul, and Donna R. Miller, Introduction, in *Texts and Contexts of the American Dream*, Bologna: Pitagora, 1993.

Ramabai, Pandita. *Pandita Ramabai through Her Own Words: Selected Works*. Ed. and trans. Meera Kosambi. New Delhi: Oxford University Press, 2000. [Contains *Stri Dharma Niti* (trans. 1882); *The Cry of Indian Women* (1883); *An Autobiographical Account* (1883); *Indian Religion* (1886); *The High-Caste Hindu Woman* (1887); *Religious Denominations and Charities in the USA* (trans. from *United Stateschi Lokasthiti ani Pravasavritta*, 1889); *The Condition of Women in the USA* (trans. from *United Stateschi Lokasthiti ani Pravasavritta*, 1889); *Famine Experiences* (1897); *To the Friends of Mukti School and Mission* (1900); *A Short History of Kripa Sadan, or Home of Mercy* (1903); *A Testimony of Our Inexhaustible Treasure* (1907); and *The Word-Seed* (1908).]

———. "Indian Religion," in *The Cheltenham Ladies' College Magazine* 13 (Spring 1886).

———. *The High-Caste Hindu Woman*. Introduction by Rachel L. Bodley, Dean of the Woman's Medical College of Pennsylvania. 3rd ed. Philadelphia, 1888.

Vaidya, D. G., ed. *Pandita Ramabai Yancha Englandcha Pravas* (1883), 2nd ed. Bombay: Maharastra State Board of Literature and Culture, 1988.

Daisy Bates

(1859–1951)

to wander over these great distances in company with the Aborigines and hear the wonderful legends of this and that star. . . .

(Daisy Bates, *Tales Told to Kabbarli*, 5)

She preferred "dream time" to chronological time; the Far East to
the West; Aboriginals to Caucasians. Nonetheless, Daisy May
O'Dwyer, born in Ballycrine, County Tipperary, was Irish to the
roots. Although her fascination with myths and legends, her ultra-white
complexion and brilliant blue eyes, and her strikingly positive attitude
toward life could hardly be considered unique in her homeland, the role
she carved out for herself in the world was strictly her own.

Her mother died when she was five, and although her father lived on
for ten more years, she and her brother, Jim, were packed off to their
grandmother's farm near the small town of Rosecrea. There they spent
much of their time wandering into mysteriously exciting caves and scam-
pering over the hills of Caraig and Knockshegowna, fantasizing as only the
Irish can. At the right time, Daisy buckled down to her studies, acquired
a secondary education, and in the process discovered she had a gift for
languages, particularly French and German (*Tales Told to Kabbarli*, 3).

Little is known about her early life: apparently she was given free passage on a ship sailing to Australia in 1883 and, upon arrival at Townsville,
found employment at Charters Towers in North Queensland. Then she

took a post as governess at Fanning Downs, a cattle station near Charters Towers, in 1884 (Daisy Bates, *The Native Tribes of Western Australia*, 3). Years later, when asked her reasons for traveling such a formidable distance from home, she admitted to being prone to tuberculosis and needing a change of climate. She might also have been induced to seek new skies for economic reasons and her Irish proclivity for living out her fantasies. She claimed that a Banchee (or *Bean Sidhe*), literally "a woman of the hills," or "woman of the fairies," had been present at her birth and had wailed, signaling approaching death. In her case, the death was that of her mother (Peter Berresford Ellis, *Irish Mythology*, 40). Intrigued by Celtic lore with its "ghosties and witchies and doggerel curses," Daisy, like other Irish people, had the moxie to set off on her own to faraway Australia (*Tales Told to Kabbarli*, 3).

Although facts are scant, shortly after her arrival in Australia, she who had reveled in the crags and open fields of Ireland fell in love with pastoral life in the Australian Outback. Human love followed in swift pursuit— and, perhaps, thoughtlessly. In Charters Towers in 1884 she married the enticing Edwin Murrant, later known as "Breaker Morant," an infamous Australian swashbuckler. The marriage soured some weeks later when he was accused of theft. Charges were dropped, but Daisy left him, never to see him again (Daisy Bates, *Native Tribes*, 3).

She next took employment as governess to the Bates family, near Nowra, about one hundred miles from Sydney, marrying the eldest son, John Bates, a "drover" (driver of cattle or sheep), in 1885. Although she remained married to him for nine years and gave birth to a son, Arnold, she realized early on that once again her marriage was wrong. No matter; the independent Daisy Bates forged around Australia with her son, spending time with friends. In 1894 she left the boy with the Bates family and sailed to England, where she worked as a journalist for W. T. Stead, editor of *Review of Reviews*, *Pall Mall Gazette*, and *Borderland*, the latter focusing on the occult (*Aboriginal Perth: Bibbulmun Biographies and Legends*, vi). By 1899, she had become well versed as a reporter and returned to Australia with the intent of studying an article published in the *Times* accusing white settlers of mistreating Australian Aboriginals in the northwest of Western Australia. Her altruistic feelings for the Aboriginals had increased during her stay in London and developed still further after meeting the Catholic clergyman Dean Martelli on board ship during her return trip to Australia. Martelli undoubtedly spoke with pride about the apparent success of his church among the Aborigines in Western Australia (*Native Tribes*, 5).

Soon after her return to Australia, Bates made it a point of traveling with the Catholic bishop Matthew Gibney to the Beagle Bay Trappist Mission, where she devoted the next three months to studying the conditions of the Aboriginals in the region. Soon thereafter, she joined her husband at a station on Roebuck Plains not far from Broome. The strong-willed Bates helped him drive a large herd of cattle some hundreds of miles south from Roebuck Plains to their new property in the Ophtalmia Range, after which she decided to separate from her husband.

The now seasoned journalist settled temporarily in Perth and, although poorly paid, supported herself as a freelance writer. Dressed in strictest Edwardian fashion—tailored suit with high-neck blouse, ankle-length skirt, hat, buttoned boots, and gloves—this young and very attractive Irish lady was recognizable wherever she went. It was at this juncture that she began her serious studies of the Aboriginals and was sent by the *Western Mail* to Australia's Peak Hill district to report on the Aborigines (ibid.). Upon being apprised of a disturbing article appearing in the *Times* in April 1899 claiming that the Aboriginal tribes living on pastoral stations in Western Australia "were worse off than the American Negro slaves had been," she set about investigating the claim (ibid., 6). In her May 4 reply to the allegations made in the *Times,* she not only "defended the settlers" but labeled the accusations "ridiculous" (ibid.). In due course she would modify her opinion. For the present, she was determined to learn more about these Paleolithic tribes.

To say that a new sense of excitement and purpose had entered Bates's life would be to minimize the fervor she felt during the years she spent researching the conditions, customs, myths, and languages of these ancient peoples. To this end, she began working in May 1904 for the state government in the Department of the Registrar-General at a salary of eight shillings a day. Her work consisted of compiling a list of the languages spoken by the Aborigines and familiarizing herself with the articles already written about them. As her research took on dimension and depth, she began studying the relatively new science of anthropology. Methodical in her approach, she consulted all available books on the subject.

She set up her "tent," which became her headquarters from 1905 to 1907, on the reserve allotted the Aborigines at Mamba, around six miles from Perth. Living at close range allowed her to speak directly with the people, to visit with them, and to know them. After carefully noting her initial research work, she continued her travels in South and Western Australia, visiting reserves such as Katanning, north of Albany. In 1907 she traveled east to Esperance and south to the Goldfields, interviewing and talking to the Aboriginals (ibid., 6). Her compulsive search for information remained unassuaged. In 1908 she visited seventy towns, traveling over 5,400 miles to talk personally with and question Aboriginal tribal peoples, gathering untold quantities of information concerning their customs, totems, tales, foods, and more (*Tales Told to Kabbarli*, 5).

The great Bibbulmun race that occupied the whole of the South-West, from beyond Julien Bay . . . to Esperance [was] the largest homogeneous group in all Australia. The residents of the Kalleep were Kallep-gur, "home people" or "townies," who wandered hither and thither over their group areas at all seasons of the year, visiting their relatives at Northam, Toojie (Toodyay), according to the time of year when the special totem food product of each group was in season. As we pass by the hollow where the old banana gardens were afterwards planted we stand near a spot that was the scene of many a kangaroo battue in Bibbulmun days. The Kalleep-gur chased the Yong-gar and Warr male and female kangaroos . . . driving the animals with shouts and yells into the hollow. . . . At its foot were other Kalleep-gur ready with spear and club to give the killing blow. There was no escape for the animals that tumbled into the hollow, and there was much feasting and fighting, and furstring and skin cloak-making after . . . a kangaroo battue. (*Aboriginal Perth*, 1)

Bates moved her tent to different Aboriginal camp sites in Western and South Australia, coming and going from one to the other at will, posing questions to those she interviewed, then noting their responses with care and method. She knew only too well that since the coming of the white man many tribes were dying out, so her work would be a race against time. Upon her return to Perth, she sent a host of papers to learned journals, now greedy for her work, even while continuing her travels and reportages for newspapers and lecturing as well to various scholarly groups.

In 1909, she returned to her office in Perth to collate the masses of information she had gleaned from her interviews with South and Western Australian tribes living on reserves in Perth, Guilford, Bunbury, Vasse, Capel, Victoria Plains, and other districts (*Native Tribes*, 11). She was made a fellow of the Royal Anthropological Society (Australasia) and invited to become a member of the Natural History and Science Society of Western Australia, all of which added to her luster (*Aboriginal Perth*, vii). Accolades increased when, in 1910, she was called upon to join an anthropological expedition from Cambidge University directed by A. Radcliffe-Brown. The two, however, were soon at odds with each other.

Although Honorary Protector of Aborigines for the Eucla district and the author of a large number of publications, Bates felt extreme disappointment in 1912, when, following the submission of her "huge rambling" manuscript titled "Aboriginal Tribes" for publication to the Australian government, the premier informed her that the necessary funds for such a vast venture were unavailable (ibid., viii). Nonetheless, her spirits were buoyed in 1934 when she was made a "Companion of the British Empire" (ibid., 7).

Despite arduous conditions during her forays into tribal territories—intense heat in the summmer, and polar cold during the winter months—Bates continued her "tent life" until 1935, glorying under the moon and the stars on the Nulla-bar Plain. At night, when not listening to the Aboriginals relating their tales, she looked into her telescope, trying to fathom the stories of the evolving constellations that had been recounted to her: the manner in which animals, birds, humans, and constellations had acquired their physical characteristics, most notably, the Moon God, Yaggin, a male, who had lived long ago with his wife, Ngan-garu, the Sun. At Eucla, Bates was "instructed in the mysteries of the Aboriginal zodiac."

The Commonwealth government gave her an office and a secretary in 1936, for the purposes of copying and cataloging the immense collection of disparate handwritten notes she had collected throughout the years. After completion in 1940, she gave the work to the Commonwealth, along with other writings. In return she received a weekly pension of two pounds a week, later increased to five. She was so poor that she could not even afford to live in Adelaide. She moved to another camp at Pyap on the Murray River, continuing her research.

Following her retirement from government employment, Bates moved to Rottnest Island, used at the time as a prison for Aboriginals. She used the opportunity to interview the prisoners, as she had the ill ones during her stay on Dorre Island. Although in her seventies, her productive years of research continued. Her sense of fulfillment burgeoned at the thought that she had been instrumental in expanding the fund of knowledge about her beloved Aboriginals, and she fully hoped that her book on them would one day be published.

Nor did the onset of old age halt her traveling days. After a year in Eucla interviewing Aboriginals from the far southeast of the state of Western Australia, she moved further east, to Fowlers Bay, then to Ooldea in South Australia. Kind to a fault throughout the years, the desperately poor Bates still visited the ill in her tribes, frequently paying for their medications. If food was scarce in tribal communities, she cooked sweet porridge and *damper* for them, even clothing them when necessary. When she went hungry, her Aboriginal friends brought her a snake they had roasted, which she ate with gusto. She died at Adelaide on April 18, 1951.

Bates's passion for travel, triggered by her love for the Australian Aboriginals, became a lifelong affair. Her many studies and articles published in the Australian government's *Year Book*, its *Agriculture Journal*, *The Royal Geographical Society*, and other learned journals, included a compilation of vocabularies of native dialects of Western and northwestern Australia. About her research work, she wrote:

> It having been found that, beyond a few works written in the early days of the Colony, West Australia possessed no standard literature of her fast fading aboriginal population, it was deemed desirable that a work should be compiled from all the existing records which should stand as a book of reference for ethnologists and philologists in their study of our interesting aborigines. My offer was accepted and I commenced work on the 3rd of May, 1904. (*Native Tribes*, 10)

Once her vocabulary was completed and distributed to the postmasters, police officers, and settlers, Bates began consulting library books, governmental records, and the works of the Scientific Societies of Tasmania, Victoria, N.S.W., and Queensland, with the goal of preparing her own study of the manners, customs, totems, languages, and myths of the Australian Aboriginals. At the end of a year she had consulted over 250 volumes and written 800 pages. Because of the conflicting information gleaned in the reference works she had read, she determined, with government agreement, not to rely on secondary information, but to go directly to the source: to Perth, Gilford, Bunbury, Vasse, Capel, Augusta, Gingin, York, Beverley, and Victoria Plains. Thanks to her straightforward but gentle interviewing method, she discovered that much of the previous information gathered by others concerning tribal marriage laws, customs, dialects, and myths had been faulty (ibid., 10).

While pursuing her remarkable research work, she began to outline a grammar book on the southern dialects of Aborigines. To accomplish her task, she continued her "tent life" that permitted her to note as much as possible of "their everyday talk" (ibid., 11). Slowly and punctiliously she wrote down the words she heard and, in time, created her own linguistic maps (ibid.). That she became fluent in several Aboriginal languages does not come as a surprise.

Turning to anthropological matters, she probed questions of maternal descent in districts such as Perth, enabling her to verify the conclusions of others: "the child of a white cockatoo woman was a white cockatoo, the father being a Crow man." Farther south, however, "the child of a White Cockatoo woman was a Crow child, thus the descent was made through the father" (ibid., 12). Upon further travel, this time to Southern Cross in Swanland, Bates discovered "a little isolated tribe having special divisions of their own . . . these having no relation to the tribes of the north, south, east or west of them" (ibid., 12).

Thrilled by the information she gleaned during her eight months of travel and investigation, she made up her mind that despite the physical hardships involved she would continue to answer her calling. Her method would be the same everywhere: never to rely on information gathered by others, but to carry out her own personal research on tribal organization, marriage laws, physical characteristics, food, initiation rituals, religious beliefs, magic, disease, legends, folklore, totems, hunting, mourning rituals, song, dance, bodily decorations, and ritual objects (ibid., 19). Her deeply emotional involvement with the tribal members whom she consulted impelled her to accomplish her groundbreaking work:

sitting by their fires at the hour of storytelling . . . it is impossible to convey the dramatic gesture, the significant "flick" of fingers or features which accompanied the narration . . . the flash of eye as the spear is driven home, the tracks made in the sand of the hand or footprint of the bird or animal of the story. . . . Only those who have watched the storyteller can fully apprecate the dramatic recital. . . . (*Tales Told to Kabbarli*, 8)

Bates's meticulously researched chapter on "Tribal Organisation and Geographical Distribution" in her volume *The Native Tribes of Western Australia*, revised by the author from 1899 to 1911 and again in 1917, was memorable for its gleanings of the topographical makeup of the Eucla district in the south of Western Australia. Her discussions of terrain, rainfall, droughts, and passable barriers, including those of the Darling Ranges almost 4,000 feet high in the southwestern part of the state, impact on the reader.

The mountainous ranges and rugged precipices of North Kimberley, she discovered,

possess native highways as yet unknown to the white man, but traversed for untold generations by their native inhabitants, and the so-called desert areas and spinifex wastes of the central areas have highways along their water-holes, springs, soaks, etc., over which friendly tribes have travelled for initiation and other ceremonies. (*Native Tribes*, 37)

Writing about "The Karratjibbin Groups," which differ from other known tribes in the West, Bates reports that they "possess a two-moiety system, which in this respect links them with their southwestern neighbors, but with the important difference amongst the Karratjibbin people of each moiety marrying within itself and producing the other moiety" (ibid., 55).

Of great interest to contemporary readers is Bates's innovative and lively account *Aboriginal Perth: Bibbulmun Biographies and Legends*, originally published in newspapers and magazines of her day. First she situates the Bibbulmun territories—in the southwest of Western Australia—and then recounts their tales of *old*, when this Paleolithic people ruled the day. At night, after she and members of the Bibbulmun tribe had eaten, danced, sung, and drunk slightly fermented water, they would sit, she wrote, around a fire, listening in rapt silence to tales of magic and witchcraft.

> Now it is night—night indeed for the Bibbulmun race—and our ramblings are over and we sit by the fire and hear the folklorists' tales of magic and witchcraft; of the powers of woggae (magic snake) and the jang-ga, and the spirits who returned from the dead and lived in the caves and shelters and were sulky, always torturing many whom they caught by half cooking them and making them alive again and again for their sport; of standing stones and rocks that held the spirits of little babies waiting for the mothers to come to them; and of the birds and beasts that spoke Bibbulmun speech, and helped or hindered as the case might be. Kower, the red parrot, showed the Bibbulmun how to make fire, and the dried flower stems of the balga (blackboy tree) with which he drilled the fire were called kowerduk ever afterwards by the Kalleepgur whom Kower had taught. (*Aboriginal Perth*, 4)

On other occasions, she related tales that probed this tribe's history, their haunted places, nomenclatures, and father-son relationships. She also singled out for study their famous members, particularly Fanny Balbuk-Yoorel, who died at sixty-five, and was "The Last Swan River (Female) Native." Her tribe's territory had once extended from near Gingin in the north, to beyond Fremantle in the south (ibid., 76).

> The peculiar system of relationship existing amongst the West Australian aborigines, which roughly speaking, makes all the father's people "relations-in law," while the mother's people are "blood relations," rendered it possible for Balbuk to pass, not only from one end of her own people's country to the other, but the "relations" that might be found in every camp along the foot of the hills through which she desired to pass. (ibid., 76)

In the old days, Balbuk used to gather "the seasonal scarlet fruit of the zamia, 'by-yoo' as it is called, and buried it to rid it of its poisonous properties and here she collected the many roots and fruits growing on the slopes of Karr'gata, as the area hereabouts was named" (ibid., 76ff.). Her first marriage was a happy one. After her husband's death, her second marriage, to her brother-in-law, according to custom, was an unhappy one. Each time she ran away from him she was dragged back by her relatives until they finally allowed her to remain. She married again—a "wrong class marriage"—and became involved in a fight with her husband's sister.

> The two women fought with their only weapon, a wanna or digging stick, about three or four feet in length, nearly an inch in diameter and pointed at one end. After some clubbing, Balbuk, at that time a young woman of unusual strength, suddenly caught her wanna "spear fashion," and drove it right through the heart of her opponent, killing her instantly. (ibid., 77)

Understandably did she flee her opponent's relatives, wandering from one camp to another until she reached the barely inhabited Moore River district, where she remained for around seven years, traveling to certain centers "where initiation and friend making" ceremonies would benefit her. It was during a period of wandering that Balbuk stayed with some cannibal natives in the Murison district. Although she was present when they ate human flesh, she maintained that she had never indulged in such eatingfests. She finally married a Tondarup of her class and gave birth to a boy child, who died at age seven. After having finally "served her voluntary banishment of seven years from her own home, she returned to the Swan River, and resumed her wanderings hither and thither amongst the 'fires' of her own people, having now, owing to the influx of population into and around Perth, no resting place or permanent camp of her own" (ibid., 78).

Music, dance, and thematic representation were implicit in Bibbulmun culture, for occasions of "mourning, rejoicing, inciting to battle, mimicry, eulogium of personal prowess, jealousy, revenge, challenge, and abuse." Music, better than words, underscored feelings of harmony and discord, love and hatred. Tones and sounds, expressed instinctively or purposefully, or heard in dreams, were implicit in tribal repertoires. As Bates noted:

> In extempore songs, the words are easily understood by singer and audience, and will be either representative of a visit paid to a distant tribe, and the wonders in there, or they may be illustrative of some event witnessed during the day. . . . Their "dream-songs" have frequently become sufficiently popular to be carried to far distant parts, although perhaps, neither the dreamer nor the hearers can understand a word of the song. The "melody" will doubtless be the attraction in many of these dream songs. (*Aboriginal Perth*, 31)

The accompaniments to the Western songs are

> the kylee (or boomerang); the meero, or throwing-stick; hand-clapping;
> beating the ground with . . . [a] (club), or a tightly-folded kangaroo-skin
> rug will be beaten by the closed fists of the women. Music evolved from
> such rude instruments has not much to recommend it to European ears,
> but to the natives themselves such music represents the very perfection of
> art. (ibid., 32)

Fascinating to the observer are the dressing rooms used for Bibbulmun
performance.

> The ground was arranged in a broken circle, one half of which was the
> "stage," the other half forming the "auditorium." A path ran through the
> centre of the circle, at either end of which and at a distance of about two
> or three yards from the ring a "green room," "dressing rooms," also of
> boughs and saplings, were put up, in which the performers prepared their
> decorations, made the nyetta or yanjee of shavings, that were to do duty as
> head dresses, armlets and anklets; spun the wog-arree or human hair string
> for the noolburn or waistbelt, and the katta wog-arree or head string; made
> the beendee beendee (shaved sticks) for head ornaments, and also to use as
> a sort of "thyrsus" in the hand during the movements of the dance; pre-
> pared the wom-mooloo or birds' down for the decoration of the body and
> face, sharpened the moolyert or nose-bone. (ibid., 32)

Details for makeup, decorations, stance, and other performing techniques
are intricate and precise. Understandably so, since theater was a gift of
the Gods.

Tales Told to Kabbarli is a collection of Aboriginal myths and legends that
Bates began noting in 1919, during her meetings with the Aboriginals at
Ooldea, short for "Yooldil Gabbi," referring to an underground lake, near
the Nullarbor Plain. Thanks to this supply of drinking water, existing for
thousands of years prior to the emergence of the white man, the area had
become a favorite tribal meeting ground. Bates would yoke two buckets
around her shoulders, carry them daily a mile and a half, fill them with
water, then carry them back to her tent. Since she had been living for

sixteen years in a tent among the Aboriginals, a loving maternal bond existed between her and her "black children" (*Tales Told to Kabbarli*, 1).

The Aboriginals narrated to Bates their tales of wonder and marvel that they had heard from their parents and grandparents. As if enacting a dramatic performance, these narrators projected the thoughts and feelings of the animals or humans involved in a hunt, or the interchanges between constellations, or other fantasy figures and situations, via the pose of a finger, a facial expression, or an eye movement, each making contact with *the other*. Nearly all the legends related in *Tales Told to Kabbarli* begin with "In Dhoogoorr," meaning "Dreamtime," the word with which the Aboriginals identified their supernatural domain. Underscored in her collection of tales are the Aboriginals' exceptional powers of observation, as demonstrated by their identification with animals. Their great humor and zest for life—its splendors and its horrors—are somewhat reminiscent of Aesop's *Fables*.

For the Aboriginals, the Moon is masculine, and the Sun feminine, as in Japanese cosmogony:

In the Nyitting or ice-cold times of long ago, Meeka the Moon was the husband of Ngangaru the Sun, and they lived together in a cave called Meeka Darrbi, the place where the Moon goes down, with their daughters and sons and a great pack of hunting dogs. (*Tales Told to Kabbarli*, 11)

Who better than Bates understood these narrations as primordial—or archetypal—experiences, sometimes personal, but more often transcendental. Although invoked on occasion for the sake of entertainment, more often they reflected a living and burning reality that existed in the psyche and culture of their people.

The recounting of myths, like original revelations of the preconscious psyche, are not simply allegories representative of the outer and inner lives of people but, like religion, are psychic realities. Every voluntary or involuntary mental construct related by Bates in her volumes of legends and myths may be envisaged as phantasms, dreams, visitations, hallucinations, or apparitions. They were real to the Aboriginals as they were at some level in Bates's psyche. They were fragments of some unknown mystery that had occurred either consciously or unconsciously to her as a child and throughout her adulthood.

Daisy Bates traveled and researched for posterity so that the mysteries of life, as known to the Aboriginals, might be saved. She left us to question the following thoughts:

> Kindly men and women tried to civilise and christianise them [the Aboriginals], but how could they absorb the ethics of either while their teachers held possession of and fenced in their kalleep (homes, fires)? How could they venerate a religion while its teachers destroyed their religious shrines, cut down their sacred trees and trod upon the sacred slope or hill that held the spirits of those who had made their laws and had given them their totem foods and waters since Jang-ga Nyitting times . . . of long ago? (*Aboriginal Perth*, 191)

Bettina L. Knapp

BIBLIOGRAPHY

Bates, Daisy. *The Native Tribes of Western Australia*. Ed. Isobel White. Canberra: National Library of Australia, 1885.

———. *The Passing of the Aborigines*. London: John Murray, 1944.

———. *Tales Told to Kabbarli*. Retold by Barbara Ker Wilson. Preface by Elizabeth Salter. Illustrated by Harold Thomas. New York: Crown Publishers, 1972.

———. *Aboriginal Perth: Bibbulmun Biographies and Legends*. Ed. P. J. Bridge. Victorian Park, Carlisle, Western Australia: Hesperian Press, 1992.

Ellis, Peter Berresford. *Irish Mythology*. Oxford: Oxford University Press, 1991.

Reed, A. W. *Aboriginal Fables and Legendary Tales*. Frenchs Forest, NSW, Australia: Reed Books, 1984.

CHAPTER 10

Edith Wharton
(1862–1937)

> . . . we had the road to ourselves, except for the flashing past
> of dispatch-bearers on motor cylces and of hideously hooting
> little motors carrying goggled officers in goat-skins and woolen
> helmets.
>
> (Edith Wharton, *Fighting France*, 48)

E dith Wharton is usually identified with the upper-class New York society into which she was born and that she satirized in her best-known novels (e.g., *The House of Mirth*, 1905, and *The Age of Innocence*, 1920), yet she lived more than half her life in Europe. Her fondness for automobile travel was celebrated in *A Motor Flight through France* (1908). By 1910, prompted by growing alienation from her husband, she moved permanently to France. The outbreak of World War I roused her to passionate support of the French cause, which she described in a series of hastily written articles first published in *Scribner's* magazine (Alan Price, *The End of the Age of Innocence: Edith Wharton and the First World War*, 43) and then as a book, *Fighting France* (1915).

It is striking that Wharton, the tireless traveler, approached her account of the opening days of the war as a travel writer, describing the disappearance of peacetime transport, the new conditions of wartime travel, and the epic size and speed of a modern motorized army. Like her friend Henry James, she believed that unchecked German aggression would mean "the crash of civilazation" (Price, 37), and she conceived

Fighting France to generate American support for France and contributions to French relief. She was, of course, an established travel writer, and in *Fighting France* she first appears as a peacetime tourist, "motoring north from Poitiers" to Paris on July 30, 1914, admiring "the noon-day quiet" and "distinctively French" look of "ruled-off fields and compact grey villages" (3), returning to the midsummer city, a place "made for peace and art," lying in "a sun-powdered haze" like "a princess guarded by the watchful giant of the Eiffel Tower" (6). Two days later Germany and Russia were at war. Within a few more days Germany declared war on France, occupied Luxembourg, and prepared to move through Belgium to invade France.

The picturesque peace Wharton described en route from Poitiers through Chartres to a fairy-tale Paris was shattered by the "General Mobilisation" (8), which brought a "break in the normal flow of traffic, like the sudden rupture of a dyke." Suddenly, the streets were "flooded by the torrent of people sweeping past us to the various railway stations. All were on foot, carrying their luggage, for since dawn every cab and taxi and motor omnibus had disappeared" (9). Wharton spent the first two nights of Mobilization at the Hotel Crillon (Price, 13), and the crowd passing her window seemed to be "chiefly composed of conscripts, the mobilisables of the first day" (9–10). Since it was August, there were also "little clusters of bewildered tourists, labouring along with bags and bundles, and watching their luggage pushed before them on handcarts— puzzled inarticulate waifs caught in the cross-tides racing to a maelstrom" (10). Those vacationers who did not leave immediately had to stay in partially emptied hotels, without porters or waiters, since "the army of midsummer travel" had been "immobilised to let the other army—fighting men—move" (12). Wheeled traffic ceased, and foot traffic increased: "[T]he middle of the Boulevards was as thronged with foot-passengers as an Italian market-place on a Sunday morning. The vast tide swayed up and down at a slow pace" (15–16). It was, Wharton adds, "a mixed throng, made up of every class, from the scum of the Exterior Boulevards to the cream of the fashionable restaurants." But, deliberately composing the most affecting picture, she notes that the "'people' luckily predominated; the faces of workers look best in such a crowd, and there were thousands of them, each illuminated and singled out by its magnesium-flash of passion" (16–17).

As motor traffic stalled, Wharton recalled "the gradual paralysis of the city": "motors, taxis, cabs and vans . . . vanished from the streets," "the lively little steamers" left the Seine, "and the canal-boats too were gone, or lay motionless" (13). Without transport, visitors and residents had to see the city on foot, and there was much "walking of the beautiful idle summer streets. . . . Never had such blue-grey softness of afternoon brooded over Paris . . . never, above all, [had] so rich a moon ripened through such summer evenings" (20). Vistas changed: "Every great architectural opening framed an emptiness; all the endless avenues stretched away to desert distances" (13). Public spaces were vacated and untended: "The fountains slept in their basins, the worried sparrows fluttered unfed, and [in] the parks and gardens no one raked the paths or trimmed the vague dogs, [who,] shaken out of their daily habits, roamed unquietly looking for familiar eyes" (13). Emptied, the city grew silent. In her "quarter, always deserted in summer," Wharton wrote, "the shuttered streets were mute as catacombs. . . . I could hear the tired tap of a lame hoof half a mile away, and the tread of the policeman guarding the Embassy across the street" (25). Paris, she concluded, seemed to have had "curare injected into all her veins" (13).

In September, the city changed again: "[T]he streets were made picturesque by the coming and going of English soldiery, and the aggressive flourish of British military motors. Then the fresh faces and smart uniforms disappeared" (32), and in their wake, "in the dark September days" came the "great army of the Refugees" (probably from Alsace), "men and women with sordid bundles on their backs, shuffling along hesitatingly in their tattered shoes, children dragging at their hands and tired-out babies pressed against their shoulders." Such people, she wrote, cannot foresee the "eventual triumph," for they belong "to a class whose knowledge of the world's affairs is measured by the shadow of their village steeple. . . . They were ploughing and sowing, spinning and weaving . . . when suddenly a great darkness full of fire and blood came down on them. And now, they are here, in a strange country, among unfamiliar faces and new ways" (33–34).

Concluding her first chapter, "The Look of Paris," Wharton noted that after six months of war, "all the early flush and shiver of romance is gone" (31), and, characteristically, she describes the city's revival in terms of its means of transportation: "The vanishing of all the motor-buses and of the huge lumbering commercial vans" had left "many a forgotten perspective open" and revealed "many a lost grace of architecture; but the taxi-cabs and private motors" remained, and "those unrivalled engines of destruction, the hospital and War Office motors," by "incessant dashing to and fro," kept "the peril of pedestrianism at its normal pitch" (32, n. 25). Commerce returned and shops reopened, for "women, however valiant . . . and self-denying, must eventually . . . begin to shop again." Parisiennes were sucked through the "swinging doors of the department stores" that drew them "irresistibly into their quicksand of remnants and reductions" (37).

Wharton herself was unusually busy in the first months of the war, setting up two large charities, a sewing room for unemployed women and the American Hostels for Refugees (Price, 37). In February 1915 she made the first of the five trips to the front that she describes in *Fighting France*. In all she went to the Argonne and Verdun once in February and again two weeks later in early March, to Lorraine and the Vosges in May, to Belgium ("the North") in June, and to Alsace in August (Price, 40). Although she characterizes herself modestly as a "traveller" (72) with "permission to visit a few ambulances and evacuation hospitals behind the lines" (45), Wharton's visits to the front were in fact "officially sanctioned by the French Red Cross and the government." She "carried medical supplies in her own car to distribute to ambulances and hospitals" (Price, 44). Nonetheless, her acount in *Fighting France* of these semiofficial trips says little of her relief work.

In a more touristic vein, she emphasizes landscape and panorama, living conditions in the towns she visits, the general impressions of a sophisticated traveler. Leaving Paris for the Argonne, "as we turned out of Meaux," she observes "the curious absence of life in the villages through which we passed," where "many of the fields were fallow and most of the doorways empty" (46). Yet while the old ways had faded, the new energies that the war had awakened—and the vehicles it employed—are notable. Going toward the Argonne, there are just "few carts driven by peasants" and "the 'civilian motor' had disappeared," so "all the dust-coloured cars dashing past us were marked with the Red Cross or the number of an army division" (47). Even more exhilarating is "the descent of the first hill beyond Montmirail [where] there came the positive feeling: This is war!" What excites Wharton is the panorama of armies on the move:

Along the white road . . . the army motors were pouring in endless lines, broken now and then by the dark mass of a tramping regiment or the clatter of a train of artillery. In the intervals between these waves of military traffic we had the road to ourselves, except for the flashing past of dispatch-bearers on motor-cycles and of hideously hooting little motors carrying goggled officers in goat-skins and woolen helmets. (47–48)

Exhilirating as they are, khaki and camouflage are, of course, "no substitute for the glitter of helmets and the curvetting of chargers" found in older wars, "but once the eye has adapted itself to the ugly lines and the neutral tints of the new warfare," she writes, "the scene . . . becomes positively brilliant." She revels in the vision of war "in all its concentrated energy" (49). Through all her tours at or near the front lines, Wharton remains a genteel traveler, particular about her "accommodations" and society. At a well-kept hotel in Chalons, where "even the grey motors and the sober uniforms seemed to sparkle" (50), she finds the scene in the restaurant "inexhaustibly interesting" (51). In peacetime she might have described local customs or, in Paris, ladies' fashions. Now there is the question of military dress: "Within the last two years," she notes, "the question of colour has greatly preoccupied the French military authorities, who have been seeking an invisible blue" (presumably for camouflage) and there is an "extraordinary variety of shades, . . . ranging from a sort of greyish robin's-egg to the darkest navy, in which the army is clothed." There is also "the poppy-red of the Spahis' tunics and various other less familiar colours—grey, and a certain greenish khaki" (52). There are also differences in cut, "from the old tight tunic to the loose belted jacket copied from the English" and the various military insignia—the "aviator's wings, the motorist's wheel" and "the doctors and the stretcher-bearers, the sappers miners, and heaven knows how many more ramifications of this great host which is really all the nation" (52–53).

Like most travelers, she is surprised to meet a friend in an unfamiliar place: at Chalons she runs across a "young man who in Paris drops in to dine with me and talk over new books and plays" and "for a blissful moment the whole fabric of what I had been experiencing . . . slipped away. . . . I seemed to see behind it the reassuring face of things as they used to be" (88–89).

In *Edith Wharton: A Woman in Her Time*, Louis Auchincloss comments on "the dependence of Edith's generation on well-organized, well-arranged, good, proper things—all frustrated by the war. . . . One may smile at it, but there is a kind of power and strength in it nonetheless" (118). Wharton's shortcomings as a war correspondent are all too evident. She is an unshakeably genteel "traveller," with cultivated taste and gracious manners, who keeps a careful, charitable distance even as she visits hospitals and trenches. The frontispiece of *Fighting France* shows her well dressed for this part, in a well-tailored traveling outfit—a tiered ankle-length skirt, jacket, and white blouse, round puffy hat, and pointed high-heeled shoes. Her right hand is gloved. In her left, she holds a tightly wrapped parasol, upon which she leans slightly. Behind her, about as high as her waist, there is improvised fencing and a barricade, interrupted by a peephole through which two soldiers, with their backs to the camera, may be scanning enemy lines. Shari Benstock comments that "[n]othing in the picture betrays the horror taking place some hundred yards beyond the fencing" (Shari Benstock, *No Gifts from Chance: A Biography of Edith Wharton*, 315). But that, it seems to me, is exactly the point. There are in *Fighting France* pictures of graves and bombed buildings, a trench lined with very clean sandbags, and a street "covered with stones from shelled buildings," but they are viewed from a polite distance as if we, like Wharton, come to the front as well-dressed charitable tourists entering a rather alien place.

Few personalities leap from Wharton's pages in *Fighting France*: one is M. Liegeay, a former mayor of Gerbeviller, who, although his house ("of the sober old Lorraine pattern") had been destroyed by German shelling, did not fail to present Wharton with pink peonies from his garden (99–100). Yet, if memorable people are rare, towns and houses are frequently personified. In May 1915, for example, Wharton sees a "ruined house . . . calcined and convulsed" (93) at Gerbeviller; in the Lorraine she passed through "streets and streets" of "murdered houses," and towns in their "last writhings" (93). Ypres had "been bombarded to death"; although "the outer walls of its houses [were] still standing, so that it presents the distant semblance of a living city," yet, seen from nearby it resembles "a disembowled corpse" (152–53). "The towns of Lorraine were blown up, burnt down, deliberately erased from the earth. At worst they [were] like stone-yards, at best like Pompeii" (152). Again, "[m]odern Nieuport seems to

have died in a colic . . . the contractions and contortions of the houses
reaching out the appeal of their desperate chimney-pots and agonized
girders."

From one angle Wharton sees "a line of palsied houses lead[ing] up
like a string of crutch-propped beggars" (167). At Dunkerque she finds a
"poor little house that reminded one of some shy humdrum person suddenly exposed in the glare of a great misfortune" (174). These residential
tragedies are highlighted by evidence of the French people's domestic passion and skill. In makeshift hospitals and villages she visits, Wharton
praises picturesque, homely arts: at a "Colonel's 'dugout'" she sees, for
example, "a long table decked with lilacs and tulips . . . spread for tea,"
and "cheery catacombs" with "neat rows of bunks, mess-tables, sizzling
sauce-pans over kitchen-fires" (126). She finds a "sod-thatched hut 'At the
sign of the Ambulant Artisans,' where two or three soldiers were model-
ing and chiseling all kinds of trinkets from the aluminum of enemy
shells." She admires "the severe, somewhat archaic design" of their work
as "a proof of the sureness of French taste" (128–29). She also remarks on
the skillful "mysteries" of "military housekeeping" when she finds shirts
"drying on elder-bushes, kettles boiling over gypsy fires, men shaving,
blacking their boots, cleaning their guns" and "on all sides a general cheery
struggle against the prevailing dust, discomfort and disorder" (150).

There is no doubt that Wharton means to praise French decency and
valor, though her tone is often that of a politely patronizing "lady visitor"
at a village school. In fact, individual lives of the "people," either in Paris
or at the front, do not attract her. She is vivified by the color and variety
of transport and uniforms, the grandeur of the armies, and, quite probably, the nearness of battle. Leaving Alsace, for example, she celebrates a
"happy accident that caused us to leave the main road," as "surging toward
us [came] a mighty movement of British and Indian troops . . . regiment
after regiment of slim turbaned Indians" and then "a long train of artillery;
splendid horses, clattering gun-carriages, clear-faced English youths."
The "never-ending stream" was slowed now and then "by a train of ambulances and supply-wagons." As the parade of troops halted in a congested
village street, children and girls appeared to greet the soldiers with bunches of flowers. Wharton's car is slowed, but when "we had extricated our
motor from the crowd," she writes, "and climbed another hill, we came
on another cavalcade surging toward us through the wheat fields. For over

an hour the procession poured by," a panoramic vision of "the long wall of armies guarding the civilized world from the North Sea to the Vosges" (178–79).

How original was Wharton's treatment of the war? Certainly, her relief work in 1915 and 1916 brought her close to the front lines, but her treatment of these visits is restrained and decorous, as were other accounts published by *Scribner's*, in part because the publisher chose not to alarm readers about the still distant war (Price, 46). What is unique in Wharton's account is her celebration of the epic force and unleashed energy of large armies on the move and the gigantic panorama of modern motorized combat. Twenty-first-century readers, familiar with wars waged on many fronts and armies sent to fight far from home, will appreciate her early recognition that war forces men, women, and families to take to the road—to travel. Inevitably, war correspondence is a form of travel writing, recording the movements of an observer and of the armies, the wounded and the refugees he or she describes.

Jane Benardete

BIBLIOGRAPHY

Auchincloss, Louis. *Edith Wharton: A Woman in Her Time*. New York: Viking Press, 1971.

Benstock, Shari. *No Gifts from Chance: A Biography of Edith Wharton*. New York: Scribner's, 1994.

Price, Alan. *The End of the Age of Innocence: Edith Wharton and the First World War*. New York: St. Martin's Press, 1996.

Wharton, Edith. *Fighting France*. New York: Charles Scribner's Sons, 1915.

Gertrude Bell

(1868–1926)

> To those bred under an elaborate social order few such
> moments of exhilaration can come as that which stands at the
> threshold of wild travel. The gates of the enclosed garden are
> thrown open, the chain at the entrance of the sanctuary is low-
> ered . . . and you step forth, and, behold! the immeasurable
> world. . . . So you leave the sheltered close, and, like the man
> in the fairy story, you feel the bands break that were riveted
> about your heart.
>
> (Gertrude Bell, *The Desert and the Sown*, 1)

In Baghdad, they called her Umn al Muminin, "Mother of the Faithful." The last one to be called that was Ayishah, the wife of the
Prophet. And the man she loved in her later years baptized her
"Queen of the Desert." She was an intrepid traveler, gifted writer, linguist
fluent in Persian and Arabic, archaeologist, and expert on Turkish Arabia.
In the 1920s, she became Oriental Secretary to the British High Commissioner in Baghdad, and in that capacity played a vital role in the formation
of modern Iraq.

Who was this Englishwoman whose name still appears almost daily in
twenty-first-century newspapers and articles, who broke down the barriers
of gender and class of Victorian England to reach fame in the Middle
East and to become the most powerful woman in the British Empire after
World War I?

Gertrude Margaret Lowthian Bell was the sheltered daughter of a county Durham baronet whose fortune came from ironworks and coal. Her mother's death when Gertrude was three years old brought her very close to her father, who recognized and fostered her superior intelligence. Although girls of Gertrude's class were tutored by governesses at home and trained to be wives and mothers, she was sent to Queen's College, a girls' school on Harley Street in London. In 1886 she went to Oxford, where a handful of women were segregated in Lady Margaret Hall. Gertrude thrived in this misogynistic atmosphere, where one of her history professors made the young women sit with their backs to him facing the wall, and where shortly before her arrival Dean John Burgon had sermonized: "Inferior to us God made you [women], and inferior to the end of time you will remain." But Gertrude was certain that she was the equal of any male and proved it by earning a first-class degree in modern history.

Still, marriage remained the ultimate goal, and Gertrude returned reluctantly to the boring London social season. During the three seasons allotted to each debutante to find a husband, Gertrude found no one to meet her intellectual standards. Depressed and fearful of life as a spinster, Gertrude was rescued, as she would be throughout her life, by travel. She was invited to go to Persia in 1892 to visit her aunt, Lady Mary Lascelles, and uncle, Sir Frank Lascelles, the newly appointed British envoy to Shah Nasiraddin.

Persia was Gertrude's introduction to the East. She was enthralled by the country, its language, culture, and above all the beauty of the desert. The desert would never lose its hold on her—it would draw her back time and again. In a letter to her parents, she exclaimed:

> Oh the desert round Tehran! miles and miles of it with nothing, *nothing* growing; ringed in with bleak bare mountains snow crowned and furrowed with the deep courses of torrents. I never knew what desert was till I came here; it is a very wonderful thing to see; and suddenly in the middle of it all, out of nothing, out of a little cold water, springs up a garden. Such a garden! trees, fountains, tanks, roses and a house in it, the houses which we heard of in fairy tales when we were little . . . echoing with the sound of running water and fountains. (quoted in Josephine Kamm, *Daughter of the Desert: The Story of Gertrude Bell*, 64–65)

Everything about the East excited her, bringing back the magic of her childhood reading of the *Arabian Nights*. She wrote in 1894:

Many, many years have passed since the ingenious Shaharazad beguiled the sleepless hours of the Sultan Shahriyar with her deftly-woven stories, and still for us they are as entrancing, as delightful as they were for him when they first flowed from her lips. Still those exciting volumes keep generations of English children on wakeful pillows, still they throw the first glamour of mystery and wonder over the unknown East. By the light of our earliest reading we look upon that other world as upon a fairy region full of wild and magical posssibilities. (*Safer Nameh, Persian Pictures*, 133)

In Persia she met and fell in love with a young junior diplomat named Henry Cadogan. In the sensual atmosphere of Persia they became engaged, as they recited to one another the passionate lyrics of the qua-trains of *The Rubaiyat* of Omar Khayyam:

> *A book of verses underneath the bough,*
> *A jug of wine, a loaf of bread—and thou*
> *Beside me singing in the wilderness*
> *Oh, wilderness were paradise enow!*

Gertrude's father found Cadogan unsuitable as a husband for his daughter and called her back to England; she returned immediately. Her unquestioning obedience was consistent with her upbringing and class—she always remained within the boundaries of tradition. However daring her own behavior in the East, her ideas on the role of women were those of her class and explain her active support of the antisuffrage movement.

Back in England, as she waited and hoped for a change in her father's interdiction, Bell wrote a series of essays about her experiences in the East, titled *Safar Nameh, Persian Pictures*, published anonymously in London in 1894. In this early work, as she had in her letters, she demonstrated her acute powers of observation and her gift for vivid descriptive writing, whether describing, in "The Tower of Silence," "the first stage in the weary journey of the dead; here they come to throw off the mantle of the flesh before their bones may rest in the earth without fear of defiling the holy element, before their souls, passing through the seven gates of the planets, may reach the sacred fire of the sun" (31); or, elsewhere, in the essay "In Praise of Gardens":

There was, indeed, a part of his domain where even his hospitality would not have bidden us enter. Behind the house in which we were received lay the women's dwelling, a long, low, verandaed building standing round a deep tank, on whose edge solemn children carry on their dignified games, and veiled women flit backwards and forwards. . . . So in the wilderness, behind high walls, the secret, mysterious life of the East flows on—a life in which no European can penetrate. (41)

A few years after the publication of *Persian Pictures*, Bell's translation of the poems of the Persian poet Hafiz, *Poems from the Divan of Hafiz* (1897), were published.

Any hope of marriage vanished with Cadogan's untimely death nine months after Bell's return to England. Her trip to Persia had provided an escape from the routines of everyday life, but her search thereafter for adventure, whether mountain climbing in the Alps or engaging in the "wild travel" she embraced (*The Desert and the Sown*, 1), would be a means to forget her personal sorrows.

Bell returned to the Middle East in 1899 to study Arabic in Jerusalem and to visit the surrounding area. In 1900 she managed to evade the Turkish authorities to visit the Druzes, a secret Muslim sect that for two hundred years had been fighting the Ottoman Turks in the Djebel Druze, a region running through the Galilee, Lebanon, and southern Syria. From there, she continued on to Damascus and then to the town of Jarad to the house of Sheikh Ahmed. "I lay on his cushions, and ate white mulberries and drank coffee," she wrote to her parents (quoted in Janet Wallace, *Desert Queen*, 54). In another letter, she described her first night in the desert:

The smooth, hard ground makes a beautiful floor to my tent. Shall I tell you my chief impression—the silence. It is like the silence of mountain tops, but more intense, for there you know the sound of wind and far away water and falling ice and stones; there is a sort of echo of sound there, you know it, Father. But here nothing. (ibid.)

In January 1905—just as she had predicted in a letter written to her father on her previous visit: "I shall be back here before long! One doesn't keep away from the East when one has got into it this far" (quoted in Susan Goodman, *Gertrude Bell*, 28)—Bell embarked on a long expedition, the first European woman to travel into remote parts of the Syrian desert. She recorded her travels in the book *The Desert and the Sown*; the title comes from verse 10 of *The Rubaiyat* of Omar Khayyam: "With me along the strip of herbage strown / That just divides the desert from the sown." In the preface to the work, Bell announces that her book differs from traditional travel literature:

> I desired to write not so much a book of travel as an account of the people whom I met or who accompanied me on my way, and to show what the world is like in which they live and how it appears to them. And since it was better that they should, as far as possible, tell their own tale, I have strung their words upon the thread of the road, relating as I heard them the stories with which shepherd and man-at-arms beguiled the hours of the march, the talk that passed from lip to lip round the camp-fire, in the black tent of the Arab and the guest-chamber of the Druze, as well as the more cautious utterances of Turkish and Syrian officials. (preface to *The Desert and the Sown*, xxi)

"You must go alone into this world of adventure," she wrote, "[t]he voice of the wind shall be heard instead of the persuasive voices of counsellors, the touch of the rain and the prick of the frost shall be spurs sharper than praise or blame" (*The Desert and the Sown*, 1). As she rode along on camelback, she learned how "to read the desert, to mark the hollow squares of big stones laid for the beds of Arab boys and the semicircular nests in the earth that the mother camels scoop out for their young." She learned, too, "the names of the plants that dotted the ground," and found that "though the flora of the desert is scanty in quantity, it is of many varieties, and . . . almost every kind has been put to some useful end by the Arabs" (*The Desert and the Sown*, 55).

Wherever she traveled, with the impressive entourage of a person of great wealth, and imbued with the confidence of the British upper middle class, Bell commanded respect, reminding her interlocutors that she came from "a great and honored stock": "Listen, oh you! I am not 'thou,' but 'Your Excellency,'" she reproached one of them, who, according to her, "laughed and understood and took the rebuke to heart" (*The Desert and the Sown*, 80). The sheikhs treated her with the courtesy reserved for distinguished male guests and feted her. She describes a dinner to which she was invited in the tent of Sheikh Fellah ul'Isa, where the encampment

> was already alive with all the combination of noises that animates the desert after dark, the grunting and groaning of camels, the bleating of sheep and

goats and the uninterrupted barking of dogs. There was no light in the sheikh's tent save that of the fire; my host sitting opposite me was sometimes hidden in a column of pungent smoke and sometimes illumined by a leaping flame. When a person of consideration comes as a guest, a sheep must be killed in honour of the occasion, and accordingly we eat with our fingers a bountiful meal of mutton and curds and flaps of bread. (*The Desert and the Sown*, 55–56)

But even on feast nights, she adds, the Arab eats "astonishingly little . . . and when there is no guest in camp, bread and a bowl of camel's milk is all they need" (*The Desert and the Sown*, 56).

Not only did Bell enjoy the privileges accorded to males, but, as a woman, she also had the added advantage of access to the harems:

The harem was shockingly untidy. Except when the women folk expect your visit and have prepared for it, nothing is more forlornly unkempt than their appearance. The disorder of the rooms in which they live may partly be accounted for by the fact that there are neither cupboards nor drawers in them, and all possessions are kept in large green and gold boxes, which must be unpacked when so much as a pocket handkerchief is needed, and frequently remain unpacked. (*The Desert and the Sown*, 157)

One night, after dinner with the *kaimakan* (Ottoman deputy) of Kal'at el Husn, she was guided to the his harem, where an

old woman . . . disposed herself neatly as close as possible to the brazier, holding out her wrinkled hands over the glowing coals. She was clad in black, and her head was covered by a thick white linen cloth. . . . Outside the turret room the wind howled; the rain beat against the single window, and the talk turned naturally to deeds of horror and such whispered tales of murder and death as must have startled the shadows in that dim room for many and many a century. . . . The ancient crone rocked herself over the brazier and muttered: "Murder is like the drinking of milk here!" (*The Desert and the Sown*, 203–204)

During the last months of the 1905 expedition to Syria, Bell went through northern Syria into Asia Minor to study ancient Byzantine churches. She visited an early Christian city, called Binbirkilisse (meaning a thousand and one churches), containing the remains of churches dating from the fifth to the eleventh century. Later on, she collaborated with the famous archaeologist Sir William Ramsay on a work, *The Thousand and One Churches* (1909), describing the great archaeological discoveries that they had made in Asia Minor. She returned to Syria in 1909 and traveled down the Euphrates to Mesopotamia to visit the ancient ruined Islamic palace of Ukhaidir on the lower Euphrates, a journey she described in *Amurath to Amurath* (1911), a fascinating account of desert travel. Two years later, she made a second visit to Ukhaidir, and wrote about it in *Palace and Mosque at Ukhaidir* (1914).

It was on this second trip that she met T. E. Lawrence (Lawrence of Arabia)—one of the two men who would play an important role in her later years—in ancient Carchemish, where he worked from 1910 to 1914 as an assistant at the British Museum's excavation of the once thriving Hittite settlement on the Euphrates. In addition to his archaeological activities, Lawrence, like Bell and other English travelers of the time, was gathering information for the British government. These "travelers," like George Nathaniel Viscount Curzon, viceroy of India in the Near East, were convinced that "the British Empire [was] the greatest instrument for good the world [had] ever seen." On each of Bell's trips to the Middle East from 1900 until World War I, she observed the Arab countries under the control of the Ottoman Empire, collecting a considerable body of information on the Arabs that was to prove of great value to the British intelligence services. From the very beginning she had had a political agenda, the consolidation of British dominance in the Middle East. "Being English, I am persuaded that we are the people who could best have taken Syria in hand with the prospect of a success greater than that which might be attained by a moderately reasonable Sultan" (*The Desert and the Sown*, xxiii). In the same work, Bell remarked that

the moral is obvious: all over Syria and even in the desert, whenever a man is ground down by injustice or mastered by his own incompetence, he wishes that he were under the rule that has given wealth to Egypt, and our occupation of that country . . . has proved the finest advertisement of English methods of government. (*The Desert and the Sown*, 58)

During World War I, the British needed the loyalty of the Arab leaders in order to maintain a position of authority in the Middle East that would assure them control over the land and sea routes from the Mediterranean to India. It was possibly Bell's knowledge and connections that provided the material for T. E. Lawrence's military success. During the war, she became a vital source of information to the British and was the only woman intelligence agent in the Arab Bureau in Cairo. In becoming an expert on Oriental affairs, Bell became what she termed a "Person," an identity unavailable to her as a woman in Britain.

The second decisive encounter of this period was with Major Charles Hotham Montague (Dick) Doughty-Wylie, nephew of Charles Doughty, the famous traveler and author of the seminal travel book *Arabia Deserta*. She fell passionately in love with Dick, as she had with Cadogan years before. This love, too, was doomed, for Doughty-Wylie had a wife whom he would not divorce. And so Bell, desperately in love and miserable in her spinsterhood, sought consolation in the desert and set out on a journey to Hayyil, the capital of the Rashid tribe, in the Nejd, a desolate area in northern Arabia. The Turkish authorities, who were concerned about the dangers posed by warfare between the two major warring tribes in the Nejd, the Rashids and the Sauds, had her sign a document absolving them of responsibility for her safety. The English, too, denied her any form of protection. Undaunted, she wrote, "Everyone goes in fear, except only I, who have nothing to lose that matters" (*The Arabian Diaries, 1913–1914*, 48). Unable to communicate by mail with Doughty-Wylie from the heart of the desert, she began a diary for him: "Thus we turn towards Nejd, *inshallah*, renounced by all the powers that be, and the only thread which is not cut through is that which runs through this little book, which is the diary of my way kept for you" (*The Arabian Diaries, 1913–1914*, 45). The diary proved to be her greatest work and one of the outstanding travel narratives of the century.

In a fascinating entry of February 2, 1914, Bell tells of her days spent with Muhammad Abu Tayyi, cousin of the great sheikh, days that

> were not wasted. I had never been in a big shaikh's camp before and all was new and interesting. And very beautiful—the sandy valley and Muhammad's big five-poled tent where we sat at night, while a man sang of the deeds and days of all the Arabs, and the bowls of camel milk brought in to us when the *nagas* (female camels) came back with their calves—and not least Muhammad's great figure sitting on the cushions beside me, with the

white *keffiyye* (headdress) falling over his black brows and his eyes flashing in question and answer. . . . I heard his tales of the desert and made friends with his women, and I made friends with him. He is a man, and a good fellow; you can lay your head down in his tents, and sleep at night, and have no fear. (*The Arabian Diaries*, 62–63)

On February 10, 1914, Bell entered a desolate and unmapped part of the Nefud desert, the first Westerner to do so.

[W]hat a world! the incredible desolation. Abandoned of God and man, that is how it looks—and is. I think no one can travel here and come back the same. It sets its seal upon you, for good or ill. . . . "*Subhan Allah*": (praise be to God) said one of my Demascenes, "we have come to Jehannum (hell)." (*The Arabian Diaries*, 64, 77)

Several weeks later she arrived in Hayyil, a walled town in possession of the Rashids, where she was held captive for eleven days in a summer palace in the south wall of the town, ostensibly until the amir returned. The amir, age sixteen and the last of a line of murdered predecessors, was away raiding his neighbors.

In Hayyil murder is like the spilling of milk and not one of the shaikhs but feels his head sitting unsteadily upon his shoulders. . . . I think the Rashid are moving towards their close. Not one grown man of their house remains alive—the *Amir* is only 16 or 17, and all the others are little more than babes, so deadly has been the family strife. I should say that the future lies with Ibn Sa'ud. (*The Arabian Diaries*, 81, 91)

Gertrude's only companions were the inhabitants of the harem. In one of the most remarkable passages in travel literature, she writes about "two hours taken straight from the *Arabian Nights* spent with the women of the palace":

Here were these women wrapped in Indian brocades, hung with jewels, served by slaves. . . . They pass from hand to hand. . . . The victor takes them . . . and think of it! his hands are red with the blood of their husband and children. (*The Arabian Diaries*, 85)

After the eleven days of captivity, without explanation, her letter of credit was honored, and she was free to leave Hayyil. Despite the fact that in the desert "danger [was] always near," Bell was becoming bored. She found the rest of the trip dull and confessed to Dick that she was experiencing the same depression she felt at the end of each adventure, and that she was already looking forward to something new, whatever it might be.

World War I would present her with the new challenge she craved, opening up for her a political career. But this time there was no Dick with whom to communicate—he was killed at Gallipoli in May 1915. Ironically, his death would correspond with her political ascent, just as Cadogan's did with her emergence as a "Person." In November 1915 she was posted to Cairo to begin her career with British Military Intelligence, which now recognized the value of the mass of information on the Arabs she had collected over the preceding ten years. From Cairo, she was sent back to Al Basrah (in Mesopotamia), and in 1917, after the British took Baghdad, she was called there by Sir Percy Cox with the title of Oriental secretary, the key intelligence post. With a few interruptions she spent the rest of her life in Baghdad, writing that Baghdad was "more than a second home now—it's a new life, a new possiblity of carrying on existence."

After the war, she was instrumental in the establishment of the new state of Iraq with Faisal I as king. She also created the Baghdad Museum, one of the great antiquities museums of the world. She had successfully entered the world of male power, but she found herself more and more on the sidelines with no official function other than museum director. In ill health, lonely, depressed, and without prospects for the future, at the age of fifty-eight, she took an overdose of sleeping pills and died on July 12, 1926.

Lucille Frackman Becker

BIBLIOGRAPHY

Bell, Gertrude. *Safar Nameh, Persian Pictures.* Published anonymously. London: Bentley, 1894.

———. *Poems from the Divan of Hafiz.* London: Heinemann, 1897.

———. *The Desert and the Sown (The Syrian Adventures of the Female Lawrence of Arabia).* Introduction by Rosemary O'Brien. New York: Cooper Square Press, 2001. Originally published in London: Heinemann, 1907.

————. *The Thousand and One Churches* (with Sir William Ramsay). London: Hodder and Stoughton, 1909.

————. *Amurath to Amurath: A Study in Early Mohammadan Architecture.* London: Heinemann, 1911.

————. *Palace and Mosque at Ukhaidir.* Oxford: Clarendon Press, 1914.

————. *The Arabian Diaries, 1913–1914.* Edited by Rosemary O'Brien. Photographs by Gertrude Bell. Syracuse, N.Y.: Syracuse University Press, 2000.

————. *The Civil Administration of Mesopotamia.* London: H. M. Stationery Office, 1920.

Goodman, Susan. *Gertrude Bell.* London: Berg Publishers, 1985.

Kamm, Josephine. *Daughter of the Desert: The Story of Gertrude Bell.* London: Bodley Head, 1956.

Tinling, Marion. *Women into the Unknown: A Sourcebook on Women Explorers and Travelers.* Westport, Conn.: Greenwood Press, 1989, pp. 38–46.

Wallace, Janet. *Desert Queen.* New York: Nan A. Talese, Doubleday, 1996.

12

ᴄᴧlexandra David-Neel
(1868–1969)

At the age of fifty-four, Alexandra David-Neel became the first
white woman to enter the holy city of Lhasa (Tibet). Disguised
as a beggar, and with a revolver concealed beneath her rags, she
made her bold dash for the forbidden Buddhist citadel in 1923.

(Peter Hopkirk, preface to Alexandra David-Neel,
My Journey to Lhasa)

Alexandra David-Neel was born in Paris and died at Digne,
France, just shy of her 101st birthday. As a toddler, the precocious Alexandra ran away from her wealthy bourgeois home in
Paris, in search of adventure. She studied at the Sorbonne, but after her
parents lost their fortune, she became an opera singer. Her voice eventually failed her, and she descended to singing in a provincial nightclub in
Tunisia. Then, in Paris, a conversion to Buddhism in the Guimet
Museum, while contemplating a huge golden statue of the Buddha, set
her on an extraordinary path for a woman of her day.

David-Neel selected Digne—a couple of hours inland from the French
Riviera—as her permanent home after years of traveling in and around
Tibet. She joked that the Basses-Alpes, which rise gradually above Digne
as chalk-white cliffs, were Himalayas for pygmies. Her villa, Samten
Dzong (fortress of meditation), gave her a place to collect her travel souvenirs and to write books on Eastern themes that synthesized the knowledge gained during her extensive travels. Her final projects, a life of Jesus
and an examination of Mao's philosophy, were left incomplete.

Only a select few crossed Samten Dzong's sun-dappled threshold. David-Neel's sharp tongue sliced boors and poseurs into slivers as though they were Camembert cheese. Discipleship with a brilliant guru and an association with the thirteenth Dalai Lama spoiled her for mundane chatter. In 1964 Lawrence Durrell visited the ninety-six-year-old "sage of Digne," whom he threw off balance by giving her a present: several snapshots of herself. Flattered, although she would have denied it, she flirted with the British author, who anointed her "the most astonishing Frenchwoman of our time."

A typically Mediterranean, two-story villa seems an incongruous abode for the gypsy accustomed to lugging her belongings around. Although she settled down physically, David-Neel treated Samten Dzong as though it were a tent she pitched on the steppes. Its somber, damp, cobweb-ridden rooms crowded with travel souvenirs looked like an Asian bazaar. She lived there with Yongden, her adopted son and editorial assistant, whom she had met earlier in Sikkim and trekked with to Lhasa.

Mementos from her epic Tibetan journey—a compass that almost gave her away as a Westerner, a battered cooking pot, her pistol, a native hat she found on the trail, a leather pouch, box cameras, a Tibetan rosary made of 109 pieces of human skulls—were tangible evidence that this daredevil slightly over five feet tall had breached forbidden Lhasa. Numerous males with large retinues and government support had failed.

To those in the know, a necklace of gold coins, a gift from the maharajah of Sikkim, whom she had met in 1912, which she lost after he died mysteriously about a year later, has romantic connotations. The depth of her attachment to this memento transcended its intrinsic value. She refused to cash in the valuable coins no matter how desperate her poverty. At times she had to scrounge for her next meal, even boil up shoe leather on the way to Lhasa. Sidkeong Tulku's gift indicated what a special role the Western Buddhist occupied in his affections. He alone touched the romantic concealed beneath the rationalist disillusioned with love.

While the Orientalists of her day theorized from armchairs, David-Neel earned her spurs in the field. Her adventure story is all the more remarkable since she ploughed through ice and snow in her mid-fifties. Afterward, instead of returning to France, she contemplated settling in America—more amenable to her grand, freewheeling style. An academic colleague seduced her back to Paris, where she pitched her tent outside the Guimet Museum and lectured to enormous crowds.

Yongden joined her on the podium as he had on the trek to Lhasa, which had nearly cost both their lives. Yongden offered his mother slavish devotion, in addition to practical help in domestic chores. He also aided her in synthesizing the Eastern lore she gathered into twenty-five published books—some for laymen, others for scholars.

David-Neel's journey to Tibet counts as her most dramatic achievement, from her farthest penetration of the Gobi desert at Anhsi in March 1923 to the northwest corner of Yunnan Province, adjacent to where she designed to slip into Tibet—a distance of over a thousand miles north to south across western China. That is as the crow flies, but she and Yongden had proceeded more like turtles, maturing their plans as they went.

By the time the pair arrived at the Abbé Ouvrard's parish on the right bank of the Mekong in late October, they had probably covered at least twice that distance. They had been on the march since leaving Jyekundo in August of the previous year, traversing desert, jungle, and rice paddy, enduring scorching heat and freezing cold—often in the course of a single day. The travelers were worn out and undernourished, in shaky health. They lived on *tsampa* (a barley flour mixture), carrying a small supply, begging as they went along, for it was considered meritorious to aid pilgrims. Their kitchen equipment consisted of one all-purpose aluminum pot, a lama's wooden bowl for Yongden, an aluminum bowl for her, a case containing a knife and chopsticks, and two cheap foreign spoons over which she was nearly to kill a man with her new automatic pistol. Alexandra reluctantly let her thermos go.

If Tibetan officials had gotten wind of her intentions, they would have guarded the few roads to Lhasa with greater care. The explorers wore typical Chinese dress, while two coolies carried provisions for a week and a light tent made by Yongden. It would have been unthinkable for a European woman to carry her own pack. On the final trek to Lhasa, David-Neel had to rid herself of all the servants she had hired earlier.

Complaining that her feet were bruised and needed rest, which was true, she discharged the coolies one after the other. Paid and fed, they were sent in opposite directions to eventually meet and share their confusion. Tramping through inhabited places no longer troubled the pair, for as soon as they approached a settlement they began crying for alms. This helped to keep off the huge, fierce watchdogs and often led to a simple meal with humble folk and a berth in the corner.

Meanwhile, General Pereira, whom she had met earlier in her travels, became enthusiastic over a large blank spot on the map of southern Tibet. To reach the Po country, a dangerous route Westerners rarely attempted, David-Neel had to choose between two roads. Pereira gave her a sketch map of the first, which clung to valleys and passed by villages and monasteries. His remark that nobody had ever been there meant, of course, no white person. David-Neel decided she must take this route, for it gave her the opportunity to show "what the will of a woman can do."

There were problems with this route through an uncharted wilderness. Any travelers met on the path were likely to be brigands setting out to rob in more settled country. They might murder witnesses to shut their mouths. Worse, a high pass led into the long valley, then another out. If heavy snow fell after they managed to get in, and the second pass was blocked, the travelers would be trapped to freeze or starve to death.

They posed as *arjopas*, the mendicant pilgrims who in large numbers roam from one sacred spot to another. Many of these, while keeping back a few coins for Lhasa, begged for their supper. From monasteries the disguised beggars sometimes purchased such extravagances as molasses cakes, dried apricots, tea, and butter.

The pair headed for the Dokar Pass, gateway to Tibet proper, and at first they walked only at night through the heavily forested district. The track itself was sufficiently rough, but in the dark they knocked into trees or fell against thorny bushes. Although tortured by thirst, the power of will dulled their pain and drove them on—aided by small doses of strychnine. When taken homeopathically, this deadly poison is a central nervous stimulant and energizer. However, a slight overdose can result in a condition in which one's senses become overly acute and one sees and hears what isn't there.

A sudden blizzard of sleet arose that tested the pilgrims' endurance. They were now called upon to manage in the most extreme of environments. Both carried staffs furnished with sharp iron tips, de rigueur for treks through the Tibetan wilds. By now the travelers had donned heavier clothes more suited to the weather: Yongden dressed in lama's robes, while David-Neel put on suede boots from Kham, a coarse, heavy dress in layers with long sleeves, and an old red sash twisted about her head.

She reveled in the unbridled freedom of a pilgrim who carries all she owns on her back and is liberated from worldly cares. She perfected her outward disguise as the pair moved along: braids out of jet black yak's hair and to match that color a wet stick of Chinese ink rubbed onto her own brown hair. Her hands she blackened with soot. She wore huge earrings in native style and powdered her face with cocoa and crushed charcoal to darken it—a proficiency with makeup learned in her days as an opera singer in France.

At one point, she found an old fur-lined bonnet on the trail. It was the sort worn by the women of the Kham region and would both complete her disguise and warm her head on the cold heights rising between them and Lhasa. But Yongden warned her against touching it. Tibetans believe that to pick up a hat, even if it falls off one's own head, ensures bad luck. The Frenchwoman laughed and stuck the greasy fur onto her pack.

The people of Tibet were naturally friendly and helpful to strangers, especially pilgrims, but they had been led to believe that the *philing* (foreigner) wished to destroy their religion. David-Neel, while posing as a beggar, soon found herself a guest of ordinary Tibetans. Already she had adopted certain habits of the country, such as blowing her nose into her fingers, sitting calmly on a dirt floor spotted with grease and spit, or wiping her soiled hands on her dress.

Now, however, she would face additional affronts to her ingrained sense of cleanliness. She was to live as did the common folk and to converse with natives in a way that had never been done by a European. This became possible because she had learned several dialects of Tibetan in the field. Her fluency in the language gave her an edge over other travelers and explorers with designs on Lhasa, who had scarce preparation to make the trip.

Autumn leaves turned gold and purple were set off by the evergreens. Sometimes a fine snow sprinkled the grass to lay down a magical carpet. But this fairyland aura could be shattered by the suspicious stare of a nosy official, or the whispered rumor that a *philing*—usually taken to be Chinese—had been seen in the neighborhood. David-Neel and Yongden, fearful of discovery, generally resorted to tramping at night.

The lack of privacy among humble Tibetans caused the retiring Frenchwoman problems. Once so fastidious, a hot bath struck her as a memory from a former life. Going to the toilet in front of others remained trying. Aside from embarrassment, she couldn't afford to divulge the articles hidden beneath her voluminous dress. She had to complete her arrangements in the early morning darkness before their hosts stirred.

Privacy gave her the chance to darken her face with soot from the bottom of the cooking pot before poking Yongden awake. They would position their heavy money belts containing silver coins—accepted currency—and, in Alexandra's case, gold jewelry given to her by the late maharajah of Sikkim whose loss she still mourned. This hoard was sufficient to get them murdered many times over. Each morning they tucked away watches and maps, and finally each secured a pistol, always kept loaded.

David-Neel wanted to carry a camera in her pack, but it meant added weight and if found would have made her position very precarious. She had been turned back earlier on that score, and her precautions had grown meticulous. She recorded everything she did bring, never mentioning a camera. There exist no photos of the four-month journey, an opportunity for documentation the traveler would have seized had she not been certain it would have meant her being discovered by the Tibetan authorities.

To David-Neel must go the prize for the most frightening reported transit of a Tibetan river. On the way to the town of Zogong, she and Yongden were overtaken by two lamas acting as couriers for the governor of the Mekong district. The lamas grew suspicious, and so the pilgrims, after getting away, altered their route to traverse the sparsely populated country of the Giamo Nu River, the upper course of the Salween.

The pair reached the station on a glorious day, and because a lama and his followers also wished to cross, they found a ferryman at this out-of-the-way spot. David-Neel was not put off by the sight of the narrow band of water at the bottom of the gorge, but the crossing device looked worrisome: a single, slack cable fastened to poles fixed at an equivalent height on either bank. The Frenchwoman, still disguised as an elderly pilgrim, and a young Tibetan girl were unceremoniously bound together to a wooden hook meant to glide along the leather cable. A push sent them swinging into the void, dancing like puppets on a string. Down they went to the middle of the sag, from where ferrymen on the far bank jerked on a long tow rope to haul them in. It snapped, and the pair slid back to the dip. Their lives were not in danger—unless one of them succumbed to giddiness and, letting go of the strap fixed under the hook, fell backward. In that case both would tumble into the gorge.

David-Neel, who boasted of nerves of steel, did not waver, but her young companion, turning pale, fixed her eyes above. She was sure the strap was coming loose. David-Neel could see nothing wrong with the knots, but the girl's terror began to communicate itself. She probably knew more about these contraptions than did a *philing*. It seemed a question of whether the men would repair the rope before the knots unraveled. What a fine subject for a wager!

David-Neel refused to countenance failure. Steadying the lass by telling her she had called on secret powers for their protection, she watched a workman crawl out along the cable, upside down, the way a fly walks on the ceiling. Finally, attached once again, the couple were hauled to safety, fearing the strap might come undone with each jerk. On the far side, the ferrymen cursed the hysterical girl, and Yongden, cool as ever, demanded alms for his old mother, who had been frightened to death. David-Neel kept going, taking fearsome chances, driven by a will of steel and the desire to find the Shangri-La that tantalized travelers and seekers.

One day in February 1924, four months after starting from Yunnan, the sojourners crossed into Lhasa territory. Here, the year before, General Pereira had been greeted by officials bearing cakes and peaches. Luckily no one took notice of this pair of dusty, weary pilgrims, no different from scores of others come for the New Year festivities.

The two found lodgings during the crowded holiday season in a narrow cell in a beggar's hostel. Remote from the center of town, it would make a perfect hideout. It even provided a fine view of the Potala, the Dalai Lama's palace. Once inside, Yongden dared to declaim in whispered triumph: "*Lha gyalo!*"—The gods win! The joyous pilgrims settled into holy Lhasa.

David-Neel was delighted to have arrived during Monlam, the great festival to celebrate the New Year, and she was determined to keep her incognito and to enjoy herself to the full. The first of her sex to crash the gates of the Forbidden City, she would see everything beautiful, unique, or holy.

The triumphant traveler exulted in the panorama of Lhasa, its temples and monasteries, which she imagined to be a carpet rolled out at her feet. Scattered among the surrounding mountains were what appeared to be toy monasteries, some clinging to rock cliffs like eagles' nests. The two peasant lads, her escorts, were anxious to depart; so the foreign pilgrim trailed after them, reminded that her stay would be limited.

Despite her artistic reservations, she decided to visit the Potala first: she admitted its imposing appearance but sincerely felt that its architects had expressed power and wealth rather than beauty. Disguised as a *dokpa*, a nomadic herder, she entered the Potala in a group of similar folk. Once atop the palace—which, including its mount, reaches to two-thirds the height of New York's Empire State Building—she took in the domain before her. She viewed the doings of its lamas and officials as though she were just one of the crowd. Wisps of smoke rose from innumerable sacrificial altars. Colored paper dragons sent up from rooftops danced in the crisp air.

She found Lhasa to be a lively place inhabited by jolly folk who loved to loiter and chat outdoors. She described the streets as large, the squares as broad and on the whole rather clean. For the three weeks of the festivities two abbots from Drepung monastery had absolute rule over Lhasa and could reprimand even the Dalai Lama. Their rule was necessitated by the streaming into town of up to twenty thousand *trapas* (monks)—many of them so-called brawling monks, given to drinking and quarreling—from the three great monasteries, Drepung, Sera, and Ganden. Had David-Neel been slower of wit and were she caught, she would have been taken not to the civil authorities but to the abbots, who were known to be fiercely antiforeign. They might have turned the interloper over to an outraged mob. Her sex would not have protected her.

Perched on the rocky mountainside, she took in an array of splendor under the bright blue sky and the relentless sun of the Asian plateau. The colors of the crowd's dress, the alabaster hills in the distance, almost hurt her eyes to look at. Lhasa lay at the beggar's feet, and she felt amply repaid for all the fatigue and danger she had undergone. Here indeed was a scene worthy of Shangri-La, a moment that has disappeared from earth that no other traveler, Western or Eastern, would witness. Since the Chinese invasion, Lhasa's glorious festivals exist only in cans of film stored in archives—and on the pages of Alexandra David-Neel's writing.

After two months of gadding about Lhasa and its environs, David-Neel left the capital as quietly as she had entered. She supposed that she was the first Western woman to behold the Forbidden City and that no one suspected she had been there. She took the prudent step of promoting herself to a middle-class woman who owned two mounts and was accompanied by her manservant (Yongden).

In *My Journey to Lhasa*, her first major work that became a classic of travel and a best seller, she claimed that because she had bought numbers of books and intended to hunt for more in the south, she needed the horses to carry the baggage. In fact, she and Yongden had both caught influenza among the holiday crowds, and they were down to skin and bones. Fortunately, their mounts carried them, for they were in no condition to walk.

The sun shone brightly the last time the pair rode past gardens where the trees were dressed in April's pale new leaves. After she had crossed the Kyi River and ascended to a pass, nostalgia gripped her. She stole a final glimpse of the shabby, splendid capital, above which floated the Potala like a castle in a fairy tale. The pilgrim, who in six months would be fifty-six years old, knew she must exile herself from the land she loved to travel in, from her spiritual homeland.

Alexandra David-Neel was not an explorer, since she carried no measuring equipment and made no maps. But the gentlemen of the exploring profession, including superbly trained British officers, had no difficulty in accepting her as one of them.

She wrote to her husband, Philip Neel, an engineer, on her arrival at Lhasa on February 28, 1924; this was her first opportunity to communicate with the outside world since she set out from Yunnan the previous October. She boasted of her success, while admitting that the trip had been an act of lunacy. She would not attempt it again, she insisted, for a million dollars. She and Yongden were not much more than skeletons, and they had gotten by on stimulants, mainly homeopathic strychnine.

Now she set her gaze toward the snowy peaks standing between her and acclaim in the West. Burning with a long-nurtured ambition, she put aside her dream of repose. The ragged pair descended in early May on David Macdonald, the British trade agent at Gyantse, while he was calmly dozing in the fort on the hill overlooking town. She threw herself on the mercy of her old British antagonists, the ones who mainly stood in the way of her getting to Lhasa. Exhausted, she now needed British help to get her back to France.

Putting behind her the stinging plateau and the blizzard-haunted mountains, like Conway, the hero of *Lost Horizon*, she reentered the everyday world. On the way back to France, she began writing of her adventures. These she intended to serve up to the public while still warm.

The return to Paris of Alexandra David-Neel and Yongden did not go unnoticed in the press. Journalists referred to her as "the first white woman to enter Lhasa," or "the great traveler and explorer." In lectures to overflow crowds at the Guimet Museum, she relived her greatest triumph in the city she once struggled to survive in.

In 1937 the "sacred fire of adventure" flamed up again, resulting in another trip to China during the Sino-Japanese war. She warned that the serious business of vagabonding was not for the fainthearted or faddish. First, one must master the language of a country. To depart without money was a disservice to native beggars. She proposed that ten years of residence was necessary to speak of a place with real authority. Otherwise, the Buddhist set down no dicta, nor would she assign her admirers mantras to chant or exercises to perform beyond what could be found in her writings.

She retained the spirit of adventure. At age one hundred she renewed her passport, much to the puzzlement of the official in charge. This was no empty gesture but the prelude to a journey. David-Neel did not like to fly, but an itinerary had crystallized in her mind. Casually, she concocted a grandiose scheme: she would drive to Berlin, where she knew of a doctor who claimed to cure arthritis, which troubled her in later years.

Then it was on to Russia, driving the length of that vast country to Vladivostok. There she could embark for her final destination, New York. Did she envision a tickertape parade up Broadway? Although willing, David-Neel never made it to New York, for by this time her inability to walk kept her homebound.

When the French government decided to cast a bronze medal in David-Neel's honor, she refused to pose. She claimed to be too old and ugly. The medal had to be cast from a photo, without the subject's cooperation. She did choose the motto to be engraved on the reverse: "Walk Straight on Following Your Heart's Desire." It is from Ecclesiastes, and had caught the attention of the youthful rebel three-quarters of a century earlier. She often repeated an old saying: "Who knows the flower best? The one who reads about it in a book, or the one who finds it wild on the mountainside?"

Yet Alexandra David-Neel has been far from forgotten. Along with her obituary, the *International Herald Tribune* showed a photo of her riding a yak; it was captioned WOMAN ON TOP OF THE WORLD. Including posthumous works, thirty distinct titles bear Alexandra David-Neel's name. Although each is concerned with the East, at least in part, they vary from early utopian to the highly erudite, from the formality of grammar to the intimacy of private letters. Her books range over philosophy, anthropology, Orientalism, philology, geographical discovery, history, politics, and Western insights into tantric sexual practices.

George Schaller, the savior of the Himalayan snow leopard, remarked in a letter written in 1987 that David-Neel "accomplished so much more and in such [a] seemingly offhand manner than most explorers in that part of the world." Although she ranged over great unmapped distances and conquered terrain from ice-clad peaks to leech-ridden jungles, she delved still more significantly into the crevices of the human psyche.

Barbara Foster

BIBLIOGRAPHY

Bernbaum, Edwin. *The Way to Shambala.* New York: Doubleday, 1983.

Birkett, Dea. *Spinsters Abroad.* London: Basil Blackwell, 1989.

Champy, Hugette. "Quelques exploratrices." *Revue économique* 68 (1955): 32–35.

David-Neel, Alexandra. *My Journey to Lhasa* (1927). Preface by Peter Hopkirk. Boston: Beacon Press, 1986.

———. *Grand Tibet.* Paris: Plon, 1933.

———. *Sous des nuées d'orage.* Paris: Plon, 1940.

———. *Au coeur des Himalayas: le Népal.* Paris: Dessart, 1949.

———. *L'Inde hier, aujourd'hui, et demain.* Paris: Plon, 1951.

———. *Le vieux Tibet face à la Chine nouvelle.* Paris: Plon, 1953.

———. *La connaissance transcendante.* Paris: Adyar, 1958.

———. *L'Inde.* Paris: Plon, 1961.

———. *Quarante siècles d'expansion chinoise.* Paris: Plon, 1964.

———. *L'Inde où j'ai vécu.* Paris: Plon, 1969.

———. *Le Lama aux cinq sagesses.* Paris: Plon, 1970.

———. *Textes tibétains inédits.* Paris: Pygmalion, 1972.

———. *The Superhuman Life of Gesar of Ling.* Boulder, Colo.: Prajna, 1981.

Dedman, Jane. "Walker in the sky." *Quest* 78 (May-June 1978): 21–26, 90–92.

Denys, Jeanne. *Alexandra David-Neel au Tibet.* Paris: Pensée Universelle, 1972.

Foster, Barbara and Michael. *The Secret Lives of Alexandra David-Neel*. New York: Overlook Press, 1998.

Galland, China. *Women in the Wilderness*. New York: Harper & Row, 1981.

Guy, David. "Ancestors: Alexandra David-Neel." *Tricycle* 5 (Fall 1995): 12–17.

Middleton, Ruth. *Alexandra David-Neel: Portrait of an Adventurer*. Boston: Shambhala, 1989.

Miller, Luree. *On Top of the World*. New York: Paddington Press, 1976.

CHAPTER 13

Isabelle Eberhardt

(1877–1904)

The valley of Figuig [oasis village of Algeria] opened out like a
great, white flower under the sun.

(Isabelle Eberhardt, Departures, 123)

The solitary, strange, frenetic, and childlike Isabelle Eberhardt
had one goal in life: to wander through the North African desert
areas of Algeria, Tunis, and Morocco. An iconoclast, she dressed
as a man, greedily lapping up pleasures that were at once sexual and spiritual. She converted to Islam, was welcomed by the Marabouts (Muslim
priests), opted for Sufism as she understood it, and changed her name to
Si Mahmoud Essadi. Her diaries, short stories, novels, and journalistic
works, written in the florid late-nineteenth-century French literary style,
reflect her highly creative and emotional nature.

Isabelle was the product of a dysfunctional home. Her mother, Nathalie,
the illegitimate daughter of Fraulein Eberhardt and a wealthy Russian,
married the tsarist General de Moërder. They and their three children
lived a life of ease in St. Petersburg. For reasons unknown, the beautiful
Nathalie left her elegant home in 1870, took her three children to Switzerland, and moved into a villa in Meyrin, near Geneva. Although a fourth
child, born shortly after her move, was recognized by her husband, she
refused to return to Russia. In no time, the children's handsome tutor,

the Armenian-born Alexander Trophimowsky, a former priest of Russian Orthodox persuasion turned nihilist, converted to Islam, left his wife and children, and moved into Madame de Moërder's villa. Isabelle Eberhardt, born on February 17, 1877, was the product of their union.

Together with the unconventional mix of individuals in the household, Isabelle was brought up—though facts on the subject differ—along the lines of Trophimowsky's agenda. She was taught six languages (including Greek, Latin, Arabic, and Russian), philosophy, and chemistry; she was forced to do the same physical labor as her brothers and to ride a horse; she was encouraged to wear male clothing and to reject bourgeois society, thus cutting her off from the Swiss. Although everything about the household spelled love and harmony, upon closer scrutiny it became evident that the older children detested their mother's lover. One daughter, Nathalie, escaped the household by marrying the son of tradespeople, thus eliciting Trophimowsky's fury. Two sons committed suicide. A strong love, nonetheless, prevailed between Isabelle and her mother.

That Isabelle began wearing men's clothes, at Trophimowsky's suggestion or not, indicates both an early identification with malehood and a rejection of woman's lot. To distance herself from Western values, she converted to Islam and chose to lead a nomadic life. Mother and daughter left Switzerland for Bône, Algeria, in May 1897. Isabelle's fluency in Arabic impressed the natives, as did her religiosity. Dressed in a white burnoose, she melded with life in the North African scene. Her feelings of joy and utter abandon in her new and dreamed-for environment inspired her to write a novel, *Trimadeur* (*The Vagabond*), about an anarchist medical student. Her mother's sudden death from a heart attack devastated the young girl. In keeping with Madame de Moërder's new religion, she was buried in a Muslim cemetery.

The time had come for Eberhardt to carve out her dream. She bought a horse, Souf, a dog, Loupiote, and took the name Si Mahmoud Essadi. Her goal was to wander about the seemingly endless deserts of a land she had already learned to love (*Au Pays des Sables*, 24*)*. In time, however, she ran out of funds and returned to Switzerland. What she witnessed shocked and dismayed her: Trophimowsky's death from throat cancer.

Prior to her return to Algeria, she went to Cagliari (Sardinia) to meet her brother, Augustin, and his wife. On to Paris to find work as a journalist. Although Lydia Paschkoff, a Russian explorer and reporter for *Le*

Figaro in St. Petersburg, befriended her and introduced her to well-placed Parisians, nothing concrete materialized (Lesley Blanch, *The Wilder Shores of Love*, 284).

Eberhardt, now called Si Mahmoud, returned to Algeria in the summer of 1900 to realize her calling as a wanderer. The flat-chested girl traveled alone on horseback deep into the Sahara desert—from one oasis to the next, up and down plateaus, befriending outlawed Arab tribes, and fulfilling her sexual needs as well. Her strong faith and incredible courage led her to infiltrate Muslim religious societies. In time, she was inducted into the Qadryas, a Sufi brotherhood founded in the eleventh century in Baghdad by Abdel-Qader al-Jilani, and she became a *khouan* (initiate) (ibid., 108). She fantasized. She saw herself becoming a Marabout and thrilled at the thought of participating in Sufi mystical disciplines and sharing their arduous monastic existence.

But, instead, she vagabonded. Hygiene was barred from Si Mahmoud's mores. She slept wherever the spirit moved her—in filthy mud huts or in sheltered areas in the Arab quarters of the villages she traversed. At El Oued, she met the good-looking spahi (member of a military corps) Slimène Ehnni, a naturalized French Arab who was garrisoned there. They fell in love. They made love. They prayed together. They indwelled in unison. She joyed in the experience. They dreamed of settling down and of opening a grocery store. Si Mahmoud's inheritance would pay for it. Soon she learned that the mismanagement of her mother's will had left her with nothing. No matter. With the help of a pipe or two of *kif* (a hallucinogenic plant), the couple experienced the heights of physical and spiritual ecstasy.

The urge to once again venture forth took hold, and the loner Si Mahmoud went to Tripoli and Tunisia at the behest of the Marquise de Morés, who had asked her to investigate certain details concerning her explorer husband's murder in 1896. Si Mahmoud thrilled at the free lifestyle granted her. She befriended strangers, chose to make love when and how she pleased during her wanderings from one end of Algeria to the other, to Morocco, and to Tunisia. She kept a diary, *Mes Journaliers* (1923). She also wrote short stories collected in *Au Pays des Sables* (1944) during her wanderings through deserts, oases, and towns, and stops at caravan *sérails*, or joining marauding tribes in the south. She had become her own person and increasingly religious. Her fervent prayers led her to experience the

heights of mystical asceticism. Her morbid and suicidal tendencies nonetheless swelled her yearning for death.

As a member of the devoutly religious Kadryas order, Si Mahmoud
believed in the salutary need for retreats. Some wondered at the time
whether her attraction for the dashing Grand Master of the Kadryas, Si
Lachmi, whom she observed riding on his stallion, had convinced her to
withdraw to the purity of his sanctuary, away from contamination by
Europeans. Leaders of Islamic brotherhoods were considered God's
earthly agents.

Although Si Mahmoud was accepted as woman/man, or androgyne,
into the Sufi brotherhood, not everyone was in agreement. On January 29,
1901, a fanatic, Abd Allah ben Mohammed, aimed his saber at this infidel
woman. Rather than killing her, however, he wounded her severely. The
trial held by the military courts attracted Arab and French journalists.
Cover-ups, dissimulations, and rumors abounded. On the one hand, it
was discovered that the assassin belonged to the Tidjani religious sect
founded in 1782 in the Maghreb—a deadly rival of the Kadryas brotherhood. On the other hand, the Grand Master was accused of attempting
to rid himself of Si Mahmoud. While the truth may never be known, the
verdict was clear: the perpetrator of the crime was sentenced to twenty
years of hard labor, and the injured party was expelled from North Africa.

Traumatized by the event, Si Mahmoud left for Marseilles. Her life
became a sweeping torment. While her thoughts revolved around suicide,
she did not sever earthly ties. She pined for her lover Slimène. To earn
money, she worked briefly as a docker, writing short stories for the Alge-
rian newspaper *Akhbar* as well. The rest of her days she lavished in
despair.

Slimène was eventually transferred to Marseilles in 1901. The couple
was married. As a French citizen, Madame Si Ehnni was allowed to
return to North Africa. Bride and groom moved in with her husband's
family. The arrangement proved untenable. She went wandering again: to
the south, to M'zab, then on to Chebka. In the summer of 1902 she joined
her husband at Ténès, near Algiers. She spent a good deal of time at the
cafès maures, seated on a mat, relating her adventures to Europeans, Arabs,
and anyone who would listen. By 1903 she had become a *kif* and hashish
addict, weeping and wailing for the old days. Her mood swings were pre-
dictable—from grave sorrow to the ecstasy of the Sufi's Infinite. Never

happy with the here and now, she swung from the heights of jubilation to the depths of self-pity.

During the colonization of North Africa by France in 1903, Colonel Lyautey, intent on subduing hostile tribes in the vicinity of Beni-Ounif, sent Si Mahmoud on a secret mission (Blanch, 299). Rather than accomplishing her goal, she was imprisoned in the Sufi religious establishment of Kenadsa but released by its Marabout because of her bouts of fever and delirium. Si Mahmoud was not only emotionally ill; her ravaged body was physically afflicted with malaria, syphilis, and gonorrhea. Her voice had grown hoarse. Her teeth had rotted away. Although she saw little of her husband, she always maintained that she loved him.

Wandering, nonetheless, rejuvenated her. Despite her fatigue, when her fever abated she left for the south of Algiers. She aimed for the High Plateaux to Colomb-Béchar in May 1904. She kept a diary, and wrote not only for *Akhbar* but for the *Dépêche Algérienne* as well. She chose to investigate the region of southern Oranais, near Morocco's borders, for the excitement of new places. When her fevers raged, she checked into the military hospital at Aïn Sefra on the outskirts of the Sahara. She and her husband having planned to meet in the small mud house she had rented near the dry riverbed in the vicinity, she was unwilling to wait for her discharge from the hospital. She simply left, walked toward their home, but before she knew it the waters of the *oued* were rising at an unprecedented rate. She climbed to the roof of her mud house, but "a roaring torrent broke loose from the mountains, flooding the *oued,* carrying with it houses, cattle, trees, people" (ibid., 302). Because Si Mahmoud was nowhere to be found, Colonel Lyautey ordered a search for her body. It was discovered two days later. Her husband mourned. Si Mahmoud was buried in the Muslim cemetery of Aïn-Sefra.

Eberhardt's writings mirror her life. She who had become a disciple in the *zéouïya,* a Muslim religious brotherhood commemorating the destinies of "Holy Ones," was curious about everything: death, litanies, and secret investitures used to communicate with the dead (Malek Chebel, *Dictionnaire des symboles musulmans,* 451). She identified with strange and solitary places and romanticized the Maghreb. Her novel, *Rakhil,* begun in 1898 and allegedly completed in 1900, although its conclusion was lost, focuses on the prostitute, sexual mysteries, and the lower depths of Algiers. She maintained that *Rakhil* was a defense of the Koran, a "song of eternal love" (*Mes Journaliers*, 27). Ironically, it was in the Jewish cemetery at Bône, where she came across Rakhil's funeral stone, that she was moved to write her novel (*Rakhil*, 10). That she was obsessed by the premature demise of her young protagonist, anticipating perhaps her own, is understandable, given the deaths and suicides in her family. The protagonist, Rakhil, a complex of contradictions like the author, is poor, solitary, and humiliated by her profession. Her procurers are two Jews. The seat of the action is the Jewish quarter that reeks of muck. Under fire in the novel is women's incarceration and infantilization by Muslim men. Far from being a work of art—due in part to its overly melodramatic sequences, its subjectivism, its flagrant Orientalism—Isabelle's novel nonetheless yields insightful images of the times.

The vignettes that make up the sections of Eberhardt's diary (*Mes Journaliers*) entitled "Impressions du Sud Oranais" (1903–1904) center on the Sahara bordering Morocco, on native soldiers with whom Isabelle had traveled, on life in oasis villages such as Tafilalet and Figuig, on nomadic tribes, colonization, war, Colonel Lyautey's politics, and her own travels to the religious retreat at Kenadsa. Her depiction of Figuig mirrors her solitude, despair, and still fragile hopes:

> The valley of Figuig opened out like a great, white flower under the sun. I was sitting on the parapet of a high, crumbling tower made of gold-colored earth, so old and fragile that it seemed ready to fall into dust. The tower was mirrored in the dark water of a pool at the edge of the gardens of Oudaghir. . . .
>
> I was alone in the splendor of the dawning day, and I was dreaming as I gazed at Figuig, queen of oases which had never looked so beautiful to me before, perhaps because I was leaving the next day.
>
> In the distance toward the South, beyond the mountains of Taghla and Melias, the red desert was climbing high into the sky, marking the horizon with a dark, clear line as on the high seas. (*Departures*, trans. and ed. Karim Hamdy and Laura Rice, 123)

Eberhardt's vision of twilight brings a more problematic side of her world into bloom.

What relief, verging on ecstasy, when the sun sets, when the shadows of the date palms and of the walls lengthen, creeping, obscuring the last gleams!

The grim indifference that grips me, throughout the long, tedious day, dissipates; and once again with avid, charmed eyes I look at the daily splendor of the landscape of Kenadsa, already so familiar, with its simple beauty of strict lines and warm, transparent colors that quickly relieve the monotony of the foreground, while diaphanous mists drown the distant horizons.

How sweet and consoling is this rebirth of the soul each evening.

In the gardens, the last hot hour slips by gently for me, in tranquil contemplation, in lazy talk interspersed with long silences.

At dusk, when the sun has set, we go to pray in the *hamada* [stony desert] just before the great cemeteries and the white, iridescent *koubba* [sanctuary consecrated to a Marabout] of the blessed Lella Aicha.

All is calm, dreaming, smiling, at this charming hour. (ibid., 166)

Kenadsa was a place revered by Eberhardt:

Kenadsa rises before us, its great *ksar* [village] made of warm, dull *toub* [mud building material made of straw and clay], preceded, on the left, by beautiful green gardens. The *ksar* descends in a graceful disorder of superimposed terraces, following the slope of a large hill. To the right, the golden dune, with its slabs of stone, rises up almost abruptly.

A *koubba*, very white, shelters the tomb of Lalla Aicha—a Muslim saint from the family of the illustrious Sidi M'hammed-ben-bou-Ziane, founder of the Ziania brotherhood. . . .

We pass by vague cemeteries, we walk along this human dust accumulated over the centuries, abandoned and forgotten, and we take the road that follows round the town ramparts, made of dark mud walls, without crenellations or loopholes. (ibid., 153)

In *Mes Journaliers* we read Eberhardt's jottings on her thoughts, moods, desires, confidences, and dreams. Her opus begins on January 1, 1900, with comments on her sojourn in Cagliari. She focuses on her aloneness, her "world of deceived hopes, deadened illusions and memories, daily more distant, to the point of becoming nearly unreal" (*Mes Journaliers*, 3). Like those of the French Romantic poets Lamartine and Vigny, Eberhardt's verbalizations of mobile light blue sky tones alternate with darkened colorations of surrounding mobile waters. She bemoans the fact that no one has "pierced" her outer mask, and peered into her "true and pure soul." Her need to drag her body through slime, she explains, was both a reaction against conventional attitudes and her own "strange need to suffer" (ibid.). Although aware of her plight, she cannot protect herself from the pain of life and death. She recoups her energies moments later, with new plans for salvation: she must learn "to think"—to be unlike the self-satisfied bourgeois whom she despises (26).

In Geneva, on June 15, 1900, she seeks to concretize her literary plans. Suddenly, on June 16, she decides to leave for Ouargla, to cloister herself in the "great silence of the [Sahara] Desert" (29). She travels to Marseilles. On January 23, 1900, she is back in Algiers. She visions "the snowy-like flow of the old city . . . when its admirable panorama appears fully lit" (56).

On July 30, she arrives at Meroïer, goes on to El-Ferd, to Ourlana, Sid Auvrau, El-Moggar, and Touggourt (59). Her funds are running out. No matter, she had come to the desert to write (61). She personifies the Sahara: "O menacing Sahara, hiding your beautiful somber soul" (63). On to Bordj Terajen on August 1 (64): "If it pleases Allah," she hopes her health will hold out (65). At El Oued, August 4, 1900, she continues on by camel, arriving at Mouïet-el-Caïd on her way to the Maghreb. The night is white (65).

Eberhardt's brief descriptions of the towns she visits, her physical sufferings, the sheikh she meets on her way, her hounding thoughts and intermittent fevers, are touching for their simplicity and naiveté. Even the unpleasant insects that at times fly or creep up to her en masse, and animals to which she relates, are singled out for scrutiny. On February 3, 1901, she confesses to her melancholia. "I am lost more than ever in the inexpressible, in the obscure innermost depths of my soul, and I struggle in darkness. The dream is somber. What will awakening bring? And tomorrow?" (101).

Isabelle Eberhardt-Si Mahmoud traveled on in death as she had in life.

Bettina L. Knapp

BIBLIOGRAPHY

Blanch, Lesley. *The Wilder Shores of Love*. London: John Murray, 1954.
Chebel, Malek. *Dictionnaire des symboles musulmans*. Paris. Albin Michel, 1995.

Eberhardt, Isabelle. *Mes Journaliers précédés de La vie tragique de la bonne nomade.* [Includes "Impressions du Sud Oranais."] Ed. René-Louis Doyon. Paris: Editions d'Aujourd'hui, 1923.

———. *Au Pays des Sables précédé de Infortunes et ivressses d'une errante.* Ed. René-Louis Doyon. Paris: Fernand Sorlot, 1944.

———. *Rakhil.* Ed. Danièle Masse. Paris: La Boite à Documents, 1990.

———. *Ecrits intimes.* Ed. Marie-Odile Delacour and Jean-René Huleu. Paris: Payot, 1991.

———. *Departures: Selected Writings.* Trans. and ed. Karim Hamdy and Laura Rice. [Includes Karim Hamdy's "The Intoxicated Mystic" and Laura Rice's "Eberhardt as Si Mahmoud."] San Francisco: City Lights Books, 1994.

———. *Dans l'ombre chaude de l'Islam.* Paris: Actes Sud, 1996.

———. *The Oblivion Seekers.* Trans. Paul Bowles. San Francisco: City Lights, 1975.

———. *Notes de Route: Maroc-Algérie-Tunisie.* Preface by Victor Barrucand. Illustrated by Jean-Marc Durou. Paris: Actes Sud, 1998.

14

Isak Dinesen (Karen Blixen)
(1885–1962)

I hold to the belief that I am one of Africa's *favorite children*.
A great world of poetry has revealed itsef to me and taken me
to itself here, and I have loved it. I have looked into the eyes
of lions and slept under the Southern Cross. I have seen the
grass of the great plains ablaze and covered with delicate green
after the rains, I have been the friend of Somali, Kikuyu, and
Masai, I have flown over the Ngong Hills—I plucked the best
rose of life.

(Isak Dinesen, *Letters from Africa*,
trans. Ann Born, March 17, 1931, 416)

An aura of mystery, even morbidity, surrounds the heroic life of
Karen Christenze Dinesen. (Her nom de plume, Isak Dinesen,
chosen to make her reading public believe she was a man,
would allow her, she believed, to receive acclaim more readily. It was
unnecessary, for her works immediately took root with her reading public.)

Born in Rungstedlund, Denmark, where winters are long and dark, she
transplanted herself to British East Africa, where light is harsh and blind-
ing. Her eighteen-year foray into this unknown land, more specifically the
environs of Nairobi, was spent empathetically amid the Masai, a nomadic
cattle-owning tribe; the Kikuyu, an agricultural people, though some
referred to them as "squatters" (*shambas*); as well as lions, giraffes, hyenas,
zebras, rhinos, vipers, deadly insects, dogs, and a pet owl. From her

veranda she never tired of gazing at the Ngong Hills, as their variegated tints of blue rippled against clear skies (*Out of Africa*, 4).

Dinesen led a double life in Africa. As mistress of a coffee farm, she was forced to deal with the vagaries of drought, crop failure, her husband's infidelities, and his financial incompetency. As incipient writer and painter, she was wrapped in subliminal spheres. Devastating to her were her severe physical and emotional illnesses sparked partly by her husband's womanizing, and partly by her loneliness and the nearly continuous failure of their coffee farm. Even her great and healing love for Denys Finch Hatton was marked by periods of spasmodic anguish. This enigmatic woman survived the pain of existence by withdrawing into her imagination and transmuting the chaos lying fallow within her into the poetics of cosmos. When questioned about the truth of "remembrance" in her writings, she responded: "And God knows if it is always true, but it is truth in a higher sense, it is myth" (*Letters from Africa*, November 21, 1928, 395).

Dinesen's valiant soldier father, Wilhelm, had fought in several European wars and on the side of the French in the Franco-Prussian debacle. He authored a volume, *Paris under the Commune*, traveled to America, and worked there. After having lived with the Chippewa Indians in Wisconsin, he returned to Denmark in 1874 (Tania Parmenia Migel, *A Biography and Memoir of Isak Dinesen*, 6). In time, he bought premium property between Copenhagen and Elsinore and married the gently beautiful Ingeborg Westenholz. Five children were born to them. Sadness impressed itself on the household in 1895 with Wilhelm's suicide. The extended family, with its many uncles, aunts, and cousins living nearby, buoyed up the bereaved. That same year, a fire destroyed part of the Dinesens' house and barns. By 1898 a change of scene was in order. Ingeborg took three of her children to Switzerland, where Karen was sent to school for the first time, for, in keeping with Victorian tradition, children were taught at home. Delighting in the class experience, Karen studied French and painting. At the age of eighteen, she enrolled at the Academy of Art in Copenhagen. Later she traveled with her siblings to Germany, England, Norway, and Paris. Even during her early years Karen loved regaling her siblings with stories—at times terrifying—of her own pure invention.

In addition to her passion for the arts, Karen yearned for a title, which she would gain through marriage to Baron Bror von Blixen-Finecke.

Though ill-suited to each other (she was attracted to art, literature, and the dream, and he was a high liver, a drinker, and a womanizer), they connected in their love for the oudoors. Her uncle, Mogens Frijs, advised the couple to go to Africa. The time was ripe. Land was cheap. They would soon become millionaires. Bror left for Africa and bought (the bulk of the money coming from the Dinesens) 1,500 acres of land not far from Nairobi. It was ideal for coffee planting, he concluded, the best investment at the time. Moreover, its forests, mountains, and plains resembled the topography of Denmark. A dream was to be lived.

Karen's mother and one of her sisters accompanied the future bride by train to Naples, where she was scheduled to leave by ship for East Africa in December 1914. Included in the cargo was newly bought furniture and a Scottish deerhound to provide companionship for Karen during the four solid weeks at sea. Bror met her at Mombasa, which was, she wrote to her mother, "a fiery hothouse and the sun blazing down on your head almost makes you unconscious" (*Letters from Africa*, January 20, 1914, 2). Dust, noisy street vendors, half-naked children, garbage, foods, some rotting, were also fare for the traveler. Karen and Bror were married that same day by the British district commissioner in Mombasa (Linda Donelson, *Out of Africa: Isak Dinesen, the Untold Story*, 23). After an official reception held at the governor's house, she and Bror left for their new home by car. Only then did she begin to see "the real Africa, vast grass plains and the mountains in the distance and then the incredible wealth of game, huge flocks of zebra and gnu and antelope" (*Letters from Africa*, ibid., 3). Although the altitude of 6,000 feet made her somewhat giddy, the cleanliness and transparency of the air invigorated her.

A surprise awaited her at the farm. About 1,200 natives, their faces painted with white stripes, were gathered around to welcome the newly arrived Europeans by dancing. Dinesen was captivated by the artistry of their colored patternings and by the accentuated rhythmic gyrations of their body movements.

> All the thousand boys were drawn up in ranks and after a really earsplitting welcome they closed ranks and came up to the house with us, surrounded us when we got out of the car and insisted on touching us—and all those black heads right in front of one's gaze were quite overwhelming. (ibid.)

She then stepped into her large fieldstone house, looked it over, assessed the placement of her furniture, and was pleasantly surprised to find a functioning lavatory (Donelson, 29). From her house, her eyes captured a sight that was to remain for her beloved and holy: the Ngong Hills. Her painterly talents imaged the scape.

> The Mountain of Ngong stretches in a long ridge from North to South, and is crowned with four noble peaks like immovable darker blue waves against the sky. It rises eight thousand feet above the Sea, and to the East two thousand feet above the surrounding country; but to the West the drop is deeper and more precipitous—the hills fall vertically down towards the Great Rift Valley. (*Out of Africa*, 4)

Equally arresting but etched in more subdued though splattered tones on her verbal canvas, were larger spatial spans.

> There was no fat on it and no luxuriance anywhere: it was Africa distilled up through six thousand feet, like the strong and refined essence of a continent. The colours were dry and burnt, like the colours in pottery. The trees had a light delicate foliage, the structure of which was different from that of the trees in Europe; it did not grow in bows or cupolas, but in horizontal layers, and the formation gave to the tall solitary trees a likeness to the palms, or a heroic and romantic air like fullrigged ships with their sails clewed up, and to the edge of a wood a strange appearance as if the whole wood were faintly vibrating. (ibid., 3)

Dinesen's particular brand of sensitivity enabled her to "catch the rhythm of Africa," in its syncopated sighs, groans, and songs (ibid., 14). The novice homebody, although aghast at her lack of knowledge in running a home, succeeded, nonetheless, in teaching her native servants the rudiments of housekeeping and cooking, as she knew them, including the finesses involved. She embraced some of their dishes as well. Better to relate to her servants, she learned the Swahili language (Donelson, 31ff.). Her assessment of the natives was sensitive and immediate: "They were quick of hearing, and evanescent; if you frightened them they could withdraw into a world of their own, in a second, like the wild animals which at an abrupt movement from you are gone—simply are not there" (ibid., 17). When possible, she maintained a marketing schedule: twice weekly she and Bror went to Nairobi by mule-drawn wagon to buy provisions. Spices were no problem. Bread, however, would have to be made at home. Dinesen's affinity for the natives was marked from the very outset of her stay in Africa.

> I had felt a great affection for the Natives. It was a strong feeling that embaced all ages and both sexes. The discovery of the dark races was to me a magnificent enlargement of all my world. . . . as if some one with an ear for music had happened to hear music for the first time when he was already grown up; their cases might have been similar to mine. After I had met with the Natives, I set out the routine of my daily life to the Orchestra. (ibid., 17)

Unique to her temperament and metaphysics were her philosophical appraisals of people in general, and natives in particular. Could her reactions to those she met be labeled religious—from the Latin *religo* (to tie, fasten)—underscoring the ease with which she connected with people?

> The Natives have, far less than the white people, the sense of risks in life. . . . I have met the eyes of my native companions, and have felt that we were at a great distance from one another, and that they were wondering at my apprehension of our risk. It made me reflect that perhaps they were, in life itself, within their own element, such as we can never be, like fishes in deep water which for the life of them cannot understand our fear of drowning. This assurance, this art of swimming, they had, I thought because they had preserved a knowledge that was lost to us by our first parents; Africa, amongst the continents, will teach it to you: that God and the Devil are one, the majesty co-eternal, not two uncreated but one uncreated, and the Natives neither confounded the persons nor divided the substance. (ibid., 18)

As to practical matters, she was accurate and methodical, noting that 1,200 Africans, under the supervision of Bror's foreman, were needed to prepare the land to plant coffee. By April 1914, to Dinesen's delight, several hundred seedlings had been planted. She shared her elation with her mother:

> Time seems to pass so quickly here. . . . It is interesting to watch the plantation and quite remarkable when I think that the thick dark forest, with a

narrow little green path through it, that I was walking along on 15 January when I came out here with Bror, has turned into a smooth peaceful coffee field, which is kept in exactly the same orderly way as the kitchen garden at home. (*Letters from Africa*, April 10, 1914, 7)

A sense of accomplishment, of fulfillment in the positive growing process, provided moments of intense joy. So, too, did her love for Bror burgeon. Setbacks, however, were in the offing—illness in particular. She was stricken with malaria. The high fevers and quixotic tremblings she now endured led to a pronounced loss of weight and anemia. Bror was solicitous, but much to her sorrow she was to experience his other side. In the throes of her illness, unthinkingly, he invited friends to the house—women as well as men. The smoke and the chatter plagued the ailing patient. Her distaste for the whites as a group came to the fore. To make matters worse, when she tried to relate to Britishers, her English was so poor she could barely carry on an extended conversation. Two months later the doctor told her she was suffering from depression. A change of scene was recommended (Donelson, 36ff.). Bror suggested a safari to the southern Guaso Nyiro River. She agreed.

The preparations were complex. Wagons were readied. Servants prepared the food. Bror taught his wife how to shoot, to protect herself from the ever-present dangers of lions, cheetah, and leopards. The six-week camping trip under starry nights and fresh mountain air worked as a curative agent. Her pleasures, nonetheless, were shortlived. World War I was declared. Wagons were requisitioned by the army, and an end was put to work on the farm. Terror struck her when she learned that English settlers might consider her a German sympathizer. She also heard the rumor that white women would be put in a concentration camp to protect them from the natives: "If I am to go into a ladies Concentration Camp in this country for months—and who knows how long the war is to last?—I shall die" (*Out of Africa*, 255). Fortunately, she was offered the opportunity to go to Kijabe with a Swedish farmer, and "there to be put in charge of a camp to which the runners from the border brought in their news, which had then to be telegraphed on to Headquarters in Nairobi. . . . In those days the Germans were supposed to be everywhere, and we kept sentinels by the great railway bridge of Kijabe to prevent them blowing it up" (ibid.).

Even though Dinesen's travails were harrowing, in times of crisis she paradoxically radiated strength. Verbally replicating an onerous task, she tints her images with cosmic grandeur.

> And in the early morning, while the old constellations of the stars were still out, we set off down the long endless Kijnabe Hill, with the great plains of the Masai Reserve—iron-grey in the faint light of the dawn—spread at our feet, with lamps tied under the waggons, swinging and with much shouting and cracking of whips. I had four waggons, with a full team of sixteen oxen to each, and five spare oxen, and with twenty-one young Kikuyus. . . . My dog Dusk walked by my side. (ibid., 256)

Activity contained her fears; solitude invited them. Only her husband could calm her. One of her servants in whom she had utmost trust, the Somalian Farah, also exerted a soothing influence. "I talked to him about my worries as about my successes, and he knew of all that I did or thought" (ibid., 377). For nearly eighteen years he organized her house, her stables, and her safaris.

Concerns over which she had no control began plaguing her: the coffee plants were not thriving for lack of rain, and the land was in itself a little too high for coffee. "But a coffee-plantation is a thing that gets hold of you and does not let you go, and there is always something to do on it" (ibid., 7). Bror's mismanagement of funds, the death of some of their livestock, and his schemes, such as charcoal making, were impractical. Worse, his borrowings of enormous sums of money seemed mindless to her. How could he possibly pay his creditors back? After awakening to the fact that he was a compulsive spender and a philanderer, misunderstandings between the two arose. The death knell to their relationship sounded early in 1915. Dinesen was like the young bride in "The Pearls," a short story she was to write years later: a bride whose husband had given her a string of pearls that had once belonged to his grandmother and which, on their honeymoon, caught on her bracelet and "sprang all over the floor, as if she had burst into a rain of tears. . . . She sat in a kind of mild panic" ("The Pearls," *Winter's Tales*, 114). Traumatized by the volley of bad news that broke out daily, she suffered insomnia, fevers, and head pains. She consulted a doctor. The diagnosis: syphilis. Karen quaked. She left for Europe with her secret.

Traveling was both arduous and dangerous in time of war. In Paris a physician told her she would never be cured. On to Zurich for more consultations, arriving in Denmark in June 1915. During her three-month hospitalization in the Royal Hospital in Copenhagen, she was given injections of arsenic and bismuth. Nausea, headaches, and cramps ensued (Donelson, 59). Although cured, no physician could predict the long-term effects of this virulent disease. Would she go insane in twenty years?

Bror arrived at Rungstedlund in the spring of 1916. The war had spurred economic growth. So dithyrambically did he speak to his wife's relatives about the remarkable business opportunities in Africa that her family borrowed money and, this time, set up a corporation which Bror was to manage, but that would be named Karen's Coffee Co. Ltd. Was it wishful thinking on Dinesen's part to believe that Bror would or could change? After a trip to London, the two returned to Africa. "At last we are home again!" she wrote her mother. "It seems like a dream to be here, and like a dream to walk around and look at everything again" (*Letters from Africa*, January 2, 1917, 39). While pleased to see that her devoted servant Farah had kept up the house and the flower beds, she worried that heavy rains and frost would be deleterious to the coffee plantings. Bror had plans to go into the cattle-raising business. To this end, he attended a cattle auction at Naivasha. On his agenda as well was an investment in a flax farm at Gil Gil. Dinesen's letter to her mother relates optimistically that "yesterday after we had been over to Hopcraft's farm to look at his cattle, on the way home we shot from the car partridge, guinea fowl, dik-dik waterbuck and *serval* cat" (ibid., February 7, 1917, 40).

Bror, the eternal *puer*, started anew. This time he was certain things would go well. The couple moved to Swedo, to another farm with a more spacious and elegant house. It had its veranda looking out on Karen's beloved Ngong Hills. She took time to refurbish her already extensive library and had some of the fields cleared for a better view of the Ngong Hills. Little went as anticipated. The drought in the Athi River valley caused coffee crop failures. Unable to deal with these negative constants, Bror left for the Uasin Gishu farm, where the weather was less inclement (Donelson, 77). The emotionally devastated Dinesen, forever fearing to be alone, suffered nights of insomnia. She developed rheumatism. Her weight loss of thirty-five pounds was worrisome. Her solitude palled. She was concerned for the natives who might starve to death for want of crops.

Armistice having been declared on November 11, 1918, husband and wife sailed for Europe in August 1919. During Dinesen's stay in Denmark it was decided that she would take over the management of her family's entrerprise. The divorce from Bror that she requested in January 1922—a virtually unheard-of step in her milieu—was granted in 1925.

In complete control of the farm by June 1921, she worked assiduously to make it profitable. Were she to succeed, she would prove her capabilities. The rains and the sight of the nine-year-old coffee bushes growing taller and taller buoyed her feelings. She knew, nonetheless, that

> coffee-growing is a long job. It does not all come out as you imagine, when, yourself young and hopeful, in the streaming rain, you carry the boxes of your shining young coffee-plants from the nurseries, and, with the whole number of farm-hands in the field, watch the plants set in the regular rows of holes in the wet ground where they are to grow, and then have them thickly shaded against the sun, with branches broken from the bush, since obscurity is the privilege of young things. It is four or five years till the trees come into bearing, and in the meantime you will get drought on the land, or diseases, and the bold native weeds will grow up thick in the fields—the black-jack, which has long scabrous seed-vessels that hang on to your clothes and stockings. Some of the trees have been badly planted with their tap-roots bent; they will die just as they begin to flower. You plant a little over six hundred trees to the acre, and I had six hundred acres of land with coffee; my oxen dragged the cultivators up and down the fields, between the rows of trees, many thousand miles, patiently, awaiting coming bounties. (*Out of Africa*, 7)

Meanwhile, she enjoyed the visits of the tall and handsome thirty-one-year-old Eton and Oxford graduate Denys Finch Hatton, flying for the Royal Air Corps and living off and on in Africa since 1911. He was conversant in Latin, Greek, Shakespeare, French and English poets, opera, ballet, and so much more (Donelson, 78). Their talks and exchanges were fulfilling and thrilling. She felt overjoyed in his presence. Was she living a dream? They saw each other during each of his stays in Nairobi. When visiting her in the spring of 1922, he encouraged her to pursue her art work. It would take her out of herself. They talked literature and music. He soothed her anguish. Theirs was a meeting of the minds. She had found a soul mate. That he spent much of his time in England, nonetheless, saddened her. During his trips to Africa he led safaris to Tanganyika.

The days he spent camping and hunting in the Ngong Hills, he was there for her and she for him. He taught her how to drive his new Hudson car. They hunted together. She thrived on his companionship and on his love, a theme she conveyed in her short story "The Dreamers" (Donelsen, 145). When she became pregnant with his child, she was overjoyed. But her miscarriage brought her to tears. She blamed herself for the loss. In Denys's company, however, she felt calmed and inspired, and a sense of pleasure enveloped her being. His departures left her virtually bereaved.

Although an excellent farm manager, Dinesen had no power over the weather. Frequent droughts were destroying her coffee crops. If financial losses were to continue, she would be forced to abandon her farm and return to Copenhagen. The very thought of leaving Africa—and Denys— not only increased her already ingrained fears of being cut off from him, but her own deeply rooted sense of personal *"Failure, failure, failure"* that had always plagued her (*Letters from Africa*, March 23, 1923, 149). Yet there were days when, after looking down at her small coffee crop that she planned to have weeded, a glimmer of hope shot through her body. She would then have shade trees planted to protect it from the sun. Donning her khaki pants, smock, hat, and clogs, she who had learned to use a tractor ploughed the land herself, then joined the natives in picking the ever sparser coffee plants, making certain the beans were sent to the factory for processing.

One day, she happened to notice that many women in Kenya ran their own farms, tending to their livestock and plantings. Unlike herself, they were hardy and self-confident. She was different. Farm management was not her forte. She had no options.

A few times, Denys and I spoke as if I was really going to leave the country. He himself looked upon Africa as his home, and he understood me very well and grieved with me then, even if he laughed at my distress at parting with my people. "Do you feel," he said, "that you cannot live without Sirunga?" "Yes," I said. But most of the time when we were together, we talked and acted as if the future did not exist. (*Out of Africa*, 329)

Little by little Dinesen began selling her furniture and dismantling her home. She frequently joined Denys when he repaired to his home on the coast, thirty miles north of Mombasa on the creek of Takaunga.

Here were the ruins of an old Arab settlement, with a very modest minaret and a well—a weathered growth of grey stone on the salted soil, and in the midst of it a few old Mango trees. He had built a small house on his land and I had stayed there. The scenery was of a divine, clean, barren Marine greatness, with the blue Indian ocean before you, the deep creek of Takaunga to the South, and the long steep unbroken coast-line of pale grey and yellow coral-rock as far as the eye reached. (ibid., 331)

Each time her Dionysian Denis left for England, or elsewhere, and he failed to write, she feared for the years to come. Was she going mad? Recurring weight loss, anemia, severe panic attacks again plagued her. Could her syphilis have returned? No, it had not. When alone on starry evenings, accompanied only by the sound of hyenas and buzzing insects, she was moved to compose her stories, to create not one child, but many children. In this manner, she assuaged the lingering pain and humiliation of her failed marriage, of her failure to bear a child, and of her failed business ventures.

To help her cope with disaster and in a spirit of altruism as well, she became involved in the movement of educating Africans, helping them to cure their diseases and heal the accidents they suffered. Such charitable work imbued her with a sense of accomplishment and helped her work through her own painful fate.

Painting, one of her creative palliatives, encouraged her to ask Africans to pose for her. At other moments, she focused on landscapes. She also busied herself entertaining. Her animals—dogs, pet owl, birds, who had always come and gone in her house as they pleased—cheered her. She planned a *ngoma* ("evening of dance")—an important tradition of the past, but now a rarity. The arrival of the old dancers was a rare, sublime sight:

There were about a hundred of them. . . . The old Native men are chilly people, and generally wrap and muffle themselves up well in furs and blankets, but here they were naked, as if solemnly stating the formidable truth. Their finery and war-paint were discreetly put on, but a few of them wore, on their old bald skulls, the big head-dresses of black eagle's feathers that you see on the heads of the young dancers. They did not need any ornament either, they were impressive in themselves. . . . As I stood and looked at them a fancy came back to me that had taken hold of me before: It was not I who was going away, I did not have it in my power to leave Africa, but it was the country that was slowly and gravely withdrawing from me, like the sea in ebb-tide. Just as the dancers had ranged themselves for the dance, an Askari from Nairobi arrived at the house with a letter for me, that the Ngoma must not take place. . . . During all my life in Africa I have not lived through another moment of such bitterness. . . . [W]hen it was over, everything was over. (ibid., 365)

Dinesen never learned why the government had forbidden the *ngoma*, but her disappointment was deep.

After five continuous years in Africa, she sailed in 1925 to Paris, where she had planned to take painting lessons, visit museums, order a new wardrobe, and travel to the Riviera. Because the City of Lights was so cold and damp and her own *état d'âme* so disjointed, she kept to her room for three long weeks, then left for Hamburg and Denmark. Her mother's presence comforted her. The feeling that she was being cared for released her from her habitual responsibilities and anxieties. It was during her visit to Denmark that she finally met one of the most influential literary critics—and her idol—George Brandes (1842–1927), "an intellectual genius, one of the greatest minds of my country," who had "revealed literature to me" (*Letters from Africa*, April 19, 1924, 209). When she met Brandes in the summer of 1925, he encouraged her to revise a play—*The Revenge of Truth*—that she had written years earlier. It was then accepted for publication by *Tilskueren*, the Danish literary magazine (Donelson, 216). She could barely cope with her joy. She visited with friends, walked through the Danish woods, was in awe, perhaps for the first time, of the beauties of her land, its merchandise, niceties, museums, ballets, and theater.

Although she dreaded the thought of the responsibilities awaiting her in Africa, she boarded a ship with her Scottish deerhound in Antwerp shortly after Christmas 1925. Rough waters, the pitchings of the ship, and a sinus infection made her ill. That Denys was not at her farm when she arrived in February 1926 troubled her. She developed a throat infection. Upon her recovery, she was determined to set herself on the right path, which meant riding horseback through the fields, marveling at the wildebeest, zebras, lions, giraffes, antelopes, ostriches, and acacia trees. Then Denys appeared as if out of nowhere. His presence comforted her, his conversation excited her, and his love fulfilled her.

She again devoted time to social work, visiting Kiyuku villages, bringing medicine to the ill and those dying of blackwater fever, malaria, tuberculosis, and so forth (Donelson, 237). Her spirits, however, catapulted in 1926, following another coffee crop failure. Bankruptcy was imminent. A love letter from Denys helped restore her equanimity. Upon his return to Africa, he began sharing his hobby of flying with her. In 1927 she nursed Denys during his bout with dysentery. When they were up to it, they went on safaris together. Denys shot two lions for her. Life was idyllic. Now that she had been in Africa for fourteen years, she considered Africans her people.

At the end of March 1929, having received news that her mother had fallen seriously ill, she made arrangements to return to Rungstedlund, but arriving in May she found her well again. After further travel to London and Copenhagen, news reached her of another coffee crop failure. She finally understood that her company's financial collapse was in the offing. The stock market crash had international ramifications. Dinesen boarded ship in Genoa for Kenya at the end of December, arriving in Mombasa in January 1930. She had time to wrestle with the idea of selling out, which would mean betraying her African people. Denys, fully aware of her dilemma and in an attempt to distract her, invited her to see his airplane, which he kept in Nairobi, but could land on her property as well. The Africans who flocked to see this incredible metallic object were awed by its magical powers. As for Dinesen, she had come to understand Denys's passion for flying: it melded with the airiness, purity, and transparency of his temperament. He was "a kind of Arie," she wrote a friend, "he moves spiritually in three dimensions" (ibid., October 12, 1930, 413). Elation was, nonetheless, blended with concern for his safety. When she flew with him, she, too, experienced the pellucid skies, assuaging momentarily her guilt toward the natives for leaving them. "I definitely believe that people who think wings are one of the attributes of the blessed are right, or: the capacity of moving in three dimensions is a part of bliss, or at least of transfiguration" (ibid.).

Reality kept Dinesen grounded. Her debts were so serious that the bank threatened foreclosure of her farm. Disease again dominated the scene: weight loss, amebic dysentery, anemia, numbness, tingling of the hands and feet, and severe depression. The millions of grasshoppers that had swooped down on her property, decimating the leaves on the trees, added to her despair. No other way out was left. She sold her property, blaming her own incompetence for her loss. Denys planned to fly to Takaunga, his home on the coast, in May 1931. Shortly after takeoff, his plane fell to earth. Karen refused to believe he was dead. She brooded. She slit her wrists. Denys now lay buried in those Ngong Hills she had rhapsodized upon her arrival as a young bride. There he remained, a transcendent power to watch over her land, awakening her to a new world and vision of life. She sailed to Denmark in June 1931. Her brother Thomas met her in Marseilles. After a brief stay at the Montreux Clinique, she arrived at Rungstedlund. Her mother was there for her.

Writing, the heart of Dinesen's new world, invited her to travel in a different sphere, refurbishing her old world via her art. Her dense, taut, and poetic sentences vibrated with a new magic, emerging from her melding of Viking enchantment with African poetics. Her masterpieces, *Out of Africa*, *Seven Gothic Tales*, and *Winter's Tales*, among other works, met critical acclaim and earned her world renown. Twice she was nominated for the Nobel Prize for Literature, in 1954 and 1957. Her antagonists, however, were the formidable Ernest Hemingway and Albert Camus.

In 1956 Dinesen began complaining of abdominal pain. She underwent surgery for a stomach ulcer. The surgeons cut out a third of her stomach. She could barely eat, lost weight, and became a virtual invalid. Mood swings became prevalent. Nervousness was frequent. By 1960 she was on amphetamines. Heavy smoking added to her ill health. She died on September 7, 1962. Or is she simply dreaming?

> For we have in the dream forsaken our allegiance to the organizing, controlling and rectifying forces of the world, the Universal Conscience. We have sworn fealty to the wild, incalculable, creative forces, the Imagination of the Universe. (*Out of Africa*, 439)

Bettina L. Knapp

BIBLIOGRAPHY

Brantly, Susan. "Isak Dinesen (Karen Blixen)." *Multicultural Writers from Antiquity to 1945*. Ed. Alba Amoia and Bettina L. Knapp, Westport, Conn., and London: Greenwood Press, 2002, pp. 87–90.

Dinesen, Isak. *Letters from Africa: 1914–1931*. Ed. Frans Lasson. Trans. Anne Born. Chicago: University of Chicago Press, 1981.

———. *On Modern Marriage and Other Observations*. New York: St. Martin's Press, 1986.

———. *On Mottoes of My Life*. Copenhagen: Ministry of Foreign Afffairs, 1962.

———. *Out of Africa* (1937). *Shadows on the Grass* (1960). New York. Vintage International, 1965.

———. *Seven Gothic Tales*. New York: Modern Library, 1939.

———. *Winter's Tales* (1942). New York: Vintage Books, 1961.

Donelsen, Linda. *Out of Africa: Isak Dinesen, the Untold Story*. Iowa City, Iowa: Coulsong List, 1995.

Parmenia Migel, Tania. *A Biography and Memoir of Isak Dinesen*. New York: McGraw-Hill, 1987.

Thurman, Judith. *Isak Dinesen: The Life of a Storyteller*. New York: St. Martin's Press, 1982.

Whissen, Thomas. *Isak Dinesen's Aesthetics*. Port Washington, N.Y.: Kennikat Press, 1972.

15

Freya Stark
(1893–1993)

> This is a great moment, when you see, however distant, the
> goal of your wandering. The thing which has been living in
> your imagination suddenly becomes a part of the tangible
> world. It matters not how many ranges, rivers, or parching
> dusty ways may lie between you: it is now yours forever.
>
> (Freya Stark, *The Valleys of the Assassins*, 170)

Dame Freya Madeleine Stark, a woman with little formal education, triumphed over neglect, sickness, poverty, loneliness, and a
terrible childhood injury that left her slightly disfigured, to
become one of the most celebrated women explorers and travel writers of
the twentieth century. At the age of eighty-two, she was knighted by
Queen Elizabeth for her contribution to the literature of travel.

"[T]he five reasons for travel given me by Sayyid Abdullah, the watch-
maker," she wrote, are "to leave one's troubles behind one; to earn a living;
to acquire learning; to practise good manners; and to meet honorable
men" (*A Winter in Arabia*, 157). To the above may be added Freya Stark's
desire to search for a substitute for love, husband, and children, to become
a writer, to combat fear and the fear of death, and to leave behind what
she termed "an unacceptable life."

Stark's life was not always "unacceptable." She was born in 1893, the
out-of-wedlock daughter of an American, Obediah Dyer, and Flora
Stark, an Englishwoman married to her first cousin Robert Stark.

Although the couple had been childless for fifteen years before Freya's birth, Robert Stark seems to have accepted the child and loved her as his own. Both Flora—who had been raised in Italy—and Robert Stark were artists, but, as they discovered almost immediately after their marriage, they had nothing else in common. Flora never adjusted either to her husband or to the lonely moors of Dartmoor in England; frequent moves back and forth to the Continent made her life tolerable. Freya seems to have inherited her mother's restlessness. She wrote in the first volume of her autobiography that her earliest travel adventure occurred when she was four years old, an age at which

> the joy of running away became conscious. I set out with a macintosh over my arm, my tooth brush and one penny in its pocket, walking down the road to Plymouth to get into a ship and go to sea. . . . The beckoning counts, and not the clicking latch behind you: and all through life the actual moment of emancipation still holds that delight of the whole world coming to meet you like a wave. (*Traveller's Prelude*, 37)

When Freya was ten years old, Flora left her husband and took Freya and her younger sister Vera to the town of Dronero in Italy to open a carpet factory with Mario di Roascio, an Italian count seventeen years her junior, removing the girls from a comfortable life in England and condemning them to a life of poverty and loneliness. In Dronero they were ostracized by the other children because of the family's unorthodox situation. Shortly before Freya's thirteenth birthday, the girls were taken to visit the factory, where Freya's hair became caught in the machinery. Mario wrenched her free—half of her scalp was ripped off, including her right ear. This disfiguring accident was particularly disastrous for Freya, who had suffered even before then from her lack of beauty. She wrote in *Traveller's Prelude* that want of a regular education had never caused her any regret, but that the absence of beauty had always been disappointing.

In 1911, after working in the carpet factory for years, Freya escaped to attend Bedford College in London, but the school closed in 1914 with the advent of World War I, and she returned to Italy. She trained at a hospital in Bologna, where she met Dr. Quirino Ruata, to whom she became engaged. He jilted her soon after to return to a former lover. The broken engagement left her with a fear that she might never be desirable enough to find a husband. It was only in 1947, when she was fifty-four years old, that she married the forty-six-year-old Stewart Perowne, naively unaware of his homosexuality. When they divorced a few years later, she returned to her maiden name, but kept the coveted status and was known thereafter as Mrs. Freya Stark.

When World War I ended, Stark's father bought her a house on the Italian Riviera, where she eked out a living for her mother and herself by growing and selling flowers and fruit. From 1920 to 1927 she studied Arabic, and in November 1927, thanks to a sum of money left to her (most probably by her biological father), she embarked on a cargo ship for French-controlled Lebanon. In a letter to a friend dated April 7, 1928, she exclaimed: "Yesterday was a wonderful day for I discovered the Desert! . . . And then the wonder happened!" She continued:

> Camels appeared on our left hand: first a few here and there, then more and more, till the whole herd came browsing along, five hundred or more. . . . The two Beduin [sic] leaders, dressed gorgeously, [were] perched high up and swinging slowly with the movement of their beasts. . . . I can't tell you what a wonderful sight it was: as if one were suddenly in the very morning of the world among the people of Abraham or Jacob. . . . I never imagined that my first sight of the desert would come with such a shock of beauty and enslave me right away. (*Over the Rim of the World*, 35–36)

During her stay in Lebanon, Stark visited the Syrian capital of Damascus and then slipped through a French military cordon surrounding the Druze—members of a secret Muslim sect who had recently revolted against French rule, as they had for 200 years before fought against their previous occupiers, the Ottoman Turks—in the Djebel Druze, a region running through the Galilee, Lebanon, and southern Syria. Comparisons were often made between Freya Stark and Gertrude Bell, who years before had managed to evade the Turkish authorities to visit the Druze (see p.150)—and indeed there were many similarities between them—but Stark was unwilling to concede that Bell had been a trailblazer in the Middle East. In a letter of January 6, 1929, she wrote: "I am rereading Gertrude Bell's *Syria* [*The Desert and the Sown*], comparing her route with ours. She, however, travelled with three baggage mules, two tents and three servants, so I consider we were the more adventurous" (*Over the Rim of the World*, 41).

While Stark and Bell were both intrepid travelers and gifted writers, Stark differed from Bell in that she looked for underlying universal truths in everything she saw. This can be seen, for example, in an anecdote about her muleteer, Aziz, who had taken a second wife, as was customary in his country, filling his first wife with grief.

> [S]he held up to him with tactless reiteration the mirror of the past with all his faults recorded ever since their wedding sixteen years before, when she was fourteen and he sixteen. . . . [T]he poor woman's grief was so deep that it was useless to point out how much worse she made the matter by railing. Love, like broken porcelain, should be wept over and buried, for nothing but a miracle will resuscitate it: but who in this world has not for some wild moments thought to recall the irrecoverable with words? (*The Valleys of the Assassins*, 223–24)

Stark took notes during her adventures in Syria—which she hid from the French authorities—and incorporated them into an article for the English *Cornhill Magazine* when she returned to Italy. The diary of this trip was later published in 1942 as *Letters from Syria*. Her experiences among the Druze marked the beginning of her fascination with secret Islamic societies and led her eventually to the ancient Assassins, a phenomenally successful terrorist group with whom the Druze were connected in some obscure way.

Stark returned to the Middle East in 1929 and spent the winter in Baghdad, where she shocked the British community by wearing Arab dresses at times and living in the home of a native shoemaker, a choice of dwelling dictated by financial necessity. "The East affected me on this second arrival," she wrote, "with a rapture such as I have never known except on my rediscovery of the Alps after the . . . war" (*Over the Rim of the World*, 41). Now she needed to find a justification for her travels as well as a subject for travel writing that would produce the income needed to supplement her modest means. She wrote to her father that she intended to "combine a sort of history with travel notes to the fortresses of the Assassins . . . [who] had a series of castles between Aleppo and the Persian borders" (ibid., 42).

And so, in 1930, Stark set out on the first of two trips to a remote area of Persia to locate the ruins of these fortress castles. For over 200 years, until their defeat by the Mongols in 1273, the Assassins, a branch of the Ismaili Muslims, had ruled by murder throughout the Near East under the Old Men of the Mountain, the first of whom, according to legend, dominated them with hashish, from which their name was derived (*hash-ishiyyin*, hashish-takers or assassins). At the end of her first trip, Stark located the ruins of the Old Men's impregnable fortress, called the Rock of Alamut, described by Marco Polo in his *Travels*.

During her second expedition, Stark explored other valleys of the Assassins and later went in search of Neolithic bronzes buried in graves in Luristan, one of the most remote and dangerous parts of western Persia. The Lurs were known as bandits and murderers—even the Persian authorities were reluctant to go into the area—but Stark would not be deterred. Although she found no treasure and was ultimately expelled by the Persian police, she did bring back a description of the graves and maps of the region that were to prove indispensable to the British government. She was the first European woman and one of very few Europeans to travel through this dangerous area, demonstrating extraordinary courage. She felt secure and was without fear in the Middle East. All that had troubled her previously, her lack of beauty, money, and social position, did not matter.

Stark incorporated the experiences of the two trips into her most entertaining travel book, *The Valleys of the Assassins and Other Persian Travels* (1934). In this account of her Persian and Luristan adventures between 1930 and 1932, she displayed her gifts as a writer, evoking the atmosphere of distant lands and exotic peoples with extraordinary skill.

> The valley was now full of loveliness. A last faint sense of daylight lingered in its lower reaches, beyond the village houses whose flat roofs, interspersed with trees, climb one above the other up the slope. Behind the great mountain at our back the moon was rising, not visible yet, but flooding the sky with gentle waves of light ever increasing. . . . Here was more than beauty. We were remote, as in a place closed by high barriers from the world. . . . A sense of quiet life, unchanging, centuries old and forgotten, held our pilgrim souls in its peace. (*The Valleys of the Assassins*, 235)

In Stark's work, the people of these remote lands come to life:

> I watched the beauty of the two girls—a fine beauty of an old race with small hands and thin lips and long oval faces. On their heads they wore

little skull caps embroidered with beads round which they wound the voluminous dark turban. There were beads around their ankles too, where the
scarlet trousers were fastened tightly and ended in a woolen fringe over the
little bare beads. This is a good and decent costume for women who sit
about on the ground all the time. Over it they wore loose gowns of printed
cotton. (ibid., 61)

She demonstrates her narrative skill in countless anecdotes—here in
her description of a wedding:

In one corner, apart from it all and completely hidden under a pale blue
chadur, or veil, stood the bride. She stands motionless for hour after hour,
while the stream of guests goes by, unable to sit down unless the chief guest
asks her to do so, and taking no part in the general gaiety. (ibid., 224)

And then the author enters into the picture:

I went up and lifted the veil to greet her, and was horrified to see large tears
rolling down her painted cheeks. The palms of her hands and her finger-
nails were dyed with henna, her hair was crimped with cheap green cellu-
loid combs stuck into it: she wore a pink machine-embroidered shirt in
atrocious taste, and a green velvet waistcoat brought specially from Qazvin;
and all this splendour, covered away under the blue *chadur*, was weeping
with fright and fatigue, thinking who knows what thoughts while it stood
there like a veiled image at the feast. (ibid, 224–25)

Stark's account of her travels into dangerous, remote areas of Persia, as
well as the successful mapmaking she did for British Intelligence, won her
the Royal Geographical Society's Back Memorial Prize. During the
period of her Persian adventures, she was based in Baghdad, where she
worked for the *Baghdad Times* correcting and rewriting Reuters dis-
patches. She also wrote a series of articles about her experiences in the
Middle East, published in Baghdad under the title *Baghdad Sketches* (the
British edition of the work appeared in 1937).

By chance, Stark had embarked upon a fabulous career, the second
phase of which began in December 1934, when she left for her first travels
in South Arabia. "I wanted space, distance, history and danger and I was
interested in the living world," she wrote (*Over the Rim of the World*, 105).

Her goal was to penetrate Yemen's interior to follow the frankincense route to Shabwa, capital of the ancient kingdom of the Hadhramaut and one of the cities that had flourished along the trade route. It was from Shabwa that Bilqis, the queen of Sheba, had departed to visit King Solomon. No European explorer before Stark had ever reached this city buried in the sands, nor did she, but her account, in *The Southern Gates of Arabia: A Journey in the Hadhramaut*, of her adventures in this colorful world of sheiks and harems, of holy men and bedouins, received excellent reviews. Her joy is palpable as she describes her experiences at the bedouin camp at the Gate of Makalla, where she stayed for five days, and where she spent many hours looking from the windows of her room on the city wall to the camping place of caravans outside the gate, "watching the picture of life below." And then,

> [w]hen the evening came, and the sweet shrill cry of the kites, that fills the daylight, stopped, Awiz appeared with three paraffin lanterns, which he dotted about the floor in various places, and, having given me my supper, departed to his home. The compound with its dim walls, its squares of moist earth planted with vegetables and few trees, grew infinite and lovely under the silence of the moon. The gate of the city was closed now, a dim glow showed where the sentries beguiled their watch with a hookah in the guard house. (*The Southern Gates of Arabia*, 31)

When she felt tired, she continued,

> I would withdraw from my verandah . . . and retire to my room. . . . As I closed my eyes in this security and silence, I thought of the Arabian coasts stretching on either hand . . . [and that] within these titanic barriers I was the only European at the moment. A dim little feeling came curling up through my sleepy senses; I wondered for a second what it might be before I recognized it: it was Happiness, pure and immaterial; independent of affections and emotions, the aetherial essence of happiness, a delight so rare and so impersonal that it seems scarcely terrestrial when it comes. (ibid., 31–32)

The Southern Gates of Arabia met with widespread critical acclaim; the maps and appendix, titled "Notes on the Southern Incense Route of Arabia," were hailed by the Royal Geographical Society as an extraordinary summation of material on the ancient southern Arabian incense route. Two years later, Stark wrote an introduction to a book of her Hadhramaut photographs, *Seen in the Hadhramaut*, the first pictorial portrayal of this remote region.

Stark took a second trip to Yemen in 1937–38, this time in the company of two scientists, Gertrude Caton-Thompson, an archaeologist and paleohistorian, and Elinor Wight Gardener, a geologist, to conduct a scientific examination of Hadhramaut archaeology. The expedition had an impressive list of sponsors, including the Royal Geographical Society, the Ashmolean Museum, and the Cambridge University Museum of Archaeology and Ethnology. Stark wrote in her memoirs that the purpose of the trip was to be archaeology, but, as always, her interest lay in native life and customs. In the preface to *A Winter in Arabia* (1940), the story of the expedition, she wrote: "The scientific and more serious records of this venture are to be found elsewhere: this is but a record of actions and reactions that might occur in any small Arabian town unused to Europeans and of a journey from Hureidha to the sea" (v).

The first part of *A Winter in Arabia* consists of a diary of three months spent in what is now Yemen, in which she portrays the life of the veiled women, the complicated rules governing social and business affairs, the palace of Sultan 'Ali of Qatn, and the hostility among rival tribes. The second part is an account of the journey she undertook on her own when the dig was completed in an effort to locate the ancient port of Cana, maritime outlet of a major incense route tributary; such a discovery would compensate for her not having found Shabwa on her previous expedition. As in all of her works, Stark expressed her happiness among simple people far from the pressures of European society:

> The perpetual charm of Arabia is that the traveller finds his level there simply as a human being: the people's directness, deadly to the sentimental or pedantic, likes the less complicated virtues; [to which may be added] the pleasantness of being liked for oneself. (ibid., 157)

During World War II, Freya became important to the war effort as the British government recognized her skills—she had spent considerable time in the Middle East and knew much of the area intimately, she spoke a number of Arabic dialects, and she was fluent in Italian, German, and

French. As the authorities had turned to Gertrude Bell during World War
I to maintain the loyalty of the Arab leaders (see p. 153), so did they enlist
Stark to help keep the Arab peoples in the Middle East on the Allied
side and prevent them from supporting the Germans. Both women played
significant political roles during the two wars. In 1939 Freya was sent to
northern Yemen, where a seventy-six-year-old imam was an absolute
ruler, to determine the extent of Italian influence there. Jane Geniesse
writes that during Freya's two-month stay in the ancient walled city of
Sana'a she was excluded from the imam's weekly receptions because of her
sex, so she sent her cook in her stead to listen and report back to her
(Geniesse, *Passionate Nomad*, 251). Later, Stark set up a series of secret
committees or cells to promote British interests in the Middle East; the
Brothers and Sisters of Freedom, which began in Cairo and then spread
throughout Egypt and into Iraq, had more than 40,000 members in
Egypt, Iraq, and Palestine by the end of the war. In 1941 there was a coup
d'état in Iraq by Rashid Ali, which opened with the massacre of Baghdad's Jews, the oldest Jewish community in the world, and was marked by
a monthlong siege of the British embassy, details of which can be found
in the fourth volume of Stark's autobiographical works, *Dust in the Lion's
Paw* (1961).

As part of the British government's effort to cultivate the Arabs, this
time by working against the establishment of a Jewish state in Palestine,
Stark was sent on a speaking tour to America in 1943. Her work entitled
East Is West (1945), published in America as *The Arab Island*, was written
to give a comprehensive picture of the Arabs and provide the background
to explain their opposition to the creation of a Jewish state. The unsur-
prising lack of an enthusiastic reception in the United States was not
understood by a woman who was capable of writing, even after having
witnessed the Baghdad massacre:

> I thought that the Jews have now for the *second* time the chance of a *spiri-
> tual kingdom*, and for the second time are throwing it away because their
> understanding is only material: when their Messiah came, they did not rec-
> ognise him, and now they could live in perfect peace in Jerusalem if they
> did not want the political control. (*Over the Rim of the World*, 205)

The third phase of Stark's travels and travel writing began in 1952. Having published eleven books on the Arabs, and discouraged both by the

loss of British influence and power in the Middle East and by the failure of her marriage, Stark again sought to forget her problems in travel, this time to a different area, Turkey. During the 1950s, she wrote four indispensable travel books on Turkey, but these were different from her works about Arab societies. Now she was no longer interested in describing Arabian people and customs, but explored the historical background of the areas visited in order to find relationships between the past and present. *Ionia: A Quest* (1954) and *The Lycian Shore* (1956), the first of her travel guides, were followed by *Alexander's Path* (1958), in which Stark explores the trails on which Alexander and his army marched from Phrygia to Pamphylia. *Riding to the Tigris* (1959) tells of her travels in Kurdish Anatolia.

Almost until the end of her life, Freya traveled continually to the Far East, Persia, Central Asia, India, and North Africa. Her last travel book, *The Minaret of Djam* (1970), was an account of her journey to an almost inaccessible part of Afghanistan. When she died at the age of one hundred, Freya Stark left behind a priceless body of work, including thirty books of her travel adventures, four volumes of autobiography, and eight volumes of published letters.

Lucille Frackman Becker

BIBLIOGRAPHY

Geniesse, Jane Fletcher. *Passionate Nomad: The Life of Freya Stark.* New York: Modern Library, 2001.

Maitland, Alexander. "Dame Freya Stark: Journeys through Space and Time." *Blackwoods Magazine* 328 (1982): 532–43.

Moorhead, Caroline. *Freya Stark.* New York: Viking Penguin, 1985.

Stark, Freya. *The Valleys of the Assassins and Other Persian Travels.* New York: Modern Library, 2001. Originally published in London: John Murray, 1934.

———. *The Southern Gates of Arabia: A Journey in the Hadhramaut.* New York: Modern Library, 2001. Originally published in London: John Murray, 1936.

———. *Baghdad Sketches.* London: John Murray, 1937.

———. *Seen in the Hadhramaut.* London: John Muray, 1938.

———. *A Winter in Arabia.* New York: The Overlook Press, 2002. Originally published in London: John Murray, 1940.

———. *East Is West.* London: John Murray, 1945. Also published as *The Arab Island.* New York: Knopf, 1945.

———. *Letters from Syria.* London: John Murray, 1942.

———. *Perseus in the Wind.* London: Wyman & Sons, 1948.

———. *Traveller's Prelude* (vol. 1 of autobiography, 1893–1928). London: John Murray, 1950.

———. *Beyond Euphrates* (vol. 2 of autobiography, 1928–33). London: John Murray, 1951.

———. *The Coast of Incense* (vol. 3 of autobiography, 1933–39). London: John Murray, 1953.

———. *Ionia: A Quest.* London: John Murray, 1954.

———. *The Lycian Shore.* London: John Murray, 1956.

———. *Alexander's Path.* New York: Harcourt Brace, 1958.

———. *Riding to the Tigris.* London: John Murray, 1959.

———. *Dust in the Lion's Paw* (vol. 4 of autobiography, 1939–46). London: John Murray, 1961.

———. *The Minaret of Djam.* London: John Murray, 1970.

———. *Over the Rim of the World: Selected Letters.* Ed. Caroline Moorehead. London: John Murray, 1988.

Tinling, Marion. *Women into the Unknown: A Sourcebook on Women Explorers and Travelers.* Westport, Conn.: Greenwood Press, 1989, pp. 265–71.

16

Hayashi Fumiko
(1903–51)

> I was destined to be a wanderer.
>
> (Hayashi Fumiko, in Ericson, *Be a Woman*, 123)

Hayashi Fumiko—wanderer and traveler—was the first Japanese woman writer of modern times to compete successfully with male authors and enjoy popularity as well.

Since her earliest years Hayashi accompanied her poverty-stricken mother and peddler stepfather from town to town in Japan. There were days when they went without food. Never did she know the meaning of a stable home environment. Rootlessness and loneliness were an intrinsic part of her childhood and adolescence (Yukiko Tanaka, *To Live and to Write*, 100). Her lifestyle was not unconventional; it was aconventional. Nor did she find herself struggling against any family-imposed moral or religious restrictions. In time, her ambition and compulsive need to pursue her own destiny as a writer helped her overcome the impediments of her nomadic upbringing. Writing became a constant in her life, a raison d'être, the food of her existence. It filled her solitude, her poverty—life's ever-gaping maw.

Born in Moji on the Shimonoseki Strait, Hayashi was the illegitimate daughter of Hayashi Kiku and the peddler Miyata Asataro (Susanna Fessler, *Wandering Heart*, 1). In 1910 her father rid himself of Kiku, the mother of several children by different men, preferring the company of a geisha. Kiku left the household with her latest lover, Sawai Kisaburo, also a peddler. When given the option of living with her father or with her mother, Hayashi chose the latter. The threesome moved to Nagasaki. In time, Sawai adopted Hayashi.

The ups and downs of business forced Sawai to continue peddling his sundry wares and Hayashi to uproot herself. On the move to Karsuyama, Saseno, Shimonoseki, Onomichi, Kagoshima, and elsewhere, Hayashi's education was at best desultory. During her attendance at the Second Municipal Elementary School in Onomichi in 1916, one of her teachers, detecting her writing talents, inspired her to pursue her studies. Since she would have to earn her way, she took a job at a sail factory and another at a noodle shop (ibid., 4). Unluckily, Hayashi fell in love with Okano Gun'-ichi, a student at Onomichi's Commercial High School. Upon graduation, he enrolled at Tokyo's Meiji University. Hayashi wisely remained in school until she graduated, spending whatever free time she had in the library tasting American, German, French, and English literature. Some of the poems she wrote at this time saw print.

By 1922 Okano had prevailed upon Hayashi to move to Tokyo, where she supported herself by working at numerous jobs: bath attendant, office worker, electric factory worker, and other sundry jobs. They were to marry upon his graduation in 1923, but his parents were averse to the union, causing him to break off his engagement. Deeply disappointed, Hayashi remained in Tokyo, where her parents had relocated. Following the devastating earthquake of 1923, she left for Osaka, on to Onomichi and Shikoku, where she once again joined her parents. That same year she began writing her first great work: *Diary of a Vagabond* (published in completed form in 1930).

Hayashi set out to grab the world. Her emotional highs and lows, her arduous work schedule, her need to learn—nothing seemed too much for her. She became involved also in the women's liberation movement, protesting against the regressive way females had been treated in Japan for centuries. She slept little, ate even less, subsisting on the small sums her menial jobs brought her. Unheeding of her physical state, she was increasingly devoured by a single, all-consuming passion—writing.

Her innate sense of freedom, coupled with her sexual energy and promiscuity, a replica of the Japanese male's comportment, invited the pleasure principle to hold sway. Unfortunately, she sometimes chose the wrong man with whom to cohabit. Nomura Yoshiya, a case in point, was a brutal woman beater, whom she discarded in 1926. That same year Hayashi married—and remained married to—the painter Tzuka Rokubin, a steady and genuine being. In no way did he hinder her sexually promiscuous lifestyle nor any of her other impulses. He did, however, bear the burden of handling her financial matters. His love, stability, and understanding of Hayashi's needs and talents gave her the freedom necessary to fulfill her creative dreams.

Hayashi's self-imposed educational agenda was demanding. She made it her mission to cultivate avant-garde writers: anarchists, leftists, liberals, Dadaists, Surrealists, train of thought stylists, and revolutionaries such as Ono Tozaburo, Hirabayashi Taiko, and Okamoto Jun. Inspired by these movements and their members, and by her own readings, Hayashi poured out poems such as "A Factory Worker Sings," some appearing in print. Just as fervor marked her personality, so it did her creative world.

She was uninterested in political, religious, and ideological themes; freedom of thought and of expression were her bywords. Nor did public opinion matter to her. What imported was the liberty to express her ideas and poetic mode. Like her lifestyle, so her poems were unconventional in their openness and allusions to her sexual encounters and relationships. If readers considered her a tramp, so be it. To the prissy, she certainly was one. Her creative appetite pointed the way. Even while continually enlarging her frame of reference, never once did she betray her roots, nor her living language, glistening with its unreflective, blisteringly blunt, brash, and bold style. Unwilling to make concessions, she spat out her words in rhythmical patterns. At all times, she was unmistakably herself. Her promiscuities, she will confide to her readers, sometimes led to abandonment by her lovers. On one occasion, she stayed overnight "at a rooming house in the Asahi area of Shinjuku." There "I was able to rest my mud-caked body. I had no guarantee of seeing the next light of dawn. . . . I wrote a long letter to the man on the island who had abandoned me" (*Be a Woman*, 123). Anger and violence mark the narrator's elegiac verses in this, her "dead-end world" (ibid., 32).

Hayashi's anthology of poetry, *I Saw a Pale Horse* (1930), won accolades from critics and the reading public alike. A year later her *Diary of a Vagabond* delineating her wanderings throughout Japan became a best seller. Her seemingly unreachable goal—popularity as a writer and financial security—became a reality. Kindness and generosity, being attributes of hers as well, led her to support her parents. Following her stepfather's death, her mother, to whom she was always devoted, moved into Hayashi's and her husband's home (Fessler, 19).

Although writing was her way of filling a gnawing sense of solitude, it was, she confided in her essay "Every Day Life" (1935), a lonely and arduous art:

> When the clock strikes ten, everyone in the house says their goodnights. I find it scary with everyone in bed, so I make a midnight snack in the kitchen and take it upstairs. . . . It's been chilly lately, and there's nothing I can do about the cold taking its toll on my body. I long to write a verse . . . and as dusk comes, I end up sitting in front of my desk, savoring the pain and joy writing brings to me. (quoted in Fessler, 29)

Diary of a Vagabond was based to a great extent on a journal she kept from 1923 to 1928. The depiction of her wanderings through Japan, nonetheless, pointed up a whole fanciful and fictitious side of her personality, said by some to have been fabricated by her to titillate her readers (*Be a Woman*, 77). Her art, however, maintained its clearly defined parameters: the brutal frankness of her language, the raw ferocity with which she conveyed her thoughts and feelings, and the randomness of her nomadism. Her knack for making fragmented sequences cohere during her wanderings were all hers. That she considered her continuous displacements throughout her life the norm was understandable. That is all she knew. As a child, she was required to cope with newness: changing faces, altering circumstances, varieties of schools, fleeting friendships, and the chill of irresolution and anticipation. Paradoxically, her moves from city to city created a certain kind of permanence, continuity, and pleasure.

Diary of a Vagabond, as travel literature, is in keeping with Japanese tradition, examples of which are the *Man'yoshu* (*Collection of Myriad Leaves*) in the Nara period (710–83); the *Tosa Diary, The Gossamer Years,* the *Tales of Ise,* and, to some extent, the *Diary of Sarashina,* in the Heian era (784–1191). These fascinating documents were a blend of prose and poetry, focusing mainly on the aristocracy. Hayashi's work, in contrast, concentrated on the working class and the poverty-stricken. Her truth and reality were not self-serving. Nor did she lament her lot or seek pity.

Rather, she sang her plight with vigor and determination, communicating to her readers the pathetic sense of vacancy inculcated by destitution.

The choice of the word "vagabond" in *Diary of a Vagabond* underscores its leitmotif: wandering, vagrancy, change, and transiency. Her writing technique follows suit: words move, bounce, and float aimlessly about in poetic strands, until, as if magnetized in some strange fashion, they begin to cohere. Action being Hayashi's byword, unmotivated locomotion her way, her shifting nouns and pronouns fashion her imagery in rhythmic echoings.

Although *Diary of a Vagabond* is divided into months, thus endowing it with greater authenticity, Hayashi had no fixed agenda. She simply continued her peripatetic life in and out of Japanese cities, enacting and reenacting her needs and desires, be it with the array of men she chose for her one-night stands, or for longer periods of time, or in the performing of servile tasks she undertook to stave off starvation. She was hired and fired; her uprootedness and her cries of desperation accentuate her moods of melancholy and are declaimed in successions of distilled vignettes.

I was destined to be a wanderer. I have no home. My father was an itinerant peddler of cotton and linen cloth. He came from Iyo on the island of Shikoku. My mother was the daughter of the owner of a hot springs inn on the island of Sakurajima in Kyushu. People say that since she took up with an outsider. . . .

I first entered school in Nagasaki. Dressed in a discarded muslin frock altered to fit me, I would walk from our rooming house, the Zakkoku Inn, to the school near the Nankin precinct. From there we moved on to Sasebo, Kurume, Shimonoseke, Moji, Tobata, and Orio, in that order. I did not have a single close friend, since I changed schools seven times in four years. . . . I was about twelve when we were living in a coal-mining area in Nogata. . . .

The sky in Nogata was dark and smoky day and night. It was the kind of town where the water curled your tongue, even though sand filters were supposed to remove the heavy iron. In July we settled into our lodgings, the Umaya in the Taisho neighborhood. My parents would just leave me behind, as usual, at the rooming house and rent a cart. Filling their large straw containers with knitted goods, socks, muslin, belly warmers, and whatnot, they would head off for the coal mines and the pottery works. . . .

To me, this was a new, unfamiliar place. . . . The streets were not alive as they had been in Moji, nor were they beautiful like those of Nagasaki.

In this neighborhood, sooty eaves yawned darkly, sandwiching alleys encrusted with coke. (*Be a Woman*, 123–24)

Plagued by joblessness, she went to the Italian embassy in Kojimachi to look for work as a maid. "No matter where I went, I felt alone. My heart was in turmoil" (ibid., 133). Yet, her very solitude and homelessness—these constants—comforted her, endowed her with warmth, with, paradoxically, a sense of security in the sameness of her anguish. A deeper understanding of herself and the world were nurtured by the very act of withdrawing into her solitude. Inexplicably, she lived apart from others, yet bonding with humans collectively. Reclusion and seclusion into self, in addition to the hum of her graceless digressions, liberated her. She burst into poetry:

> *They say that, at night,*
> *Impoverished maidens*
> *Throw their lips like fruit*
> *To the wide sky.* (ibid., 136)

> *The light-pink cherry blossoms tinge the heavens.*
> *But these "lovely" women's*
> *Kisses of obligation*
> *Leave traces without emotion.* (ibid., 137)

She worked as housekeeper, then as a bathhouse attendant. She despised authority. She found it more oppressive to "kowtow to the traditions of a wealthy family than to commit harakiri. I wept at the sight of Mother's forlorn face" (ibid., 139). How could it be otherwise when fantasizing about "a plump steamy pork cutlet."

Elsewhere she writes:

I was happiest when I ambled along the boulevards in Shinjuku. Boarding the street car, I saw scenes that might as well have included banners declaring "All the world is at peace." The sight of these gracious thoroughfares wiped away my painful experiences. (ibid., 139)

Boarding a train and traveling in third class to Akashi, she allows her tears to flow, her heart to break—humiliation to override all else in another love affair gone sour. The outside world that she surveys from her window mirrors her mood: "It was pitch black outside. As jumbled scenery rushed by the glass window, I pressed my eyes, nose, and mouth against it and cried, sticking to it like a too-salty pickle" (ibid., 153). She questions: "Where exactly did I think I was going? Each time I heard the vendors calling at one station after another, I opened my eyes in panic. If this life was so impossibly difficult, I preferred to be a beggar and wander about from place to place. . . . I caught my strangely shifting countenance—my hundred comic faces—in the window" (ibid.). Hayashi's reference to "comic faces," like those of a clown, identifies her with the most tragic of beings—those glimpsing utter pain (ibid.).

The variety of moods captured in *Diary of a Vagabond* range from tempestuousness to listlessness. Highlighted as well are love and hatred, each distilled in stark, vibrant images. Nor are the vagrant's contrasting visceral and cerebral inclinations omitted. As she points out the countless towns through which she passed, or in which she remained for a period of time, the richness of Hayashi's discourse becomes increasingly evident. No longer the outpourings of an untutored child, *Diary of a Vagabond* becomes a stimulating poetic experience in which diversity, maturation, and understanding explode and implode in time and with time.

As an important novelist, Hayashi was solicited by newspapers and magazines to write on-the-spot travelogues. This allowed her to earn money and indulge her passion for travel. From 1930 to 1943, she took more than twelve trips abroad. When possible, she chose to travel alone, which not only excited her intellectually, but stimulated her emotionally. Her first trip abroad, in January 1930, was on a lecture tour with other women writers, at the invitation of the governor general of Taiwan. The travelogues she composed during this foray—"The Taiwanese Landscape," "A Souvenir from Taiwan," and "Traveling in Taiwan"—highlighted her impressions of the country, but were of little lasting moment (Fessler, 17). Her later, more extensive, and sometimes dangerous, trips abroad not only tested her endurance, courage, and will to experience the cultures of different lands, but underscored her ingenuity and direct approach to the people she met en route. Her trip to mainland China in August took her to Shanghai and Manchuria: Harbin, Changchun, Mukden, Fushun, Jinzhou, Sanshili, Dalian, Oindao, Nanking, Hangzhou, and Suzhou. She returned to Japan in September 1930, after which she traveled around Japan with her mother, with whom she was very close.

November 4, 1931, must be singled out as a day to remember for Hayashi. Who would have thought that this once poverty-stricken girl would be stepping on board a train of the Trans-Siberian railway to begin an arduous but momentous trip to Paris? Although her third-class accommodations were less than desirable, she spent most of the time looking out of the window, glimpsing the sights as the train sped through Korea, Manchuria, Siberia, and Eastern Europe. She arrived in Paris on December 23. Her travelogues—"Third Class on the Trans-Siberian Railroad" and "Clear Skies All the Way to Paris," among others—describe the wretchedness of the conditions both on the train and during the stops, and the vistas she saw from her window. Whatever illusions she might have harbored concerning Russian communism as an answer to social problems vanished when she was confronted with miserable reality. The long weeks of train travel, nonetheless, catalyzed her heightened sense of discovery and wonderment.

After her arrival in Paris, Hayashi studied French in night school, hoping to become conversant in the language so she could make friends. Although her linguistic skills failed her, she did meet Jean Cocteau, among others, whom she again saw in Japan during his visit there in 1936. To keep abreast of the latest French and Japanese publications, she cultivated Paris's Japanese enclave, but most of the time Hayashi, who treasured solitude, ambulated alone.

> Walking alone [along the Champs-Elysées] gives me a vague feeling like the tedium experienced on the open sea during a long voyage. But, for me, this voyage is an adventure. While I think about how I'd like to return to Japan and get on with my work, I take pleasure in the feeling that comes from the pain and joy that I experience by myself in this strange land. (Fessler, 84)

Her days were filled to capacity—reading, strolling, attending theater, concerts, and visiting museums—with the goal of broadening her education and fulfilling her search for novelty. Among the articles she sent back for Japanese consumption was "A Walk in the Latin Quarter" (1932), depicting daily life in the City of Lights. Then, after a month of sightseeing in rainy but charming London, she produced "A London Boarding House and Other Matters" (1932) (ibid., 80).

Hayashi returned to Japan, traveling always in third class, but this time by ship. To her delight, she found one that anchored at Naples and at Shanghai, thus allowing her to visit two extra cities. She arrived home to an admiring public in June 1932. A slew of travel writings—including "Paris Diary" (1932), "Literature, Travel, Etc." (1936), "Idle Thoughts on Travel" (1936), "Sunday in Naples" (1936), "Memories Abroad" (1936), and "Literary Fragments" (1936)—would feed her devoted readers. They particularly delighted in reading about the people she had met during her peregrinations, the entertainment of the day, and her reactions to certain customs. Rarely, however, did Hayashi describe landscapes in her travelogues: "A Landscape without people is boring" (ibid., 82).

Danger accompanied her every moment on her next foray: an assignment for the *Mainichi Shinbun* took her to Shanghai, then to Nanking. After the fall of the latter city to the Japanese in December 1937, Hayashi not only remained with the Japanese troops at the front for one month, but was the first Japanese woman to "enter Nanking after its fall" (Ericson, 80). No mention of the atrocities perpetrated by the Japanese on the Chinese was made in her articles. Omitted as well was virtually all information about the city itself (ibid., 80). Lest we forget, restrictions on wartime reportages were severe.

In November 1938, Hayashi the war correspondent again made history as the first woman to enter Hankow following its fall to the Japanese. Her article "Battlefront" (1938) understandably lauded the Japanese army and their heroic ethos. She did not, however, spare her readers certain unnerving details.

War has a painful, barbaric side to it, but also has plenty of truly splendid aspects, aspects which are excruciatingly beautiful. Once I was passing through a village, I heard the following conversation between two soldiers who had captured a member of the Chinese resistance:

"I'd like to see him burn at the stake."

"Nah, when I think about the image of [our fellow soldier] who died in Tianjia village it makes me sick to my stomach. That's really offensive. Let's kill him like a man, with a single strike of the sword." And with that, the captured Chinese soldier died instantly, without a moment of suffering, at a single, splendid, strike of the sword. I listened to the soldiers' conversation with a feeling of concurrence. I do not feel that this is in the least bit brutal.

What are your thoughts? I'd like you to understand these soldiers' pure state of mind. The strong memory of their fallen comrade called forth their sentimentality and aroused great indignation in these soldiers' hearts. (ibid., 133)

A second article, "The North Bank Unit" (1938), covering the same story, added poetry and brief vignettes about individual Japanese soldiers and their dedication to the cause (Ericson, 81). At the assignment's conclusion, Hayashi contracted malaria during an epidemic, but she soon recovered.

As a reporter for the Japanese News Corps, she traveled to French Indochina (today Vietnam), Singapore, Java, Borneo, and Sumatra from October 1942 through May 1943. Her mission was to spread goodwill between the Japanese and the native populations. Her reactions, as expressed in "Below the Equator" (1943) and "Sumatra—Island of the Western Wind" (1943), were, understandably, virtually divested of political statements and innuendos.

Conditions during these war years were dangerous, and censorship stringent. Even Hayashi's *Diary of a Vagabond* was banned. She and her family were evacuated to the countryside near Tokyo in 1944. Not until the war's conclusion did they move back to the city.

Floating Cloud (1953), Hayashi's last completed novel, considered by critics to be one of her finest works, intertwines travel to Dalat and other cities in French Indochina with trips in Japan, following this country's defeat in World War II. Hayashi's taut, alert, and succinct style invites readers to share privileged moments with her nihilistic protagonists. Stripped of veneer, the creatures of her fantasy tap into the complexities of eroticism in their controlled, slow-paced, and dirgelike thoughts and actions.

Although *Floating Cloud*, a metaphor for wandering and aimlessness, is reminiscent in its thrust of *Diary of a Vagabond*, a vast gap separates the two. The autobiographical elements in her early work, conveyed in harsh, brutal, and stark language, are based on the belief that hard work, talent, perseverance, and choice may alter one's future circumstances. Such positive thinking is absent in *Floating Cloud*. Its interior monologues, like litanies of sorrows, are dark, despairing, and nostalgic.

The novel explores the world of a young and attractive typist, Koda Yukiko, who, upon graduating from typing school in Tokyo, is sent by the Japanese Ministry of Agriculture and Forestry to the highlands of Dalat. At first, her mood is hopeful. The weather in Japan was chilly when she left, she comments. Upon journeying "southward from Haiphong, Hanoi and Tanh Hoa, the season has gone back to summer" (*Floating Cloud*, 8). Comforting to her as well is "the monotonous chorus of the bull-frogs which sounded like *samisens* or heavy raindrops" (ibid.). She justifies her trip to Dalat:

> I was fed up at home. So I came here to work. . . . How could a young woman keep going amidst that spirit of fight to the last man and die in honor? I didn't come so far on a mere whim. I wanted to get away, float adrift, just anywhere. (ibid., 20)

En route to Dalat, she stops at Hue, a beautiful ancient town in French Indochina. "The rows of camphor-trees on the roads glittered with their golden powder shining under the bright morning sun. . . . The Hue River flowed by, with gay-colored flowers lining its banks, wafting a fragrant river-breeze" (ibid., 11).

Tension rises. She would have preferred to stay in Hue instead of going on to what she considered that unknown and unheard-of town of Dalat. She begins denigrating the commonplace job awaiting her. Yukiko longs for Japan and for the people she knew. Seconds later, Dalat's backdrop of mountains and its lakefront dispel her "uneasiness and melancholy" (ibid., 13).

She is ill at ease when she first meets Tomioka Kengo, a minor official from Japan, who is also to be employed by the Department of Agriculture and Forestry. Both seem to foresee the emptiness of their affair before it has even begun. Like mobile pawns of destiny, beings shunted here and there by an unknown, invisible mechanism, the two are drawn together. Their sexual relationship, and others indulged in with different partners, will, they believe, alter their negative state of mind. Tomioka, however, is less than polite to Yukiko. Moreover, he drinks heavily. He picks up women whenever the urge moves him to do so. He suffers. His head is frequently "empty of thought, only gnawing loneliness, like a wet towel, hung heavy over his forehead" (ibid., 22). To dispel his sense of loneliness, he visits the forestry patrol station about four kilometers away.

> Leaving Dalat he passed several lumber-mills from which the shriek of trees being torn into pieces came to disturb his ears. The forests of thick evergreen trees endlessly flanked the road, their branches and leaves twining, embracing each other, forming a dense gloomy thicket against the bright morning sun. (ibid., 25)

When she and Tomioka visit the tomb of the ancient Anamese king, the scenery replicates the protagonists' inner worlds:

> Thick, dense forests spread all over along the foot-way. The air was endowed with something sweet, enthralling. . . . The trees became thicker in the neighborhood of the tomb. . . . [T]he woodland was of no attraction to her. What interested her was the advancing back of Tomioka's tall body that pulled her like a thread. Caught by a piece of sweet, romantic, dreamlike fantasy, she kept on walking, skillfully assuming the solitary look of a traveling woman veiled in melancholy. (ibid., 26)

With the end of World War II, Yukiko and Tomioka are sent home. Their memories of Dalat, which in retrospect seem so beautiful, intrude into their present realities. Following the death of his wife, Tomioka finds a job in the forestry department on the distant island of Yakushima, south of Kyushu. Yukiko is intent upon joining her lover, but his words spell doom. "If you're with me, you'll rot. Since returning to Japan we should have different paths. Things change with the passing of time. I think it's best that you go your way and I, my way" (ibid., 86).

She insists. In mid-February, the two leave Tokyo on a night train, arriving at Hakata in Kyushu at dawn, and at Kagoshima the next morning. Despite the pouring rain and her discomfort, Yukiko feels unmitigated joy upon hearing her lover register her at the hotel as his wife. Although assailed by a pulmonary disease, she insists on accompanying him by boat to his new workplace at Yakushima Island, south of Kyushu. They will take a later boat, she tells him. Four days elapse. Regardless of the doctor's warning against settling in a climate of crags and clouds, of endless dampness and daily rains, the couple travels on to Yakushima, then to Anbo. Since the circular-shaped island has virtually no inlets, the ship continues on, anchoring the following morning off Miyanoura, whereupon the couple feasts on an otherworldly sight.

> In the center of the mountainous island towered 6,000-foot Mt. Miya-noura, the highest peak in the Kyushu area, whose base was densely covered with Yaku cedars. Tomioka stepped out on the deck to be exposed to the cold sea breeze and viewed the island. Skiffs coming out to the ships tossed like leaves in the rough sea near the shoreline. (ibid., 103)

At the inn, Tomioka does not discount the possibility of Yukiko's dying. She knows she is to die and has no regrets. Returning from work the following evening, Tomioka sees Yukiko's lifeless body lying on the bed like a frozen fixture. She had finally been "liberated from her loneliness" (ibid., 110). Unencumbered in life, Tomioka's goals have vanished, his future is nonexistent, and he, like so many of Hayashi's protagonists, will drift along, like floating clouds, for the rest of his dark earthly sojourn.

The morbid nature of *Floating Clouds* replicated its author's chilled appraisal of Japan's postwar society. No longer ebullient as she was in her earlier works, she now sees hopelessness and a sense of pathos marking each individual's life. In every area of the globe earthly beings are transformed into pawns of destiny. The hopes that formerly accompanied Hayashi in her travel sequences allowed the wanderer to speculate, keeping her vigorous and alive. It was no longer to be.

The intensity of Hayashi's hunger for work, for travel, and for achievement, as well as her inability to rest and relax, allowed her to produce voluminously, but also contributed to her increasingly dangerous heart condition aggravated by pressure from her editors and a smoking habit of over two and a half packages of cigarettes a day. She died of cardiac arrest on June 28, 1951. She was forty-eight years old.

Her funeral was held in her home. One of Japan's most famous writers, Kawabata Yasunari, officiated. The literati attended and offered incense. Two thousand people, mostly women from the working underclass, came to pay their respects (Ericson, 97).

Bettina L. Knapp

Bibliography

Ericson, Joan R., trans. *Be a Woman: Hayashi Fumiko and Modern Japanese Women's Literature.* Honolulu: University of Hawai'i Press, 1997.

Fessler, Susanna., trans. *Wandering Heart: The Work and Method of Hayashi Fumiko.* Trans. Susanna Fessler. Albany, N.Y.: State University of New York Press, 1998.

Fumiko, Hayashi. *I Saw a Pale Horse (Aouma wo mitari) and Selected Poems from Diary of a Vagabond* (1930). Intro. and trans. Janice Brown. Ithaca, N.Y.: East Asia Program, Cornell University, 1997.

———. *Floating Cloud (Ukigomo)* (1953). Trans. Y. Koitabashi. Illustrated by Sho Tanaka. Tokyo: The Information Publishing Ltd., 1957.

Lippit, Noriko Mizuta, and Kyoko Iriye Selden. *Japanese Women Writers.* Armonk, N.Y.: M. E. Sharpe Inc., 1987.

Tanaka, Yukiko, ed., *To Live and to Write. Selections by Japanese Women Writers, 1913–1938.* Seattle, Wash.: The Seal Press, 1987.

CHAPTER 17

Anaïs Nin

(1903–1977)

We travel, some of us forever, to seek other states, other lives,
other souls.

(Anaïs Nin, *Diary*, Vol. 7, 98)

Travel is seeking the lost paradise. It is the supreme illusion
of love.

(Anaïs Nin, *Diary*, Vol. 7, 96)

Anaïs Nin's diaries span her life from the age of eleven, when her
father deserted the family, until she died in 1977. As a meta-
phoric vehicle, they enable their readers to accompany Nin on
her many journeys, to ride alongside her, and to view inner and outer
landscapes as if seeing them with her eyes, feeling and sensing atmo-
spheres and aromas, immersing their beings in the sacred waters of her,
now our, spiritual transformation. For Nin was to learn that travel is an
important remedy for our diseases, both physical and spiritual. Henry
Miller wrote:

> The diary is full of voyages; in fact, like life itself it might be regarded as
> nothing but voyage. The epic quality of it, however, is eclipsed by the meta-
> physical. The diary is not a journey towards the heart of darkness, in the
> stern Conradian sense of destiny, not a voyage *au bout de la nuit*, as with
> Céline, nor even a voyage to the moon in the psychological sense of escape.

It is more like a mythological voyage towards the source and fountain head of life—I might say an astrologic voyage of metamorphosis. ("Un Etre Etoilique," in *The Critical Response to Anaïs Nin*, 147)

Having lived a vibrant cultural life in Europe as the child of Joaquin Nin, a well-known Spanish concert pianist and composer, Anaïs's move to New York in 1914 with her mother, her two brothers, and her diary (as her constant companion) was the first major journey of her life. This move imprinted upon her soul the theme of cross-cultural migration, its profound losses as well as its rich possibilities for transformation. During the decade that she lived in New York, until she married Hugh Guiler, a banker (who later became the filmmaker known as Ian Hugo), she continued writing and learning the art of transforming ordinary reality into a chosen world vibrant with creativity, love, and devotion to family and friends.

In 1924 Nin and her family returned to France and resided in a house in Louveciennes outside Paris. It was during this period that she met Henry and June Miller, that she consulted Dr. René Allendy and began to explore the unconscious and the dream world. Eventually, she worked with Dr. Otto Rank, and was then trained by him to practice lay therapy. During this period she published a book on D. H. Lawrence and developed her aesthetic philosophy by critiquing Miller's excesses of realism and embracing the passionate and mystical qualities of writers such as Lawrence and Marcel Proust. She also befriended the surrealist Antonin Artaud, and expanded her friendships in the Parisian world of literary and artistic culture. After giving birth to a stillborn child, she recovered her connection with spirituality and her communication with God.

What was to become typical of Nin's life of travel was the pattern of pulling up roots just after she had become rooted in a new life. Thus, she made the decision to move back to New York in 1934, accompanying Dr. Otto Rank, in order to work with him and become a lay analyst. She had begun to settle down in New York, but true to her transmigrational pattern, she soon decided to return to Paris, where she would devote her life to her literary creation. In Paris she lived out her dream of a passionate creative life, but with the outbreak of World War II she again moved back to New York, where yet another new life was to begin.

Thus, as we see, a pattern of migration has been set in place in Nin's transcontinental life, whereby she would reside in one country, speak and write in its language, move in its literary circles, and then journey to another world to which she would transplant her entire family, where she would reroot, and develop new and ever-expanding circles of friends—always writing in her diary and recording the insights for posterity. These transcultural migrations permitted her to live out different aspects of herself via the diverse languages and cultures with which she became conversant. Migration and knowledge of languages taught her how to perceive nuances of the exterior life of a people that revealed their deep inner lives, their spiritual moorings, and their aesthetic expressions. This constant metamorphosis of the self from one "homeland" to another was to prepare her for her dual lives as the wife of Hugh Guiler (Ian Hugo) in New York and of Rupert Pole in Los Angeles (beginning in 1948). Like an aerial trapeze artist, she would fly cross-country, from home to home, from beloved to beloved, always creating the illusion that each was her only partner and her only home. It will be my contention that the multiplicity of selves that Nin displayed in her cross-cultural and bicoastal lives is characteristic of the shape shifting that shamans perform in order to ensure safety in their own spiritual journeys to "otherworlds." They often have to take on the mask of a different persona so that the true nature of their journey will not be perceived until their goal is reached.

Nin's traveling began in April 1936, when she visited Morocco and fell in love with Fez, which symbolized for her the cities of the soul. "The layers of the city of Fez are like the layers and secrecies of the inner life. One needs a guide." It was in Fez that she came upon travel as a cure for the pain of the past—the insecurities and separations that had wounded her, and the introspection that had eaten away at her psyche. Travel became the chosen antidote for suffering and neurosis.

> The last vestiges of my past were lost in the ancient city of Fez, which was built so much like my own life, with its tortuous streets, its silences, secrecies, its labyrinths, and its covered faces. In the city of Fez I became aware that the little demon which had devoured me for twenty years, the little demon of depression which I had fought for twenty years, had ceased eating me. I was at peace. Walking through the streets of Fez, absorbed in a world outside of myself, a past which was not my past, by sickness one could touch and name, leprosy and syphilis. . . .
>
> [I]t was in Cadiz that I stood up and broke the evil curse, as if by a magical act of will, I broke the net, the evil curse of obsession. I learned how to break it. It was symbolized by my going into the street. . . .

It seemed to have happened suddenly, like a miracle, but it was the result of years of struggle, of analysis, of passionate living. Introspection is a devouring monster. You have to feed it with much material, much experience, many people, many places, many loves, many creations, and then it ceases feeding on you. (*Diary*, Vol. 2, 79–81)

Here I wish to note the use of the verb "feed," which I see as a key to the nature of Anaïs Nin's teaching about traveling. She journeys in order to nourish and to feed both the inner demons (to appease and then expel them), and the surrounding world (friends, family, readers), so that their hunger for beauty, spirituality, and new visions will also be nurtured.

Whether Nin traveled to Mexico, as she did many times, or back and forth from New York to Los Angeles, whether she returned to Europe and revisited familiar places or those that moved her to experience new ecstasies (Venice), or whether she traveled to Japan, Tahiti, Thailand, Cambodia, Malaysia, Bali, or Hawaii, she was always intent on capturing the "quint/essences" of these cultures in her diary. Here I would apply the Native American use of the word "medicine" (as in bear medicine) to Anaïs Nin's travel writing. Much like an explorer who would bring back a native plant that could be used as an antibiotic when it was transformed by scientists, Nin sought out and transformed by her writing those indigenous teachings, intuitions, visions, and forms of knowledge that could be used to heal the West of its most serious disease, the absence of the dreamworld that came with the development of modernity.

Nin's travels can best be understood in the context of what I now see as a "shamanic" vocation. When I invoke the term "shamanic" I want to allude to the roles of healer and seer that a shaman embodies in a given culture. All shamans journey to other worlds, to commune with spirits in other dimensions in order to obtain knowledge that may contribute to a healing in this world. Michael Harner refers to these dimensions as states of Ordinary and Non-Ordinary reality. He writes: "A shaman is a man or woman who enters an altered state of consciousness—at will—to contact and utilize an ordinarily hidden reality in order to acquire knowledge, power, and to help other persons" (*The Way of the Shaman: A Guide to Power and Healing*, 26). Harner refers to the shaman's journeys to other dimensions via ecstatic trance states as Core Shamanism. He maintains that this is the basic shamanic practice that is common to shamans of all cultures, whereas the other functions of the shaman vary from culture to culture, for the shaman must give guidance and advice in almost every area of life. The shaman performs the roles of psychologist, priest/ess, doctor, lawyer, economist, educator, political leader, and so forth, as well as that of healer. Harner affirms that the "shaman operates in nonordinary reality only a small portion of his time, and then only as needed to perform shamanic tasks, for shamanism is a part-time activity" (ibid., 59).

Anaïs Nin's life and journeys may be viewed as those of a person born in the West without a shamanic lineage from which to receive official initiation, who was intuitively in touch with what might be called "the archetype" of the shaman, and whose life was spent reaching out through both ordinary and nonordinary means to discover and experiment with the techniques that would permit her to embody the mission implied in that "call." Her life was that of an autodidact shaman, who imagined a world in which her community of writers and artists would be healed by the intuitions and knowledge she gleaned from her journeys to the dimensions of the dream and visionary reality as well as through travels on earth to other cultures—to Japan, Mexico, Indonesia, Bali, Morocco, Tahiti, Europe, and America. She even experimented with LSD under the guidance of a medical doctor in order to see whether the visions she was able to obtain without the use of drugs—simply through the dream, poetry, and travel—were as extraordinary and intense as those she attained via LSD. She concluded that she had herself reached the states of consciousness and of visionary experiences that she had once accessed through LSD.

Shamans in various cultures call upon a wide variety of techniques in order to induce the trance state in which they travel to other realms. Many use psychotropic substances; some use peyote, sacred mushrooms, ayahuasca, and other hallucinogens, or none of these modalities.

Nin's techniques included the reveries she entered during journal writing, the imaginings responded to in her fiction writing, the intuitions and perceptions she cognized when engaged in intimate human encounters on every level with her closest friends—from the sharing of journals and letter writing, to the sharing of lives and of sensual and sexual intimacy. However, some of her most exquisite and ecstatic states of altered consciousness were attained during her travels, because she fell under the spell of various cities as their enchantment worked upon her like a drug. She writes of Venice: "It is like Acapulco, not a city but a drug" (*Diary*, Vol.

6, 195). Later in life, when she had already made a number of memorable journeys, and she was rewriting her diary for publication, she was able to reweave her way through her life, continually cross-indexing (as it were) themes from one trip with themes from another in order to superimpose, through a literary reimmersion-in-time, one experience upon another, and thereby approximate the joy she received when reading the works of Marcel Proust. In Volume 6 of the *Diary*, after reflecting upon Proust, she writes: "The power of the diary to re-create the emotional intensity of the relationships I describe makes it so potent that while I am copying it I am reliving them and seeking to understand the mysteries" (85).

The shaman often dons a symbolic costume and performs a ritual dance in order to communicate with the spirit world. The shaman's costumes and gestures constitute a sacred language that the deities, the energies, and powers understand. If we consider Nin's love of music and drumming, the frequency with which she sought occasions to dance, her affinity for symbolic jewelry and exotic clothing, her shape shifting (which involved leading many different and secret lives in different places), and her constant journeys to both inner and outer worlds, I think we may begin to understand the nature of her constant traveling in many modes as an integral part of the shamanic role that she intuited as her spiritual mission. For her community of writers and artists, she became the shamanic visionary whose journeys, whether they were made via the mind, the spirit, the emotions, or the dream, via dance, music, poetry, or journaling, or via steamship, airplane or train, were necessary in order to retrieve information essential to the healing of souls. Shamans are known as "wounded healers" because it is generally through a critical and life-threatening illness that they received the call to engage in journeying, healing not only others, but themselves as well.

When Nin left Paris for New York in 1939, she wrote that she "could not believe that there could be, anywhere in the world, space and air where the nightmare of war did not exist" (*Diary*, Vol. 3, 3). She seems to intuit that this radical geographic split in her life had caused a split in her soul that only a shaman would be able to heal. Her physical as well as psychic illnesses, whether brought about by the abandonment by her father or her loss of roots, as she migrated from one home to another, from one country to another, can all be viewed as a form of soul loss, that only shamans can truly heal. Nin understood profoundly that there was no official medicine in the West that could reconnect these painful splits. As she learned the practice of psychoanalysis, which was the only tool available for healing psychic disease, she understood that she had to invent another tool for healing the disease of soul loss. She craved the presence of a medicine man, and ultimately had to become that person herself.

A foundational belief of shamanism taught by the shamans of the Shuar culture of the Andes and the Amazon basin in Ecuador is that "the world *is* as you *dream* it" (cf. John Perkins, *The World Is as You Dream It: Shamanic Teachings from the Amazon and the Andes*). The shamanic world-view teaches that matter and energy are one, that the dream is real, and that everything is interconnected in the great web of life. For a shaman, the journey to a visionary realm is a real journey to a real place, a prayer is a real communication with the spirit world, and the visionary knowledge obtained from being in that place and communicating with that world is capable of providing the solution to political, psychological, social, and economic problems, as well as of healing our psychic and physical diseases in material ways.

When she went to the hospital for surgery in 1953, her friends chided her that this was one event she could not transform into something beautiful. But she was determined to do just that, and she brought with her a red wool burnoose in order to cheer the other patients who saw her dressed in red as she was wheeled into the x-ray room.

> Then the gods, who sometimes listen to the defiance of the artists, decided to listen to my prayers for a little beauty to cover the stark events. The king of the gypsies was having surgery at the same time! . . . I was convalescing in a gypsy encampment. . . . When I looked out of the hospital windows at the end of the hall, small, narrow, and barred, giving on an ugly courtyard, *I turned my mind and my will toward Yucatan* [italics added]. I wanted to see Chichen-Itza. I was reading about it. My spirit was already there. All my body had to do was to pick itself up and follow. (*Diary*, Vol. 5, 105–6)

Ultimately, Nin utilized the beauty of her travels in this world to energize a positive experience of healing during her struggle with cancer at the end of her life. When she went for radiation therapy, she closed her eyes and practiced what she called "spiritual radiation." She guided her imagery through the Colorado River and into the desert, then on to Acapulco, and

Chichen-Itza, and the next day into Cambodia, Japan, and Tahiti. As the radiation treatments continued, she used costume the way a shaman would to enhance the trance visionary journey.

> The radiation was weakening me. Each day I felt less strong. But the film lasted. The South of France, the Italian Riviera, Portofino . . . Sun. Water. Dancing. Swimming. Tahiti. I dwelt on—always with my phantom lover.
> On MacDougal Street I found long Indian velvet dresses of beautiful colors, blue and aubergine. They made the weakened body seem less ill. (*Diary*, Vol. 7, 131)

Memories of travel to places imbued with emotional, intellectual, historical, and personal memory can function to conquer depression. Nin's *Diary* is replete with the keys to such "alchemical" or magical transformations. When she revisited Paris in 1954, she was prepared for the shock by René de Chochor, who said to her: "The Paris you loved is dead. . . . I want to prepare you for the changes" (*Diary*, Vol. 5, 200). Those she had loved in Paris were now dead—of illness, of the war, or in concentration camps. To transform her vision of death into an experience that would still conjure up the pleasures of Paris she had known in the past, she wrote in the *Diary*: "I dressed my mind and my body for the present. I wore warm colors, and thought about a new Paris, an unknown Paris" (*Diary*, Vol. 5, 201).

The secret to the transformative use of travel is to shamanize, and to time-travel to the past by contextualizing a given location in its cultural history. The works of literature and art produced in a given place are similar to the chemicals in an al/chemical formula. When combined in the correct way, they produce the perfume necessary for the appropriate spell to be cast. On that trip to Paris, Nin lay on her bed in the hotel room and wrote:

> I had the feeling that I had taken a drug. That the room was full of erotic brilliance, and of past visitors. Names came to my lips, Nijinsky, Diaghilev, Madame Du Barry, Ninon de Lenclos, Marcel Proust, Jean Giraudoux, Colette. . . . All the life of Paris like an exquisite intoxication crowded in this room without need of steam heat, of electric gadgets, of anything but people who had lived richly, that the past could not erase. They remained

like a perfume in the air, in rooms that had been lived in, enjoyed, leaving psychic, voluptuous secretions. (*Diary*, Vol. 5, 201)

Nin used the power of naming to evoke the spirit-presences of those artists whose lives are imprinted in the spiritual records of the universe, sometimes referred to as the akashic records.

She also practiced the shamanic use of intent, of believing that "blood flows where attention goes" (Ross Heaven, *The Journey to You*, 48). By focusing her intent on transforming the dead Paris of the past into a living Paris of the present, Nin succeeds in drawing her attention to those aspects of the present that recall the past and that remain the same. She is drawn to scenes and images that lift her spirit, for her shamanic journeying has produced a psychic transformation. She teaches us how to use the memory of pleasurable past travel experiences to infuse productive, positive visions into the present.

Nin's shamanic use of intent and time-travel worked, as she discovered:

The Paris I loved is not dead. The lovers still love each other. The Seine still glitters with barges and boats. The fountains still play. The shopwindows are still dazzling displays of imagination and style. The galleries are crowded. The bookshops are crowded. The parks are filled with flowers, gardeners, and children. . . . It is still the capital of intelligence and creativity, enriched by the passage of all the artists of the world. (*Diary*, Vol. 5, 207)

Nin intuits correctly that it is via the voyage—spiritual and physical— that one (shamanically) makes contact with everything in the universe. She senses that there is no space and no time, because all forms of travel permit us to be in touch with multiple times and spaces almost simultaneously.

At times I do feel like a snail who has lost his shell. I have to learn to live without it. But when I stand still, I feel claustrophobia of the soul, and must maintain a vast switchboard with an expanded universe, the international life, Paris, Mexico, New York, the United Nations, the artist world. (*Diary*, Vol. 5, 237)

Time-travel can be catalyzed by traveling to a foreign country, and contemplating a specific architectural creation. On Nin's trip to Japan in the summer of 1966, a visit to Frank Lloyd Wright's Imperial Hotel enabled her to journey through civilizations by associating ancient and modern Japanese architecture, linking the richness of ancient lost memories to the sterility of present realities.

> Wright's design gave the sensation of living through many centuries; it evoked every palace or temple ever portrayed, from Egyptian to Inca. He restored to man the sense of pride and deep accumulation of experience entirely lost in modern architecture, which reduces man to an anonymous, meaningless being in an anonymous, meaningless abode, like an ant cell. Here the man who moved about in Wright's setting was a being containing memories of all the past, and strong enough to have a vision of the future, and of his metaphysical place in it. (*Diary*, Vol. 7, 5)

In Mexico during the winter of 1947–48, through the Spanish language, Nin's memories return to Spain and Cuba.

> I feel at home in Mexico, because I learned Spanish at the age of five, because the exuberance reminds me of my childhood in Spain, the singing reminds me of our Spanish maid Carmen, who sang all day while working. The gaiety in the streets, the children dancing, the flowerpots in the windows, the profusion of flowers, the liveliness of the people, all recall Barcelona and Havana. (*Diary*, Vol. 5, 38)

Thus, travel provokes the experience of déjà vu: "These memories lie dormant until aroused by a face, a city, a situation. A simple explanation of 'we have lived this before'" (ibid., 38).

Travel also functions as a potent hallucinogen for Nin. It stimulates memories from ancient civilizations and possible past lives—what she refers to as a "racial memory." Layers of a collective unconsciousness are released into present-day consciousness and cause a fusion of imagery, not only from historical epochs, but also from mythological ages and legendary times that may reside in archives of a collective past life, of a vanished civilization. As this layering of time occurs, Nin is able to voyage back and forth in diverse time zones that are accessible only in shamanic states of nonordinary reality. Not having received classic shamanic training, she has invented her own means of time-travel. Like an astronaut of inner space, she is able to make spiritual journeys to buried civilizations.

Racial memory. Is it a racial memory which stirs when I am shaken by certain scenes? I was deeply affected by the scenery of the Azores. I was disturbed in an obscure, mysterious way. Later I discovered it belonged to Atlantis; it is said to be one of its remaining fragments. It had for me the hauntingness of a dream, the ephemeral, fragile incompleteness of a dream, the black sand, the black rocks, the light, the multicolored houses.

In the same way, why was I so affected by Fez, in which I lost my individuality, where I fused with the city, the people, melted into the colors, textures, the eyes of the people?

Why was I so affected by the undersea explosions of Walt Disney's *Fantasia*, the section on the creation of the world, fire and water, the inner explosions? It is in this way that Atlantis disappeared. Why do these scenes have such strong vibrations in me whereas others leave me completely indifferent?

Atlantis has always bewitched me. It was said to be the place where people had a dimension unknown to us, a sixth sense, and a prodigious musical development. I made of this my true native land. (*Diary*, Vol. 3, 218)

Nin identified with her "people" of the sixth sense in precisely the same way that many of us, searching for our roots, identify with our ethnic or cultural origins. In speaking of "racial memory," Nin is referring to her tribe of origin—metaphysically, the people who lived according to their sixth sense in a culture where visionary knowledge was validated. Today that kind of culture is portrayed as mythic, fantastic, or unreal. For Nin, as for most indigenous populations, seership is real, and the sixth sense is a form of knowledge, not a form of mere speculation, or a delusion.

I see one of the functions of travel in Nin's life as her means of retrieving the soul or the spirit of a place that carries with it, through its actual presence or its history, legends, and culture, an essence that we are missing in our dehumanized, present-day lives. These souls of lost times and places are then transfused into us via the *Diary*. They pour into our minds and our imaginations, and they restore the dreamworld to us, liberating us to be creators and dreamers again.

Nin wrote about her travels, whether covering a trip to Mexico, Tahiti, or Bali for business purposes or for sheer pleasure, but the hidden agenda of every trip was really the recovery of the soul of the city and of the dreams that we need in order to become whole once more. She journeyed with the ulterior motive of capturing her experiences in the *Diary*, her ledger filled with the records of the magical potions that she would leave behind to teach us how to flood our mind's eye with visions of ecstatic beauty so that we might reclaim the pleasures and values of which we have been robbed since the advent of the so-called progress of Western civilization.

She has always claimed that the *Diary* was her confidante. It was the recipient of her spirit through her writing, and over the course of many years of travel and of sharing experiences with her, the *Diary*, shamanically speaking, became more than a simple personification. It came to possess its own spirit. It became a spiritual entity. She speaks of it as if it had a life of its own, and when she does so, this is not mere metaphor; it is in a shamanic sense that her spirit is alive in the book. The *Diary* also gets fatigued, like a human being. During the winter of 1950–51 she notes:

> This year the diary almost expired from too much traveling, too much moving about, too many changes. . . . Several trips to Mexico, several explorations of the West, several trips to New York for the books, a mood of instability and restlessness, and I wrote mostly letters. (*Diary*, Vol. 5, 59)

As she conceives it, the *Diary* needs the nurturance of her writing, and when she stops, because of excessive traveling without journaling, the *Diary* risks its own death.

Nin also had a shamanic sense that one nurtures one's own death experience. She had decided not to record any illness in the *Diary* and to make her last pages a diary of music. As she approached her own death, it was the knowledge she obtained from one of her journeys that inspired her to create a beatific passing, the transmigration of her soul to a new world. Rather than energize the pain of her suffering, Nin shamanically utilized the spiritual revelations she acquired in Bali to ease her transition. "Let me think of death as the Balinese do, as a flight to another life, a joyous transformation, a release of our spirit so it might visit other lives" (*Diary*, Vol. 7, 336). The *Diary*, as an alchemical ledger of travel-medicine, is like a Balinese spirit house, providing a home for the wandering soul of the artist/alchemist as traveling shaman.

Gloria Feman Orenstein

BIBLIOGRAPHY

Bair, Deirdre. *Anaïs Nin: A Biography*. London: Bloomsbury, 1995.

Fitch, Noel Riley. *Anaïs: The Erotic Life of Anaïs Nin*. Boston: Little, Brown, 1993.

Harner, Michael. *The Way of the Shaman: A Guide to Power and Healing*. New York: Bantam Books, 1982.

Heaven, Ross. *The Journey to You: A Shaman's Path to Empowerment*. London: Bantam Books, 2001.

Knapp, Bettina L. *Anaïs Nin*. New York: Frederick Ungar, 1978.

Miller, Henry. "Un Etre Etoilique." In *The Critical Response to Anaïs Nin*, ed. Philip K. Jason. Westport, Conn.: Greenwood Press, 1996, 147–54.

Nin, Anaïs. *The Diary of Anaïs Nin, 1934–1939* (Vol. 2). The Swallow Press & Harcourt, Brace & World, 1967.

———. *The Diary of Anaïs Nin, 1939–1944* (Vol. 3). New York: Harcourt Brace & World, 1969.

———. *The Diary of Anaïs Nin, 1947–1955* (Vol. 5). New York: Harcourt Brace Jovanovich, 1974.

———. *The Diary of Anaïs Nin, 1955–1966* (Vol. 6). New York: Harcourt Brace Jovanovich, 1976.

———. *The Diary of Anaïs Nin, 1966–1974* (Vol. 7). New York: Harcourt Brace Jovanovich, 1980.

Perkins, John. *The World Is as You Dream It: Shamanic Teachings from the Amazon and the Andes*. Rochester, Vt.: Destiny Books, 1994.

18

Xie Bingying (born Ming Gang)
(1906–2000)

Like a fallen leaf in the autumn wind, I would stay wherever I drifted to.

> (Xie Bingying, *The Autobiography of a Chinese Girl*, trans. Tsui Chi, 199)

No sooner had Xie Bingying reached the age of reason than she demanded to be sent to school and repudiated the Chinese custom of arranged marriage. Little did she realize the struggles that would ensue—not with her father, a writer and school principal, who secretly sided with his daughter, but with her strong-willed, traditionalist, viraginous mother, who resorted to all types of punishments, including imprisonment, to maintain dominion over her daughter. Xie's intellectual and emotional battle for the independence that would enable her to travel was poignant and dramatic. Her struggle was cumulative for its aggressiveness, combative for its physicality, and idealistic for its philosophical thrust.

Chinese women had lived in a state of quasi-servitude for over two thousand years. Many, even prior to the turn of the twentieth century, began to demand liberation from their serfdom within the family–clan complex. They sought to outlaw not only arranged marriages, but also the sale of wives and children, infanticide, and the practice of foot binding, the latter begun in the tenth century. The establishment of certain girls' schools in the late nineteenth and early twentieth centuries was one of the most significant steps China took toward the acknowledgment of women as individuals rather than as mere appendages of the husband and family. These seats of learning bred notions of nationalism, communism, and independence of spirit, and, in time—much to the horror of traditionalists—girls began demonstrating, boycotting, and striking in protest against social and political inequities.

Xie Bingying belonged to a new breed of resistant women who not only sought to change outworn, regressive, and physically deleterious customs through governmental reform, but also fought a more personal and difficult battle—against their own mothers. Understandably, many conventional mothers took pride in obtaining their daughters' compliance with customs and rituals, namely, filial piety and observance of hierarchical family relations. The dictatorial roles played by some mothers—including Bingying's—provided them with a desired sense of authority and security, which gave purpose and direction to their otherwise vacuous lives. Many mothers, moreover, were still convinced of women's so-called biological inferiority, inculcating these and other infelicitous ideas in their progeny. By contrast, some mothers taught their daughters to create an independent life for themselves and to combat the facile stereotype of the weak, self-effacing, and self-sacrificing woman.

Xie Bingying was born in the small village of Xietuoshan in Hunan Province, the youngest daughter in a household of three male children. Unlike most young girls of the time, she had had been taught to read at the age of five by her father, whose ideas were less regressive than those of his contemporaries. Though unaware as yet of his daughter's unquenchable drive for liberation, he sensed her wondrous spark of intelligence and sought to encourage its development. Even as a young child, she loved the company of her teacher father and her three well-educated brothers. Perhaps unconsciously Bingying was attempting to divest herself of inherited modes of behavior. Unlike her docile older sister, whom she loved and who carried out her mother's orders with impunity, Bingying refused to play the role of the stereotyped Chinese daughter—obsequious, ignorant, and self-effacing. She sought to direct her own life, to study, to travel, even at the cost of abandoning the family she loved.

Although she was looked upon by her family as the "Little Treasure" during her early years, she was, in keeping with tradition, to be married off to a young man who had been chosen for her when she was but a child. What Bingying's parents failed to realize was that complete obedience and subservience to the family was anathema to the independent-minded girl. Knowledge had triggered ideas, and with these, a desire to alter the course of her life. Fortunately for Bingying, her mother was not so strict with her as she had been with her older daughter. Nonetheless, in 1914 Xie was forced to endure the agony of foot binding, which she described in some detail.

> I felt as if the bones of my feet were broken and I cried and fell down on the ground. . . . [H]enceforth I spent most of my days sitting by the fire spinning. Sometimes I could manage to walk very slowly in the hall. It seemed as though my feet were fettered, and to walk was very difficult. The days of enjoying beautiful flowers and of catching fish and prawns would never come to me again. (ibid., 43)

Despite her love for her mother, Bingying began to look upon her as an "executioner." Her zest for life, and her open vibrant personality and youthful energy were now directed toward breaking out of the constrictive mother-dominated home environment, a difficult attitude, given the absence of women's formal rights in China at the time. Any exercise of power in situations outside the household was precluded, but within the family confines mothers were autocrats; their dominating presences were essential to the prolongation of the patriarchal system. In Xie Bingying's household, her mother decided the future of her three sons and of her eldest daughter, but not that of her second daughter, Bingying, whose strength grew proportionately to the physical pain she felt in her feet. Although education was instrumental in broadening her thought processes, the physical torture she endured taught her the dangers of oppression. She was now dealing with *reality*.

Constantly at loggerheads, mother and daughter faced a crucial test of strength when it came to Bingying's schooling. Predictably, her mother wanted her to remain at home, spinnning, sewing, learning the arts of homemaking, and preparing for her arranged marriage. Bingying was adamant: no matter the frightening eventualities of disobedience, she refused to yield to old ways. Only when she was ten, in 1916, and after much persuasion, did her mother reluctantly agree to send her to the village's private school for boys. After two years, however, she put a stop to her education. Young girls in China at the time, and in prior centuries as well, had but one weapon to express their opposition in family matters: that of threatening suicide. (According to statistics, many young girls actually committed suicide rather than agree to an arranged marriage or accept other impositions.) Should her pursuit of education be denied, Bingying, too, would resort to suicide. To this end, she neither ate nor drank for three days. Her mother finally relented.

The changing political, social, and ideological climate in China was to work in Xie Bingying's favor: the fall of the Ch'ing dynasty and the birth of the Chinese Republic in 1912, the election of Sun Yat-sen as president of the republic, and the creation of the Chinese Communist Party in 1921. Sun Yat-sen was the director of the Kuomintang Party, which became increasingly interested in land reforms and admitted Communists to its group, the common goal being the creation of an independent and unified China (Wolfram Eberhard, *A History of China*, 325).

Thanks to Bingying's progressive-thinking elder brother, his twelve-year-old sister was sent to the Datong Girls School. Once a cultural center and trading partner with Mongolia, and only nine miles west of the fourth-century Yun Gang Buddhist caves, Datong bore witness to a past age of imperial and cultural splendor. Inspired by both the city and the school, Bingying took full advantage of the learning opportunity offered her. One teacher in particular triggered her appetite for political reform. Not only did he believe in the equality of the sexes, but he encouraged his students to "rise against the imposition of the old moral code" (*The Autobiography of a Chinese Girl*, 59). When the school's director heard that Bingying's bandaged feet prevented her from running and jumping with the other girls and caused her great pain as well, the authorities allowed her to remove her bandages. It turned out to be a boomerang: the child's mother withdrew her from the school. Her argument was clear: what man would choose to marry a girl with big feet? At home, Bingying's feet were again bound. She would learn to embroider. Her determination to free herself from bondage at home worked particularly well on her father. In 1919 she entered the Xinhua County Girls School, which soon proved to be unsatisfactory. A year later, she was sent to Xinyi Girls School in Yi-yang. To be far from home meant traveling. The prospect thrilled her. With unparalleled joy, she wrote:

> From my home to the city of Yiyang was a journey of more than six hun-dred li [a li is equivalent to a third of a mile]. By travelling in a junk with a favourable wind it would take at least four days. It was really beyond my dreams that my mother should allow me to study in a college at such a distance. Perhaps I was destined to be an exile, for I didn't feel the least regret or sorrow when I learned that I was to leave home and live so far away. (ibid., 63)

No sooner did she discover that the Xinyi Girls School was a Christian mission school than it became anathema to her. As an atheist, she refused to be baptized. Nor could she accept the thought of transferring from one meaningless religion to another. Clearly, politics motivated Xie's actions. On May 7, a day of National Shame ("when Japan handed China the twenty-one demands regarding special rights in Shantung Province," ibid., 66), all public schools and organizations in Yiyang were closed. The school's director locked the doors to prevent the students from participat-ing in demonstrations. Turning agitator, Xie organized the students, who then paraded inside the building, screaming "Down with imperialism!" The disturbed authorities requested that Xie's eldest brother take her home. Unperturbed, she reasoned that destiny forced her to leave "the School of God." In fact, "the result of my being patriotic was to be expelled" (ibid., 68). So much the better! After passing a set of difficult entrance examinations, the determined Xie was admitted to Changsha's First Provincial Girls Teacher Training School. Her first publication, "Momentary Impression," appeared in a Changsha newspaper.

That the political climate was becoming increasingly active suited Xie Bingying. The memorable Student Movement of May 4, 1919, which began as a literary debate, not only changed the course of Chinese litera-ture in general, but Xie's taste in particular. Ts'ai Yüan-p'ei (1868–1940), chancellor of the Beijing National University, had been challenged by Lin Shu (1882–1924), a translator of Western works, to adopt a new and more convenient vernacular language for teaching, literary, and diplomatic pur-poses. Concurring that "our Chinese literary language is . . . much like

Latin," Ts'ai Yüan-p'ei recognized that the outdated and stilted Chinese classical language could not convey vital modern ideas. The Chinese diplomatic debacle at the post–World War I Versailles peace settlement that forced China to accept Japanese possession of former German concessions precipitated Beijing student protests on May 4 against the pro-Japanese government. Demonstrations were set off in university circles and other organizations; a plethora of newspapers, pamphlets, and brochures written and edited by students sprang up rapidly. Ch'en Tu-hsi (1879–1942), one of the founders of the Chinese Communist Party, in advocating literary reform, fused demands for change in all fields—philosophical and literary as well as political. The role of women in society, and fairer treatment of them at home as well as in the marketplace, were also subjects of debate.

Xie listened intently and absorbed new ideas, which in turn opened her up to a different brand of idealism. No longer satisfied with studies alone, the time had come for her to act, to travel, and to write about what she saw, heard, and felt. The incident that provoked her into action was the massacre of May 30, 1925, when Chinese demonstrators walking the Nanking Road in Shanghai were killed by British and Japanese policemen. The students at Changsha protested and demanded that the authorities look into the matter, "tackle imperialist Japan," and refuse the twenty-one demands. "We wanted the dead to be avenged" (ibid., 87). Numerous student arrests provoked further demonstrations. "Release all our schoolmates who have been arrested!" they yelled. It was a time of fervor and of hope for Xie and for other students. Her brother published magazines advocating the abolition of arranged marriages and the evils of the "domestic tyranny" characteristic of an ultra-Confucian patriarchal society. That women were becoming politically conscious and active was very nearly miraculous in a land where they had been sequestered and kept in a state of virtual ignorance for centuries. The birth of a new politically oriented literature motivated Xie to write for newspapers under a variety of pen names.

After Sun Yat-sen's death in 1925, the political climate altered drastically. Internecine fighting between right and left factions increased. Nonetheless, the Kuomintang and the Communist parties entered into an alliance in 1923, their goal being to reunify China. In 1926 they undertook a northward march, led by Chiang Kai-shek, known as the Northern

Expedition—from Canton to the central valley of the Yangtze. Its goal was to arouse peasants, workers, and women in uniting China. That year marked a turning point for Xie. The Communist Party, working with the movement for the emancipation of women, created a special army unit designed not to fight but to tend to the wounded and participate in missions to indoctrinate workers and peasants to a new way of life. Xie secretly enrolled and was accepted in the yearlong course offered by the Central Military and Political School in Wuhan (in Hunan Province) to train propagandists. Excitedly, she thought her emancipation was now a certainty. She would leave home and travel. She and other young girls bobbed their hair, donned military apparel, and looked forward to working alongside men in the struggle for the political and social independence of their land, which had been compromised by the Versailles Treaty settlement.

Together with fifty female students, Xie waited eagerly at Changsha's East Station to board the train for Wuhan. Every trip she took thereafter, in or outside China, was regarded by her as a liberating and learning experience. Each thrilled her. After being inducted into the army in November 1926, she was simultaneously enrolled in a twelve-month course in propaganda studies at Wuhan's Central Military and Political School and became editor of its newspaper. Upon completion of her studies in 1927, she was among twenty girls to be inducted in the Northern Expedition led by Chiang Kai-shek. Their orders were to repair to Tingsha Bridge to fend off a Japanese attack. Xie and her group readied to leave at five o'clock the following morning. Overwhelmed with excitement and fervor, her dream of travel was to finally be realized.

Thousands of people saw the new recruits off. Bugles sounded to shouts of "Kill the enemy and come back in victory." By the time they arrived at their destination hours later, "wounded comrades covered with blood lay on stretchers"; others had lost limbs (ibid., 118). First aid was hastily administered, after which the group was ordered on a three-day march—averaging eighty to a hundred li daily—with barely enough rice to eat. It was June; the heat was intense. Although exhausted, Xie noted the events in the diary she carried with her. Several days later, to her distress, she realized it was missing. No matter; the mental notes of the war and the suffering she had seen were again transcribed and published in Chinese in Shanghai in 1928.

Days later, upon arriving at the outskirts of Hung-Ko, Xie spied a group of farmers who had just imprisoned three men. Upon further inquiry, she was told that prior to the revolution, these rich men had oppressed the poor. It was time for retribution. That night she was ordered to keep watch over the prisoners. Despite their verbal ploys, she refused to free them. The following morning, the villagers met. Not one argued for the men's release. "Shoot them! Shoot them! Quick! Quick!" they cried out impatiently (ibid., 124). Within seconds they were dead.

That same night, orders from the divisional headquarters directed the army to repair to Chin San An, around forty li away, to rout out the enemy hiding in the mountain. The night march was hazardous. As they made their way with rifle in hand, some fell into ditches, others slipped into puddles. Torrents had to be avoided and silence maintained in order to reinforce the element of surprise on the enemy. The march lasted until dawn. They reached their objective. After another month and four days, Xie's unit returned to their base "singing songs of victory" (ibid., 129). Although casualties amounted to seventy schoolmates and one hundred comrades from the training troops, their victory, for Xie, meant the deliverance of "thousands and tens of thousands of oppressed people from the hands of military lords" (ibid., 130). After their victory, however, they learned in shocked disbelief of the demobilization of their unit. They were ordered to destroy their uniforms and return home. No reasons were given.

Military offensives between the Communists and the more conservative Kuomintang Party now led by Chang Kai-shek erupted with savage force. The climate was ominous. Xie, who had just begun her travels and was savoring the very thought of self-determination, was stunned at the idea of having to return home to confront her mother. Nonetheless, she was comforted by the knowledge that, despite the demobilization, "this great, majestic women's army" had existed, and "the seeds of revolution had already been sown all over China" (ibid., 133).

At home, Xie was obliged to go through a marriage ceremony. "What a faithful servant you are to the old system," she muttered, directing that mix of love and hatred toward her mother (ibid., 166). Not one to accept defeat, Xie chose the merriment of a crowded wedding feast to escape from bondage. No sooner had her mother's eagle eye begun to rove than Xie slipped out of the room and ran over hill and dale to Nan-Tien, her unstoppable energy seeing her to her destination. Never once did she fear. "I felt like a person who had just escaped the scaffold" (ibid., 173). She continued on her way, and just as she was about to board a boat to freedom, Xie turned around and to her horror saw her formidable mother standing before her. She was again brought home, and again tried to escape, succeeding in repairing to Changsha on her fourth attempt.

To celebrate her freedom, she rushed to buy some books on socialism but was summarily arrested. "Thousands of boys and and girls were arrested and put in prison on the charge of communism, which might mean nothing more than favoring radical ideas against the old society" (Lin Yutang, introduction to *Girl Rebel*, xiv). After her release on her brother's recognizance, she began teaching at a grade school in Hengyang. She wanted to travel. "I must not give up my struggle and surrender to the old system. Let me go forward. The world is large" (*Girl Rebel*, 199).

Wandering about China in these unsettled times was, however, perilous: the military was imprisoning anyone suspected of being a Communist. There were conflagrations everywhere. No one was safe. The still unflagging Xie took a boat to Shanghai in 1928. After docking three days later, her thrill and excitement at the thought of having finally reached this city, about which she had dreamed since childhood, was memorable.

> I looked intently on the wild rolling waves of the Yangtze River. The roar of the water seemed to me to be a new revelation.
> Flow on like this mighty river. To go forward is the only way to find your final destination. No matter what hardship you are going to meet with, shoaly sand-banks or dangerous rocks, you will overcome them all and will bring life to everything that you meet!
> There on the bank of the Woo Sung River were motor-cars, tramcars, carriages and buses moving very busily before a background of high chimneys and factories and lofty buildings. Shanghai is a sample of western civilisation. While the rich people spend their millions here seeking pleasure, I could hear labourers who were working as stevedores on the wharf singing aloud, "Yo-ho, yo-ha." This is their song, this is their groan and their war-cry. It will awaken mankind. (ibid., 216)

As a girl soldier, Xie was offered a scholarship in the Department of Chinese Literature at the Shanghai Academy of Art. She pursued a writing career as well, sending articles to newspapers and enjoying the publicity accorded the publication in Shanghai of what she remembered of her missing war diary. Although she worked long hours, she lived in poverty. Many days she went without food. Times were difficult. Tramway workers in the French Concession struck. Chaos reigned. She moved to Beijing. Her affair with Qi, a young poet whom she had met during her army stint with the Northern Expedition, concluded some time following the birth of their daughter in 1930. Qi's mother would care for the infant.

Xie again began yearning for a change of pace and a change of space. Suspected of leftist tendencies, she was advised to leave Beijing. Prior to taking a steamship north, she wrote wistfully of the city: "Beijing had left a deep impression on me. I loved it as a beloved person. I was used to a wandering life and could settle anywhere, but Beijing was very hard to leave. I cannot describe the feeling . . ." (ibid., 220). She took the train to Nanking, then a steamer to Hankou. "The placid river once more made me think of suicide. . . . I had nothing on this earth to live for" (ibid., 221). On to Wu Chang. Her third brother suggested she visit her parents. She did so. Although her mother never spoke a word to her, about midnight she lit a small lamp, entered her daughter's room, picked up her blanket from the floor, covered her, and left.

No lamenting. On the contrary, her writings had earned her six hundred dollars, sufficient to take her to Tokyo in 1931 to study Japanese. She was exuberant and fearless.

> Since childhood I had loved the joys of travel, the sights and sounds and smells of mountains and seas. When the *Empress* carried me from Huang Pu harbor into the East China Sea, I felt as full of joy as a little bird that has escaped from its cage. I watched huge waves of a boundless jade-green sea under snowy-white clouds. My heart felt like a seagull, one moment soaring, the next plunging—for though I felt sad at leaving my country and dear friends, when I thought of the bright future ahead I temporarily set aside my worries and felt infinite joy. (Xie Bingying, *A Woman Soldier's Own Story*, 223)

Xie's hopes ran high for good relations between China and Japan, but tensions between the two countries increased. The Japanese feared that the unification of China in course since the 1920s would jeopardize their interests in Manchuria. When, in September 1931, a bomb destroyed part of the Japanese railway near Shenyang (Mukden at the time), the Japanese used the incident as a pretext to take over southern Manchuria. When Xie's ship arrived at Nagasaki, she was both stunned and outraged by the Japanese newspapers' headlines: IMPERIAL JAPANESE ARMY OCCUPIES SHENYANG! ARMY OF CHINA DEFEATED!

Although her presence in Japan seemed precarious, Xie was so intent upon learning Japanese that she took the train to Tokyo, as planned, and moved into the Higashi Nabano Women's Dormitory. She made friends not only with many compatriots, but with some Japanese as well. In no time, she began to acquire a speaking, reading, and writing knowledge of Japanese. Counterproductively, she attended meetings of the Overseas Chinese Students Association for Resistance Against Japan. The meetings grew increasingly frenetic with each Japanese advance on Chinese territory. When Xie and her compatriots began shouting "Long live the Republic of China" and "Down with Japanese imperialism!" Japanese detectives arrested the Chinese students, forced them to disperse, and gave them three days to leave Tokyo. Xie had no choice (ibid., 228). Upon her return to Shanghai in the fall of 1931, she devoted her time to revolutionary causes, including relief work.

Following the landing of Japanese marines in Shanghai on Janury 28, 1932, the bombing of the city, and the launching of a full-scale attack on its civilians, leading to the deaths of thousands of Chinese, Xie joined the ambulance corps of Baolong Hospital, did propaganda work, and went to the front to observe the heroic Chinese army in action. At night she edited and wrote for a weekly magazine, *Women's Light*. Moving about virtually continuously, she went to Longyan, then to Gutian, both in Fukien Province, where she taught, then to Xiamen, where she continued her teaching and founded a monthly literary magazine, *The Lighthouse*. In Changsha, her next port of call, she began writing *A Woman Soldier's Own Story*. Her yearning to translate international literary classics—works by Tolstoy, Balzac, and Dickens—from Japanese into Chinese, encouraged her to firm up her knowledge of Japanese.

In the spring of 1935, she again left for Japan, enrolling immediately at the Literature Research Institute at Waseda University in Tokyo. Her skills were rapidly improving when, falsely charged with conspiring against the Japanese government, she was imprisoned in the Muhei Police Station (ibid., 260). Prior to her arrest, she had been asked by detectives to welcome Puyi, the last emperor of the Qing dynasty, upon his arrival in Tokyo. "Not only will I not go to welcome him," she replied, "but I fundamentally oppose him and I do not recognize the Manchurian Nation" (ibid., 260). Xie spent only three weeks in prison, but the guards tortured her by hitting her on the head with a round rice bowl. "They also inserted three square bamboo sticks between my right hand and pressed [down] with such force that the joints of my right hand were almost broken, and several times the pain knocked me unconscious" (ibid., 261). Even worse, they confiscated many of her writings. After her release from prison, she was closely watched and finally escaped to China. There she continued her travels. In July 1935 she vacationed in Guilin, after which she taught Chinese literature at Nanning Senior Middle School in Guangxi Province. The first volume of *A Woman Soldier's Own Story* was published in Shanghai in 1936. A year later, Xie visited and cared for her dying mother, recalling without rancor the difficult yet beautiful memories associated with this woman who always thought she was acting righteously vis-à-vis her daughter. Xie wept "tears of repentance" (ibid., 269).

To alleviate her sorrow somewhat, the ever compulsive Xie, living in an arduous present rather than a self-indulgent past, organized the Hunan Women's War Zone Service Corps in Changsha in four days. Nor did her hatred of the Japanese diminish after having been apprised of the "Marco Polo Bridge incident," which had taken place south of Beijing (July 7, 1937) and which had been provoked by the Japanese to extend their occupation. She bided her time. At the propitious moment, in September 1937, she left with the Chinese army for the front to nurse the wounded. It had been ten years since she had worn China's military uniform.

Her travels now took on a different contour. In the face of heavy bloodletting at the front, she managed to write her *New War Diaries*. Though her words resonated with the thrill of being in the thick of the struggle, they detailed unsparingly the excoriating suffering of the fighting men. She knew theirs and hers to be a lost cause. The Manchurian provinces had been lost to the Japanese six years earlier. Women could not bear arms, but they were trained to nurse the wounded soldiers at the front. Under what circumstances she moved from Changsha to Süchow!

September 14, [1937]. *Changsha*
    I carried high the bright red banner of the Women's Corps, and marched at the head of the line. . . . [A]nd in the street girls and

boys who were coming home from school sang with us. We shouted "Down with Japanese Imperialism! Long live the Chinese nation!" (*Girl Rebel*, 236)

September 15, "On the way."

We slept in a car used for carrying horses. There were no windows, only an iron door in the middle, and the floor was covered with hay where eighteen of us curled up together. . . . In the same car there were some soldiers and a few higher ranking officers. . . . We got to Yochow at half past eight in the morning. (ibid., 238–39)

September 17, "Nanking."

Arriving at Nanking, I got up at half past five. . . . I begin to realize that it is going to be hard for me. I have to be the leader of the corps, with a sick body. (ibid., 240)

September 19, Waikang. Mid-Autumn at the Front.

We reached Anting, at half past five; we all got out of the train and went toward the Kiating front. . . . When we had walked about one hour, we saw the first enemy airplanes . . . We hid among the bamboos. . . . Soldiers were aiming a gun at the planes. (ibid., 240)

September 23, At Field Hospital.

A certain division had fought for only two days, but seven hundred wounded soldiers filled the courtyard, the landing, the corridors . . . everywhere! . . . There was not much medicine. . . . Four or five doctors were sharing one pair of scissors. . . .

I saw many wounded soldiers lying on the floor. There was a groaning soldier, half of his hip shot away by a shell. With great difficulty three of us bound up his wound, and my hands were red all over, soaked in blood. . . .

The sound of guns came nearer every minute but we went on. (ibid., 242–43)

September 24.

There were many wounded today and our uniforms and shoes and stockings were smeared with blood. . . . There is blood even in our rice. (ibid., 244)

September 25. Scared of Airplanes.

Suddenly the enemy dropped five bombs near us. (ibid., 246)

September 26.

At half past one the officer sent an aide to take me to the trenches. . . . We passed many little villages lying in a countryside of cotton farms and winding canals. . . . "The artillery fire is severe this afternoon," said the commander. "Now it is getting nearer. We may be buried here tonight." (ibid., 247)

September 28, Kiating.

We had walked through West Gate Street . . . when we found an old woman crying, sitting among a pile of debris. She told us her little house was struck by a bomb, her husband and son killed instantly. (ibid., 248)

September 30. Advancing under the Guns of the Enemy.

When I stepped over the trenches, the hidden comrades stretched out their necks and looked. The rain fell on them; some were dozing; some were eating, and everyone covered with mud. . . . They were shivering from cold; some had not eaten for two or three days, or had not a mouthful of water to drink, except water that had floated corpses. (ibid., 249)

October 1.

I was changing my dress when with a *hung* a bomb dropped, which shook the walls of my room. The others knelt down and covered their heads with blankets, but I stood still, and wished that I could see the bombing.

"Get down!" they said. "It's too dangerous!" "No! I'd rather die standing up!" (ibid., 249)

November 12, Soochow. The Retreat.

When I arrived at the hospital they all surrounded me and kept asking why we were sent back to Soochow, and whether we were losing at the front. . . . Many severely wounded soldiers were being brought in. . . . There were some who had become ill from drinking the water in the river [which] was so full of corpses that the water had turned red, and these soldiers could not find any other water and so drank the blood of their own comrades. But blood alone could not make them sick. The enemy had thrown poison into the river, and so they were poisoned. . . .

We did not reach Soochow until dawn. . . . I heard the explosion of bombs and went out and saw houses fallen, and wounded soldiers and refugees killed by machine guns lying scattered on the ground. . . . The worst thing were the cries from under burning piles. "Help me, help me, please!" . . . At night the city is a stretch of blackness. . . . Suchow which we used to call "heaven on earth," is now in Hell! (ibid., 261–63)

Despite the retreat, Xie continued to fight on various fronts in the interior.

Our work must not stop until the enemy is driven out. . . . I know that I will be at the front again in the immediate future, and I will take more girls with me. . . . [I] urge every Chinese patriot to go forth and join in this war of defense. . . . Good-by my friends. We'll meet again at the front! (ibid., 270)

Xie married her longtime lover, Jia Yizhen, in Xian, in 1938, and gave birth to a boy (1940) and a girl (1943). She continued her rovings, moving with her family to Taiwan in 1948. She taught at Taiwan Normal University in Taipei and continued her writing. In 1957 she and her husband moved to Malaysia, where she taught, and returned to Taiwan three years later. She traveled to the United States in 1968, and moved to San Francisco with her husband in 1974. Her husband died in 1988 and she on January 5, 2000, in San Francisco.

Xie's era was turbulent—politically, economically, culturally, and emotionally. Modern values were being pitted against ancient ones, and individual freedom set in opposition to traditional interpretations of Confucian dicta. Nonetheless, in the face of harrowing ordeals, Xie never despaired. Her powerful will drove her on to succeed and to fulfill her cherished wish to travel in China and outside of her land, and to lead the life of a "wanderer," fighting all the while for freedom of mind and body. Despite her physical and emotional suffering during virtually each stage of her life—particularly during the Sino-Japanese War (1937–45)—she looked forward to China's liberation and to better times ahead. Whether she ever achieved emotional fulfillment is difficult to say. She did, however, win acclaim for her writings. Travel and wandering were Xie's mainstay throughout her life.

Bettina L. Knapp

BIBLIOGRAPHY

Eberhard, Wolfram. *A History of China*. Berkeley: University of California Press, 1977.

Xie Bingying. *Girl Rebel: The Autobiography of Hsieh Pingying. With extracts from her New War Diaries*. Trans. Adet and Anor Lin. Introduction by Lin Yutang. New York: Da Capo Press, 1975.

———. Hsieh Ping-Ying (Xie Bingying). *The Autobiography of a Chinese Girl*. Trans. Tsui Chi. Introduction by Elisabeth Croll. London and New York: Pandora Press, 1986.

———. *A Woman Soldier's Own Story: The Autobiography of Xie Bingying* (1936). Trans. Lily Chia Brissman and Barry Brissman. New York: Columbia University Press, 2001.

19

Ruth Gruber

(1911–)

I am experiencing that feeling of zest which goes with exploration. I am in the thick of an historic moment. I am in an era in
the making. . . .

(Ruth Gruber, *Ahead of Time: My Early Years
as a Foreign Correspondent*, 213)

Before Outward Bound, before Odyssey Expeditions, before
adventure travel, there were the travels of Ruth Gruber. She was
among the first of the great solo adventurers who gave meaning
to the term "intrepid traveler." The desire to travel, to see and understand
the world, came early and forcefully to Gruber. She was born into an
Orthodox Jewish family in the Williamsburg section of Brooklyn. Her
small all-Jewish world was intensely committed to its own ways, with education its top priority. The bonds of family were strong and affectionate—
Mama and Papa Gruber, two sets of grandparents, and four siblings—but
Ruth felt the pressures to be suffocating. Her way out into the larger
world was through academic achievement. She lived at home while
attending New York University, yearning all the while to move to Manhattan, home of Greenwich Village, where *real* writers lived.

Her full escape from parental pressures came with a summer course in
German at Mount Holyoke College in Massachusetts in 1928, and
another summer course the following year at Harvard University, studying
Shakespeare. Then in 1930 she won a fellowship to the University of

Wisconsin for her master's degree—an entire year away from home. An exchange fellowship to Germany awarded by the Institute of International Education to the University of Cologne followed in 1931. In Cologne, she found a room with a Jewish family, whose daughter Luisa became a close friend. Like her own parents, Mama and Papa Herz welcomed young people to their table. Gruber particularly enjoyed their informal Sunday night suppers, which she shared with her school friends.

At the university, she studied German philosophy with Ernst Bertram, the leading Nietzsche scholar, as well as modern English literature and art history. At Carnival time, she and Luisa got caught up in the rollicking pre-Lenten celebration in which young and old paraded through the medieval streets in costumes and masks, blowing horns and noisemakers and carousing until dawn. During her sojourn in Germany, she visited Goethe's house in Frankfurt and saw the room in which he had written his celebrated plays and poems. But such normal student explorations were ominously endangered by the rising ill wind of Nazism. Her first encounter with Nazism took place in a melee at the university in which Nazi and Communist students clashed. This was followed by a Christmas party in the fairy-tale village of Berchtesgaden during which anti-Semitic and anti-American remarks outraged her and provoked her to leave.

Professor Herbert Schöffler at the University of Cologne asked Gruber to stay on and work for a doctorate. Since she had only a year's support from her exchange fellowship, he persuaded her to try to complete the doctoral studies in a single year. She agreed to try. Gruber's philosophy was always to dream dreams, have visions, and let no obstacle stop her. She finished the doctoral dissertation—the first dissertation in history on Virginia Woolf—passed the oral examinations, and received the doctoral degree magna cum laude. In August 1932 the *New York Times* reported that when the steamship *St. Louis* docked in New York, an attractive twenty-year-old Brooklyn girl stepped off the gangplank bearing a coveted doctoral degree, making her the youngest holder of a doctorate in the world.

Earlier, the mayor of Cologne, Dr. Konrad Adenauer, had invited her to his office in the city hall on Judengasse Street, presented her with two magnificent art books on Cologne, shook her hand, and urged her to send many more young people like her to Germany.

Gruber's remarkable accomplishments led to further opportunities. On the recommendation of the Guggenheim Foundation, she was awarded the Yardley Foundation Fellowship for "creative research." This was opportune, as she had been hoping to travel again through Western Europe to study women's lives in democracies and under dictatorships. Immediately the *New York Herald Tribune*, for which she had been writing freelance articles, named her their special foreign correspondent, gave her credentials, and told her to cable them whenever she found an important story.

En route from Berlin to Moscow, Gruber had a short but emotional visit with her mother's family in the shtetl of Beremlya in the Wolyn Province of Poland. It was 1935, and anti-Semitism was in full cry. After entering the simple wooden hut, with her relatives crowded around her, hugging, kissing, and plying her with food, her joy was suddenly shattered. Polish gendarmes burst into the house. "Where is she?" they demanded to know. It was obvious that someone had informed them that a young foreigner, carrying a typewriter and a camera (highly suspicious objects), had entered their tiny village. The gendarmes examined her baggage, held her underwear up in the kerosene light, and demanded that she leave immediately, or they would arrest her and lock her up. In the darkness, hiding in her cousin's horse cart, covered with straw up to her chin, she traveled to Warsaw. Catching the first train out, she breathed her first sigh of relief when Polish guards stamped her passport and the train crossed the Polish border.

In Moscow, she made her way to the offices of Otto Yulyevich Schmidt, the tsar of the entire Soviet Arctic. Schmidt, in a white uniform, with a white beard and a white naval hat, was intrigued by her knowledge of the Arctic and the study she was making of women. He invited her to be the first journalist—male or female—ever allowed into the secret Soviet Arctic. Gruber believed that he had selected her not only because she was making a study of women, but because she was a woman. If she, a young woman, not yet twenty-four, could travel alone through Siberia and the hitherto sealed-off Soviet Arctic, then maybe people would realize that transportation, the biggest problem in opening the Arctic, was being solved.

She had bought a duffel bag at Moscow's Mostorg department store and, preparing for all kinds of weather and occasions, packed it with "The Compleat Explorer's Equipment": one woolen dress, one silk dress, two pairs woolen underwear, two pairs silk underwear, a bathing suit, one pair mittens, one pair galoshes, two water bottles, mosquito netting, and one Boy Scout compass (Ruth Gruber, *Ahead of Time*, 186). Soon she was aloft on her way to Siberia and the Soviet Arctic. With maps on her lap, she followed their route through several time zones. Many of the towns she landed in were a strange jumble of "low wooden blockhouses and steel-and-concrete apartment houses" (ibid., 190). From the air she saw the beautiful seaplane base of Molokov Island on the Yenisei River, shaded by pine trees and surrounded by the Stoloviyie Mountains (ibid., 194). There, on Molokov Island, she spent the night before flying on to Igarka. It was a brand-new lumber-exporting town north of the Arctic Circle, being built by pioneers and prisoners. Gruber saw freighters flying the colors of England, Norway, Belgium, and Denmark, all loading wood. In truth, Igarka was a city of wood, with little indoor plumbing. A bath in the port's bathhouse was a welcome treat, followed by a visit to the sauna. There she was flogged with heavy leaves that left her tingling and reminded her of the Turkish baths in Brooklyn that she and her mother used to frequent.

After several weeks of exploring Igarka, she watched a Russian cargo ship, the *SS Anadyr*, steam into port. Invited by the captain to board the ship, she accepted eagerly. Her intelligence, wit, and sense of adventure made such a profound impression on the captain that he persuaded her to join them to complete the journey. It was a traveler's dream voyage of firsts. Joining the *SS Anadyr* as the only woman traveler, Gruber became the first foreign correspondent aboard the first cargo ship determined to break its way through Arctic fog and wind and hazardous ice floes. Its mission was to attempt to open the historic Northeast Passage linking the Pacific and the Atlantic across the top of the world in a single summer. In wartime it was crucial for pilots; in peacetime, vital for trade and tourism. She filed the following dispatch: "I am experiencing that feeling of zest which goes with exploration. I am in the thick of an historic movement. I am in an era in the making. . . ." (ibid., 213). When the *Anadyr* reached Murmansk, she and the crew were mobbed by the press and saluted by cheering crowds. Ignoring the hoopla, they raced down the gangway to the best hotel in town and stuffed themselves with longed-for fresh fruit, caviar, and delicious food and wine.

A year later, in 1936, Gruber returned to the Arctic to explore it further, traveling aboard ships, trains, and open-cockpit planes. She interviewed miners in the Aldan goldfields and pioneers and prisoners in the gulag. One of the highlights of her trip was a women's conference in Yakutsk, where she met native women of all ages and ethnicities. Another highlight was her visit with a 104-year-old Yakut woman, the mother of twenty children. She gave Gruber a unique birchbark cradle in which she had rocked all of her babies. Years later, Gruber used it to rock her own two children.

Before returning to New York, she flew from Moscow to London to keep a date set up months earlier with Virginia Woolf: "At 6 p.m. I rang the bell at 52 Tavistock Square. A housekeeper led me up the stairs. Virginia Woolf lay curled on a rug in front of a blazing fire, like an elegant greyhound, in a long gray gown, gray stockings, gray shoes, gray hair cropped short like a boy's, puffing a cigarette in a long, gray cigarette holder" (ibid., 222).

After the publication in 1939 of her influential memoir, *I Went to the Soviet Arctic*, Secretary of the Interior Harold L. Ickes sent her to Alaska to report on how best to settle the territory and preserve its beauty. Here was an opportunity for her to travel and report to the administration on how to inspire Americans to help open a new and welcoming frontier land. In Seattle, before boarding the steamship sailing to Alaska, a soured official warned her that "Only schoolmarms and whores go to Alaska." While chatting with settlers in Alaska, she was amused to learn that she, herself, was the subject of rumors: "One incredible tale was that she was trying to bring Hebrews to Alaska; another, that she was planning to teach birth control to the Eskimos; and, still another, that she was a spy for American naval intelligence" (Ruth Gruber, *Inside of Time: My Journey from Alaska to Israel*, 44–45).

It took her nineteen months to cover Alaska by air, rail, boat, and sled, meeting the unexpected all the way. Trying to radio a bush pilot to pick her up, she would often get the reply: "Pick you up tomorrow WEAPERS," which meant "Weather Permitting" (ibid., 76). Tomorrow could often turn into weeks of waiting. Aside from weather problems, mechanical problems were commonplace, and from time to time, the pilot might be drunk. All of which taught Gruber to live and work inside of time, instead of fighting it, because she realized she could not control time.

Gruber loved Alaska. From north to south, she traversed the entire territory. In Nome, she met Sinrock Mary, the Queen of the Reindeer, who owned a herd of 4,000. Not all of her reports were sunny, however. At one point, she wrote Ickes: "One should never visit Nome. It is hard on its white settlers and disastrous for its natives. Nome is a great well of drunkenness, juvenile delinquency and disease" (ibid., 71). She was horrified to watch seals clubbed to death at a huge seal rookery in Alaska's Pribilof Islands. But she accepted the fact that when native Eskimos harpooned walruses, they were doing so to get food to eat and skins for their clothes and tents. For the most part she slept in schools and hospitals, but when no accommodations were available in Kodiak, Sitka, and Point Hope, she had no qualms about sleeping in jails. She often thought she might write a book on the Alaskan jails and outhouses she had known.

In 1944 Secretary Ickes gave her one of her historic assignments: to shepherd 1,000 Holocaust survivors, hunted by Nazi planes and U-boats, to safe haven in Fort Ontario, an army camp in Oswego, New York. Eventually, she told the story of these refugees more than fifty years later in her book *Haven: The Dramatic Story of 1,000 World War II Refugees*. The book was made into a CBS miniseries, starring Natasha Richardson as Gruber and Anne Bancroft as her mother. The television production was followed by a musical play, also called *Haven*.

Rescuing refugees became the leitmotif of her life. "Standing alone on the blacked-out deck, the wind blowing through my hair, I was trembling with the discovery that from this moment on, my life would be forever bound with rescue and survival. I would use words and images, my typewriter and my cameras as my tools. I had to live the story to write it, and not only live it—if it was a story of injustice, I had to fight it" (ibid., 163).

Gruber left the government in 1946 to return to her first love, her life as a foreign correspondent. She covered the camps for displaced persons in Germany and Austria, traveled throughout the Middle East, and covered the stories of the birth of Israel and the war of independence. By the summer of 1949 Gruber was back in Israel to cover "Operation Magic Carpet" for the *New York Herald Tribune*. She flew from Aden to Israel in an American Skymaster airplane with 140 Yemenite Jews. Assuming that these Yemenites, who had never before seen an airplane, would be terrified, she asked one man whether he was afraid to fly. He was not afraid, he said, because the Bible predicted the flight. He quoted the passage from Isaiah: "But they that wait upon the Lord shall mount up with wings as eagles; they shall run and not be weary; and they shall walk, and not faint" (ibid., 340). Fearing for the security of the mission, Gruber had the *Herald Tribune* hold the story until all 50,000 Yemenites were safely in Israel. Again, she was the first with the story of the miracle of "Operation Magic Carpet."

Like a ballerina on point, Gruber was always ready to leap into her next challenge. In her reporting for the *New York Herald Tribune*, the *New York Post*, the wire services, and the Roosevelt administration, from historic places at historic times, she developed lasting friendships. Among them were such world leaders as Eleanor Roosevelt, David Ben Gurion, and Golda Meir, who served Gruber her own home-made chocolate chip cookies in her Tel Aviv kitchen.

Now in her nineties, Ruth Gruber is still the chic, globe-trotting author, who continues to travel, visit her children and grandchildren, write books and articles, and lecture to eager audiences around the world. Blanche Wiesen Cook, Eleanor Roosevelt's biographer, in her review of *Inside of Time*, hails Ruth Gruber as "fiercely independent and powerfully talented. . . . As a photojournalist, she was mentored by the best. Photographer Edward Steichen told her: 'Think with your heart. Take pictures with your heart.' Every picture Gruber took, every word she wrote, every detail was from the heart" ("The hard-eyed witness," R12).

Rosalie Brody Feder

BIBLIOGRAPHY

Cook, Blanche Wiesen. "The hard-eyed witness." *Los Angeles Times Book Review,* May 18, 2003, p. R12.

Gruber, Ruth. *Virginia Woolf: A Study.* Leipzig: Tauchnitz Press, 1935.

————. *I Went to the Soviet Arctic.* New York: Simon & Schuster, 1939.

————. *Rescue: The Exodus of the Ethiopian Jews.* New York: Atheneum, 1987.

————. *Ahead of Time: My Early Years as a Foreign Correspondent.* New York: Wynwood Press, 1991.

————. *Exodus 1947: The Ship that Launched a Nation.* New York: Random House, 1999.

————. *Haven: The Dramatic Story of 1,000 World War II Refugees.* New York: Random House, 1999.

————. *Inside of Time: My Journey from Alaska to Israel.* New York: Carroll & Graf, 2003.

CHAPTER 20

Oriana Fallaci

(1930–)

When right minds fail to come to terms and order breaks down
into chaos, when nations face off across flat plains and oppos-
ing citizens march into fields of blood, she is there to record
the trauma.

(Kim Murphy in *The Guardian*, February 28, 1991)

Who's afraid of Oriana Fallaci? Henry A. Kisssinger and
Mu'ammar Muhammad al-Gadhafi, for two. She, for her
part, is afraid of no one.

Kissinger and Gadhafi both fell victim to her unusual and invasive
interviewing techniques: the former blundered into what he subsequently
described as the stupidest error of his life—namely, the 1972 interview
with Fallaci in Washington, in which she badgered him into a thundering
peroration about the role of the United States in the battle against evil
(communism) and induced him to describe himself as the lone cowboy of
American foreign policy—for which he was soundly ridiculed by press and
public alike (Locher, *Contemporary Authors*, 134). Ironically, just when Fallaci was receiving the honor of a doctorate *honoris causa* in literature by
Columbia College in Chicago, Kissinger was forced to refuse a professor-
ship in political science offered by Columbia University in New York
because of student and faculty objections. As for Gadhafi, she called the
Libyan leader the "new Mussolini of the Mediterranean" and made fun
of his homosexuality in a 1979 encounter in Libya described in one Italian

newspaper as the first hard-core interview in the history of journalism. To avenge the "insult" of her two-hour-long wait before the investigation-interview with Gadhafi began, she hurled a book at his press secretary, then turned to ask: "Colonel, if [the masses] love you so much, then why"—gesturing to his battalion of bodyguards—"do you need so much protection?" (quoted in Peer, "The Fallaci Papers," 54).

Fallaci defends the pugnaciousness of her interviewing techniques on the grounds that she is not simply a journalist but a historian as well:

> A journalist lives history in the best of ways, that is, in the moment that history takes place. He lives history, touches history with his hands, looks at it with his eyes, listens to it with his ears. . . . I am the judge. I am the one who decides. . . . If I am a painter and I do your portrait, have I or have I not the right to paint you as I want? (Oriana Fallaci, quoted in Locher, 134)

She tussles with history and biography, shaping real lives to her own end, fitting perfectly Milan Kundera's definition of the journalist as "not a person who asks questions, but a person who has the sacred right to ask questions, to put questions to anyone about anything" (Milan Kundera, quoted in Marco Fini, "Signora grandi firme," 32).

No holds are barred in her interviews with people in power; she documents their most intimate thoughts and political convictions, in scenarios that have made her world-famous. She corners her subjects with sharp questions filled with insight, thereby eliciting revealing answers. She delights in recording, with devastating openness, the interviewees' tics and arrogance. Mistrust of organized authority and disillusionment with social progress have reinforced her conviction that *homo homini lupus*—an awareness that conditions her essentially pessimistic view of history.

Her vast knowledge of contemporary world events and her deep understanding of the eternalness of human nature underpin her interviews, eighteen of which she conducted during 1969–73 for the magazine *Europeo* and then published in book form (*Interview with History*, 1974; Eng. 1976). The intensity of her journalistic activity during that period can be measured by the distances traveled and the scope of nine important meetings in a single year (1972)—in New Delhi, Amman, Karachi, Addis Ababa, Colombo, Jerusalem, and Washington, in that circuitous order, to interview personages of the ilk of Indira Gandhi, King Hussein of Jordan, and Yasir Arafat in the Jordanian seat of Al Fatah, the president of Pakistan Ali Bhutto, Emperor Haile Selassie, Prime Minister Sirimavo Bandaranaike of Sri Lanka, Golda Meir, Kissinger, and others.

World leaders both intrigue her and fill her with indignation because "they rule our lives, command us, decide whether we live or die, in freedom or in tyranny." General Giap's answer to her question during their 1969 meeting in Hanoi: "Is it true that 45,000 of your men died at Dien Bien Phu?" makes her tremble with rage each time she recalls it: "Madame, every two minutes 300,000 persons on this planet die. What are 45,000 in one battle? In war death doesn't count" (quoted in "Speciale," 10).

But not always was she able to drive her questions home: sometimes she was met with gelid silence, sometimes outright refusal to answer, and Emperor Haile Selassie touchily dismissed her at the end of their interview with the words "Via, basta, ça suffit! Ça suffit!" But she undauntingly faced each extenuating task of meeting with these foreign political figures, plying them with her questions, browbeating, badgering, and luring them into her traps. By her own admission, she went to these interviews "oppressed by a thousand angers, myself assailed by a thousand questions . . . hoping to understand in what way those who are in power, or who are opposed to that power, determine our destiny" (*Interview with History*, 5). In the end she realized that those who determine our destiny are really not better than we are, nor more intelligent, nor stronger, nor more illuminated than we are—they are simply more enterprising and more ambitious (ibid., 7).

Active, tenacious, and hardworking, Fallaci is both a journalist and a novelist, and she attacks both genres with driving missionary zeal, running the gamut of lexical variety and appropriate metaphors. Yet clarity and transparency are the hallmarks of her journalistic prose, whether she is covering the Hungarian revolt of 1956 or the 1968 massacre in Plaza Tlatelolco during the Olympic Games in Mexico City, during which she herself received gunshot wounds. She has relentlessly recorded the suffering of soldiers and civilians alike in Vietnam, Lebanon, Greece, Palestine, Argentina, and the Persian Gulf area, where she arrived in the desert kingdom of Saudi Arabia in February 1991 to cover that war for *Corriere della Sera*. A front line witness, tape recorder in hand, she has courageously reported from the scenes of bloody battles, dressed in bulletproof vest and the good-luck helmet that she has kept in her suitcase since the

Vietnam War. And it is with the same aplomb and command of wit that she receives threatening telephone calls at home since the publication of her political pamphlet *The Rage and the Pride* (2001; Eng. 2002) following the events of September 11, 2001 (see below). She has wrapped up the story of her stormy life in two books that were published in quick succession in 2004: *La Forza della Ragione* and *Oriana Fallaci intervista Oriana Fallaci*.

Fallaci was born in Florence into an anti-Fascist family (she describes herself as a "quarrelsome, intolerant Florentine"). Deeply committed civically and politically, she usually stands on the side of the opposition. Part of her childhood was lived during the Italian Resistance of World War II, so she bears the imprint of war and feels compulsively thrust into dangerous situations. As a child, she learned about the difficulty of crossing checkpoints and boundaries to penetrate hostile territory: she ran courier missions for her father in his clandestine activities for Florence's Justice and Liberty group of the National Action Party. One of her assignments was to take a basket of food containing a revolver to Carlo Levi (the author of the 1945 novel *Christ Stopped at Eboli*), who was in hiding opposite Florence's Pitti Palace. Levi took the food but returned the gun, so Oriana was twice exposed in her risky mission. She remembers an American plane parachuting to the Resistance in Tuscany weapons, ammunitions, and ten smiling, Italian-speaking American commandos—a recollection that perhaps rooted an early bond with America. Honorably discharged from the Italian army at the age of fourteen, at fifteen she attended her first political rally in Florence's Piazza della Signoria, then began working in order to contribute to the family's sole luxury, "culture"—that is, the buying of books on an installment plan. Of all the voices that reached her through books, she best heard Jack London's "call of the wild." He stirred her ambitions of emulating him: a novelist, journalist, adventurer, and war correspondent. When Fallaci left off her writing to go to cover the 1991 Persian Gulf War, remembering the American author she so much admired, she said she felt the need to get out of her lonely prison cell "to return to the Klondike or to the Russo-Japanese war like Jack London" (interview with Paola Fallaci, "Ma il successo . . . ," 28).

She began her career by working as a reporter for a Florentine daily newspaper. Assigned to cover local news, her first article was a damning piece about a dance hall where mothers took their daughters looking for husbands. After covering criminal and judiciary news, she obtained a regular contract with the newspaper but was fired two years later for refusing to write a satirical piece about the Italian Communist leader Palmiro Togliatti. She then worked for the widely read magazines *Epoca* and *Europeo*, succeeding often in scandalizing Italian public opinion. Her first trips to the United States began in the 1950s, when, as a special envoy for *Europeo*, she covered the golden era of Hollywood's myths and vices. Now she resides permanently in New York, the city she calls "the capital of the West," living the life of a recluse, deliberately loosening her ties with her roots. "This city gives me that feeling of freedom, trust and optimism that I never felt in Italy and in Europe," she has declared. "If Italy is mother to me, then America is my husband" (interview with Paola Fallaci, 24)—perhaps a poorly chosen metaphor inasmuch as Fallaci, rejecting any form of surrender of control over her own life, has never taken a husband.

Her pro-Vietcong sentiments during the Vietnam War were a matter of public record, but by 1988 she would declare that "perhaps the American war was not unjust." Openly recognizing that she had erred in judging events in Southeast Asia, she took the blame for having contributed to misleading public opinion (Salvatore Scarpino, "Rambo, l'ultimo amore di Oriana," 1). Later, reporting from a U.S. air base in Saudi Arabia during the 1991 Persian Gulf War, she firmly declared that she did not belong to "the antiamerikanism party" and never joined in the "Americans go home" demonstrations ("Speciale," 6, 13). She comes full swing with the very pro-American *The Rage and the Pride*, in which she declares her love for the America where she chose to live and work, and where she has spent a great part of her life not as a guest but as a citizen.

Her journalism career ended with the reportage of the Persian Gulf War and the liberation of Kuwait on February 27, 1991, in a series of articles for *Corriere della Sera* (1991). Her stated reasons for covering the war for the newspaper, despite her success as a novelist, were not so much for the sake of journalism as to "live out the adventure . . . to escape the tedium of too many years of sitting at the desk writing *Inshallah*" (interview with Paola Fallaci, 28). It was also for what she called "personal egoism"—that is, had she not gone personally to the area of conflict, she would have felt like a deserter—both of herself and of her profession ("Speciale," 9). She spent almost two months in the desert, covering all aspects of the Middle East in the throes of battle. Part of her reportage is dedicated to the ecological disaster produced by the war: the cormorants trapped in petroleum and destined, like the sea, to die; another part personifies the "Black Cloud"—smoke rising from the oil wells in flames. She comments on the chemical weapons that Saddam Hussein did not use, the almost nonexistent Kuwaiti resistance, and the slaughter of at least twelve thousand retreating Iraqis on Jaharah Road by American bombers (she calls them "avenging angels") ("Speciale," 13).

But prior to her settling in her brownstone house on East Sixty-first Street in Manhattan, where she literally confined herself to write *Inshallah* (1990; Eng. 1992) and *The Rage and the Pride*, Fallaci traveled around the world. Even travel to the moon was important to her: she made a special trip to the United States in order to write *If the Sun Dies* (1965; Eng., 1966), about the American space venture, which she closely followed. In her fictionalized diary account of this trip, she enthusiastically observes the preparations for the Apollo lunar excursion modules. She projects herself in a time capsule to the year 2026, when the Bomb has burst and Earth is dead. "And if the Earth dies, and if the Sun dies, we'll live up there" are her confident words in the concluding paragraph (*If the Sun Dies*, 1965, 491).

But travel was scarcely ever a pleasure for Fallaci. Rather, it was to investigate faraway revolutions, denounce dictators, engage in abrasive and bruising "boxing match" interviews with far-flung protagonists on the world scene, or look with horror on backward societies. Pugnacious and provocative, she rails against the inequality of the sexes that she observes during her travels: "[N]o man [in Muslim countries] has ever covered his face with a bedsheet in order to go out into the street. In China no man has ever had his feet bound and reduced to seven centimeters of atrophic muscle and broken bones. In Japan no man has ever been lapidated because his wife discovered that he wasn't a virgin" (Oriana Fallaci, *The Useless Sex*, 1961; Eng. 1964, 9).

Wherever she went, she seized the opportunity to tackle her subjects with doses of malice, venom, and irony. In Spain in 1977, for example, she placed red flowers on the tombs of patriots executed under the Franco regime and when, during a brief interview on Spanish television, prior to which she had been warned to avoid any political allusions, she was asked whom she would like to interview in Spain, her courageous answer was that she wanted to talk to "your dead, those who were shot dead" ("Los muertos, los fucilados")—at which transmission of the program was cut short. For her, as for Robert Musil, irony is not an expression of superiority but rather a form of struggle. She does not write about history; she *makes* history, and therefore she occupies a strategic position in social historiography.

Her travels for interviewing purposes may indeed have changed the course of history. She claims, for example, that her question to Pakistan's President Ali Bhutto in Karachi in 1972 (was it true that he and Indian Prime Minister Indira Gandhi really couldn't stand each other?) resulted in the delaying of a peace agreement between the two countries. After the protocol-shattering session with Haile Selassie, in which she asked the "Lion of Judah" what his feelings were in the face of the extreme poverty of his people, he recalled his ambassador to Italy (Peer, 53). South Vietnamese President Nguyen Van Thieu burst into tears during their interview in Saigon in 1973, while the Polish union leader Lech Walesa, in a trial-of-strength interview in Poland, said her difficult questions gave him a headache. Mohammad Reza Pahlavi, the Shah of Iran, under her alternative wheedling and goading in Tehran in 1973, unleashed an impolitic tirade against women; and the Ayatollah Ruholla Khomeini, the religious leader of Iran from 1979 to 1989, learned what Fallaci thought of his politics when she angrily ripped off the chador she was wearing, with the words "this stupid medieval rag," which brought the interview to an abrupt end (ibid.).

Fallaci is fiercely ironic about the chador, which she invariably calls a *lenzuolo* (bedsheet): "[W]hether you call it purdah or burka or pushi or kulle or djellabah, it's got two holes at the level of the eyes, or a thick wire-mesh two centimeters high and six centimeters wide; through those holes or wire-mesh [women] look at the sky or at people as though they were looking through prison bars. This prison extends from the Atlantic to the Indian Ocean, passing through Morocco, Algeria, Nigeria, Libya, Egypt, Syria, Lebanon, Iraq, Iran, Jordan, Saudi Arabia, Afghanistan, Pakistan, Indonesia: the immense domain of Islam" (*The Useless Sex*, 29).

The Useless Sex is a volume of travel essays surveying the status of women and the taboos that condition women's life in countries around the world. The editor of the magazine *Europeo* had temptingly invited her to duplicate the trip made by Phileas Fogg (the hero of Jules Verne's *Around the World in Eighty Days*). She was to stop mainly in Eastern cities to report on humans who "didn't count," the "useless" feminine sex. (In

Pakistan, she met a man with three wives, two at Karachi and one in Lahore, who had given him nine children in all. "Congratulations!" Fallaci exclaims naively. "Nine people make up a nice family." "Not nine, four," he corrects her. "I and my three male sons. Women don't count" [ibid.].)

The thirty-day trip took her to Pakistan, India, Indonesia, China (for which she was unable to obtain a visa and had to content herself with Hong Kong), Japan, Hawaii, the United States, and back to Italy, where she felt she had come full circle, in every sense of the word. She had followed in the footsteps of women everywhere in the world and saw that everywhere, despite a move from repression to emancipation, women are plunged in darkness and unhappiness (ibid., 255). All of her "fantasies of the rainy season and statues of Buddha and temples of Shiva and Polynesian canoes" (ibid., 12) faded in the face of the difficult task of recording what she saw, heard, and believed to have understood between Karachi and New York. Could any of her valiant attempts to explain Western standards have made any dent on her interlocutors? A "no global" before the time, she sees that the world is changing, that women are changing, and that everywhere they are

> learning to imitate our ugly European dresses, our stupid high heels, our absurd competition with men; but regardless of how much French fashion they sell in Tokyo department stores, regardless of how many feminist slogans they shout during rallies in Bombay, regardless of how many military schools they open up to girls without brains in Peking and Ankara, everywhere the female difference remains.

She concludes by saying that probably women are the same throughout the world, no matter what race or climate or religion they belong to, simply because human nature is the same everywhere.

From one end of the earth to the other, women live the wrong way:

> either cooped up in cages like animals in a zoo, looking up at the sky and at people from under a bedsheet that wraps them like a shroud wraps a corpse, or unleashed like ambitious warriors and winning medals in shooting matches with men. (ibid., 253–4)

In the end, she does not know whether she felt sorrier for the weeping fourteen-year-old child bride of Karachi being married off to a man she had never seen before, or for the ugly woman soldier of Ankara; whether she was more horrified by the old Chinese woman with bound feet or by the frenetic "liberated" American women she met in New York.

Fallaci's literary talent appears, however, mainly in her novels, in which she eminently succeeds in overcoming the limitations of her journalistic trade. She demonstrates an unquestionable linguistic capacity and wields the Italian language to perfection. Whether her novels are confessional or political, her self-identification with her work gives her writing a power sui generis. Her best-known and breathtaking novel *A Man* (1979; Eng., 1980) intermingles autobiographical memoir, historical document, and political pamphlet. It has been described as one of the most extraordinary examples of the historical and inner biography of a man ever written by a woman (Paola Blelloch, *Quel mondo dei guanti e delle stoffe* . . . , 75). *A Man* is the heartrending biography of the single, great, desperate love in Fallaci's life: the poet and Greek resistance hero Alexander Panagoulis, who had been condemned to death in 1968 after a bungled attempt on the life of the Greek military junta chief Georgios Papadopoulos. She had flown to Athens to interview Panagoulis in 1973, when he was released from prison in a general amnesty. The released political prisoner and his interviewer succumbed to what Fallaci calls "the most dangerous love that exists: the love that mixes ideals and moral commitments with attraction and emotions" (quoted in Peer, 53). Subsequently Panagoulis was killed, at the age of thirty-six, in a political assassination just as he was about to publish evidence of government corruption. Fallaci describes the novel as a book on the solitude of the individual who refuses to be pigeonholed; a book on the tragedy of the poet who neither wishes to be, nor ever can be, a man of the masses and an instrument of those who command; and, finally, a book about a hero who fought alone for truth and freedom, and who died for refusing to surrender to government repression and the acquiescence of the masses. Panagoulis has been assigned by history to the ranks of hero and political anarchist, but Fallaci has given him a higher title—that of *a man*—which in its utter simplicity, and in association with the intimacy that she brings to bear on the public and private figure, has brought the tormented Greek hero into the hearts of millions of readers. His vainglorious gestures and the needless risks he ran, betrayals by his companions and the tortures he endured, have been indelibly impressed on the minds of those who have read the novel. The author succeeds in capturing the poignancy of their love affair and the pathos of the hero's drama, as Eros and Thanatos soar far above the tragic Greek situation under the colonels' dictatorship.

Nothing and Amen (1969; Eng., 1972) and *Inshallah* are both war novels, based on the shamefully inhuman and bestial wars in Vietnam and Lebanon, respectively. (Fallaci declared in 1991 that to understand human beings' "beauty and ugliness, intelligence and stupidity, bestiality and humanity, courage and cowardice, war serves the writer more than anything else" ["Speciale," 7].) In both novels, striking foreign landscapes and natural settings serve to underscore the anger she feels in the face of wanton destruction. The mountains surrounding a military camp in Vietnam, for example, where men are now dying, are "blocks of jade and emerald"; the sky from which bombs drop is a "cornflower colored cape"; and the cool, clear waters of the river now serve only to extinguish fires. "Why must we always sully beauty?" she asks rhetorically (*Nothing and Amen*, 18), but then goes on fiercely to ironize the best-laid plans of an American representative who sees the Mekong Delta, after the war, competing with Florida in factories, skyscrapers, and highways. "The idea that the peasants in the Delta don't want to compete with Florida," she writes, "that they want only to live in peace with their hand-planted and hand-gathered rice eaten with chopsticks, is an idea that doesn't enter his mind" (ibid., 83). Hammering her point, she observes, as she flies to An Xuyen in the extreme south,

> for miles and miles beneath us an extended desert of craters and holes like those on the moon's surface, and this is what remained after bombings by Phantoms so that Vietnam might become as rich as Japan, as modern as Japan, as respected as Japan. Then we left the Moon and flew over Mars, over an extension of tree trunks and branches, naked as in winter: the remains of a forest scorched by defoliants so that Vietnam might have factories, skyscrapers, and highways, compete with Florida, and become as rich as Japan, as modern as Japan, as respected as Japan. (ibid., 85)

Beirut, once the "Switzerland of the Middle East" and one of the loveliest places on the planet with its mild climate, blue sea, and green hills, is transformed into a lugubrious stage set of stripped homes, disemboweled buildings, bullet-pocked walls, and mountains of cadavers, thanks to the

Palestinians, the Israelis, and the Christians in the east and the Muslims in the west of the divided city. On the day that truce was declared, "the bluest sky ever seen in Beirut" (*Inshallah*, 779) seems to command the machine guns and mortars to be silent, but the vitality, the imperiousness, the impetuousness, and the indomitability of war seem destined never to die (ibid., 793–5).

Fallaci knows how to probe deeply into the human psyche and give body to emotions and sensations that everyone experiences but only few can make manifest and narrate. She skillfully depicts fears, anxieties, and the most hidden contents of the unconscious. Like Pablo Picasso in his Spanish civil war mural *Guernica*, Fallaci, in *Nothing and Amen*, presents the tragedy of the war in Vietnam as a nightmare. Arriving in Saigon in November 1967 at the Than Son Nhut air terminal, her eye lines up deadly arms and miserable men: "Jet fighters, helicopters with heavy machine guns, trailers loaded with napalm bombs, stood in line with unhappy-looking American soldiers" (*Nothing and Amen*, trans. Isabel Quigley, 2). By contrast, "dying didn't occur to you" in the warmth of the glorious sun, in the well-supplied food stores, the jewelry shops glittering with gold, the open restaurants, and in the relaxed atmosphere of her Saigon hotel, where she paints in word pictures "the table [on which] there was always a bowl of fresh pineapple and mangoes" (ibid., 3). Six months later, Saigon is burning, and she is there to describe the tongues of fire and columns of black smoke as South Vietnamese Skyraiders and American Phantoms dive and rise over the city. "How ugly Saigon has become," she laments (ibid.).

Shortly after her arrival in Vietnam she went to the village of Dak To, ten miles from the Laotian and Cambodian border near the mouth of the Ho Chi Minh trail. The battle here resulted in failure and major casualties for the Americans. She records the agony, anguish, frustration, and despair of the wounded as they are prepared for evacuation, recreating atmosphere with mimetic ability and describing scenery in such sharp detail that readers experience the war as fully as possible. "Her success," in the opinion of one critic, "lies precisely in the ability to communicate directly an investigation of the war in Vietnam as if she were writing a novel" (Santo L. Aricò, "Oriana Fallaci's Journalistic Novel," 181). She spent almost a year on location in a total immersion in the Vietnam conflict, interviewing fighting men at the bloody conflict in Dak To, flying on a bombing mission in order to experience a pilot's emotions during combat, almost losing her life during the battle of Hue, and achieving a comprehensive panorama of Vietnamese society. She changed what could have been an objective record of an armed conflict into a fresh form of art (ibid., 172).

Her 1990 novel *Inshallah* (she calls it her "little modern *Iliad*") is a polyphony of dialects and foreign languages ranging from classical Latin to American slang. Fallaci's sensitivity to the role of language in human relationships is comparable to that of Elias Canetti. Besides the fact that both authors see the human condition as one in which the powerful dominate the weak and in which individual freedom and individuality are continuously compromised, both believe that a common language unites, and that one cause of unhappiness may be linguistic diversity, for it divides the human family into enemy factions.

Fallaci dedicated *Inshallah* to the four hundred American and French soldiers massacred by Beirut's "Sons of God," to all the men, women, oldsters, and children massacred in the city and in all the massacres of the eternal massacre called war. The novel offers exciting firsthand clarification of the entanglements of the Lebanese war during the Israeli invasion, even while magnifying the perversions of Italian males stationed in Beirut, the city of no escape. She, with other journalists, was in direct contact with the international peacekeeping force's Italian contingent strung out along the "green line" separating Christians from Muslims. They supply the pattern for her invented fictional characters whose stories unfold against the historical landscape of the war in Beirut. The divided city had already suffered severe damage during the civil war between left-wing Muslim and Arab nationalist groups and right-wing Christian militias, and was further devastated by the Israeli siege of 1982 to expel the Palestine Liberation Organization (PLO) guerrillas from its western sector. The multinational peacekeeping force was established after a massacre of Palestinian refugees at the Sabra and Shatila camps by Israel's Lebanese Christian allies, but France and the United States withdrew in 1984 after nearly three hundred troops were killed in terrorist attacks.

Fallaci sees Lebanon as a metaphor of our times, a country that could very well be our universe, the universe of absolute Irrationality. The book begins with the bombing of the American marines and ends with the Italians making their escape from the port without much loss, due to some intriguing with a Shiite potentate. Her characters, trapped in fear and claustrophobia, suffer all the torments of suffocating cities and stifling suburbs—themselves real characters in the novels. She transforms the vestiges of Beirut's past beauty into a stinking mass of blood, garbage, and rot. The city's bombed-out cellars and rat-infested sewers by day shelter the hundreds of stray dogs and jackals that prowl through the deserted streets and empty squares at night—but perhaps they are only the ghosts of animals that appear when darkness falls to imitate men tearing each other to pieces. We witness a Beirut that Fallaci describes as formerly a carefree, tolerant Babel of races and languages, in which Shiite and Sunnite Muslims, Maronite and Greek Orthodox Christians, Druses and Jews all coexisted, where "war didn't exist" (*Inshallah*, 49), but where now everybody shoots at everybody. Swarms of thugs are incited to action by fanatics and criminals to defend a piece of garbage-strewn sidewalk; territories are guarded by teenagers armed with Kalashnikovs; corpses and rubble are strewn everywhere. The pounding of artillery is matched by the pounding of her litanies: "everywhere rubble, rubble, rubble. Corpses, corpses, corpses" (ibid., 55). She provides vivid descriptions of massacres, lootings, bombings, grenades, and kamikaze trucks that wipe out hundreds of human beings in seconds. Condemning the senseless genocide in Lebanon, she rejects the notion that war is inevitable, and she sees male jingoism as an ingredient of all wars (a thesis supported by the contemporary French historian Georges Duby). "History doesn't change," Fallaci writes in *Inshallah*. "Eternal history, the eternal story of Man, who in war shows himself in all his truth, because nothing shows him *plain* as much as war" (ibid., 207). Parallels have been made between Fallaci's own novel and Ernest Hemingway's *For Whom the Bell Tolls* and André Malraux's *L'espoir* (Giancarlo Vigorelli, "Il racconto più umano sul dramma d'un popolo," 3).

War is a metaphor for our world: Vietnam, Lebanon, September 11th are metaphors for our times—the universe of the Irrational. The linguistic babel of Saigon, Beirut, New York are the supreme metaphors of utter Chaos, according to Fallaci. Yet all seems to move not chaotically but very slowly as death hovers everywhere to the tune of *Inshallah*'s leitmotiv: "Life is the Food of Death." She is obsessed with the concept of death, whose "faceless smile" she brought to life in her novel *A Man*. Among her purposes in writing *Inshallah* was to try to "exorcise death." One of the

protagonists of the novel is obsessed by an equation expressing the formula of Death; he tries to find the formula of Life, and does so, just one
second before dying, and intuits that Death does not exist: it is the Food
of Life (Claudio Altarocca, "Fallaci sola a New York," 15).

   The Rage and the Pride was Fallaci's first work after a ten-year silence.
Its themes, linked to the September 11th events and interspersed with personal memoirs, revolve around America, Italy, and Europe, those geographical entities that she indicts for their blindness to the threat of Islam.
Perhaps the very anger and pride of the title of her work helped to fan the
fires that raged on September 11th; perhaps she contributed to transforming America's fears into diffidence and hatred. She wrote viscerally, spew-
ing forth her repugnance of fanaticism and terrorism, and in her
denunciations she herself was violent and Manichaean, viewing only one
good civilization (Western) as opposed to other subcivilizations. She projected Rationality onto the West, and Irrationality onto Islam—which has
been seen as a dangerous oversimplification. Having vowed scorn and
"bestial hatred" for the fringe of Islam extremists, whose mounting intolerance endangers Western civilization, she writes deprecatorily of Islam
and Muslims—a disparagement that may stem in part from her earlier
experiences in Islamic countries (see interviews, *The Useless Sex*, and *Inshallah*, above). The expanse of Islam that she describes—from Afghanistan to Sudan, from Palestine to Pakistan, from Malaysia to Iran, from
Egypt to Iraq, from Algeria to Senegal, from Syria to Kenya, from Libya
to Chad, from Lebanon to Morocco, from Indonesia to Yemen, from
Saudi Arabia to Somalia—encompasses a warning that "hate for the West
swells like a fire fed by the wind. And the followers of Islamic Fundamentalism multiply like protozoa of a cell which splits to become two cells
then four then eight then sixteen then thirty-two. To infinity" (Oriana
Fallaci, quoted in George Gurley, "The Rage of Oriana Fallaci," 15).
Among the first to react to the radical changes that the very notions of
"West" and "Europe" are undergoing, she wrote:

> Europe is no longer Europe. It is a province of Islam, as Spain and Portugal
> were at the time of the Moors. It hosts almost 16 million Muslim immi-
> grants and teems with mullahs, imams, mosques, burqas, chadors. It lodges
> thousands of Islamic terrorists whom governments don't know how to iden-
> tify and control. (Oriana Fallaci, "The Rage, the Pride and the Doubt," A18)

Fallaci's representation of Islamic fundamentalism in *The Rage and the Pride* was wrongly interpreted as a desire to destroy and physically eliminate Muslims; it was seen as stirring racial hatred and as anti-Muslim racism by some who compared her book to Adolf Hitler's *Mein Kampf*. Whereas Fallaci has always opposed war, she is accused of compounding the causes of war by positing evil in Islam and thus falling prey to the very charges of intolerance and irrationality that she imputes to it. After the French publication of *The Rage and the Pride*, she was called to court in Paris (2002) at the instigation of three antiracist organizations: the MRAP (Movement Against Racism and for Friendship Among Peoples), which sought to have the work banned and withdrawn from bookshops, accusing her of having written an "Islamophobic" text and a "call for total war against Muslims"; the LDH (League for Human Rights), whose lawyer called her the "Ben Laden de l'écriture" (writing's Bin Laden); and the LICRA (International League against Racism and Anti-Semitism), which sought to have an antiracist appeal inserted in the book—that is, a warning explaining that Islamic extremists and Muslims must not be confused. The appeal for sequestration of the work was rejected by the Paris tribunal on the grounds that the book had already been widely diffused in France and in the rest of world.

Now a leader of public opinion with a worldwide reputation, Oriana Fallaci has become a myth. A long list of lawsuits and clashes with colleagues, world leaders, and human rights organizations have spun the notion of Fallaci as the prima donna of the press. Despite the notoriety of her narcissism and bad character, she is known and admired from Lapland to Romania, where women have named their daughters Oriana in her honor. Pearl Buck admired her and used to say that Fallaci's books would survive. (Fallaci, having read and admired Buck's *The Good Earth*, sought her out in Philadelphia for an interview and was incensed to learn that the *New York Times* had rejected Buck's favorable review of *If the Sun Dies* because the newspaper's literary editor was a friend of Werner von Braun, whose Nazi past Fallaci had exposed.) The American science fiction writer Ray Bradbury considers Oriana Fallaci to be one of today's most committed writers; and, in a novel by Irving Wallace, the protagonist's main ambition is to become "like Fallaci" (Franco Occhiuzzi, "Oriana dottoressa (ad honorem) del best-seller," 13).

The formula for becoming "like Fallaci"?

I was a woman full of curiosity, desirous of seeing the world: and I did, thanks to journalism. I grew up in a society where women are oppressed, maltreated: and to journalism I owe the fact that I have been able to live like a man." (Oriana Fallaci, quoted in Marco Nozza, "Guerra e amore nel 'suo' Libano," 3)

(All translations are mine, unless otherwise noted.)   *Alba Amoia*

BIBLIOGRAPHY

Altarocca, Claudio. "Fallaci sola a New York col diavolo in corpo." *La Stampa,* August 9, 1991, p. 15.

Amoia, Alba. "Matilde Serao, Oriana Fallaci, Camilla Cederna: Three Women Journalists." In Alba Amoia, *20th-Century Italian Women Writers: The Feminine Experience.* Carbondale and Edwardsville: Southern Illinois University Press, 1996, pp. 100–35.

Aricò, Santo L. "Oriana Fallaci's Journalistic Novel." In *Contemporary Women Writers in Italy: A Modern Renaissance,* ed. Santo L. Aricò. Amherst: University of Massachusetts Press, 1990, pp. 170–82.

Blelloch, Paola. *Quel mondo dei guanti e delle stoffe. . . .* Verona: Essedue Edizioni, 1987.

Fallaci, Oriana. *I sette peccati di Hollywood.* Milan: Longanesi, 1958.

———. *Il sesso inutile: viaggio intorno alla donna.* Milan: Rizzoli, 1961. [*The Useless Sex.* New York: Horizon, 1964.]

———. *Se il sole muore.* Milan: Rizzoli, 1965. [*If the Sun Dies.* New York: Atheneum House, 1966.]

———. *Niente e così sia.* Milan: Rizzoli, 1969; 60th ed. 1990. [*Nothing and Amen.* Trans. Isabel Quigly. New York: Doubleday, 1972.]

———. *Intervista con la storia.* Milan: Rizzoli, 1974; 9th ed. Biblioteca universale Rizzoli, 1990. [*Interview with History.* New York: Liveright, 1976.]

———. *Un uomo: romanzo.* Milan: Rizzoli, 1979; 19th ed. 1993. [*A Man.* New York: Simon & Schuster, 1980.]

———. *Insciallah.* Milan: Rizzoli, 1990. [*Inshallah.* Trans. Oriana Fallaci from a translation by James Marcus. New York: Nan A. Talese, Doubleday, 1992.]

———. "Speciale." Interview. *Europeo,* April 12, 1991, pp. 6–15.

———. Interview with Paola Fallaci. "Ma il successo può essere fonte di grande infelicità." *Oggi,* December 23, 1991, pp. 24–28.

———. *La Rabbia e l'Orgoglio.* Milan: Rizzoli, 2001. [*The Rage and the Pride.* New York: Rizzoli International Publications, 2002.]

————. "The Rage, the Pride and the Doubt." *Wall Street Journal,* March 18, 2003, p. A18.

————. *La Forza della Ragione.* Milan: Rizzoli, 2004.

————. *Oriana Fallaci intervista Oriana Fallaci.* Milan: Rizzoli, 2004.

Fini, Marco. "Signora grandi firme." *Epoca,* June 30, 1990, pp. 30–35.

Gatt-Rutter, John. *Oriana Fallaci: The Rhetoric of Freedom.* Oxford and Washington, D.C.: Berg, 1996.

Gurley, George. "The Rage of Oriana Fallaci." *The New York Observer,* January 27, 2003, pp. 1, 15.

Locher, Frances C., ed. *Contemporary Authors.* Vols. 77–80. Detroit, Mich.: Gale Research, 1979, pp. 133–34.

Mazzoni, Riccardo. "Oriana Fallaci risponde." *Panorama,* November 21, 2002, pp. 44–53.

Nozza, Marco. "Guerra e amore nel 'suo' Libano." *Il Giorno,* August 7, 1990, p. 3.

Occhiuzzi, Franco. "Oriana dottoressa (ad honorem) del best-seller." *Corriere della Sera,* June 9, 1977, p. 13.

Peer, Elizabeth. "The Fallaci Papers." *Newsweek,* December 1, 1980, pp. 53–54.

Powers, Elizabeth. "Elias Canetti." In *Multicultural Writers Since 1945,* ed. Alba Amoia and Bettina L. Knapp. Westport, Conn.: Greenwood Press, 2004, pp. 128–33.

Scarpino, Salvatore. "Rambo, l'ultimo amore di Oriana." *Il Giornale,* March 3, 1988, p. 1.

Vigorelli, Giancarlo. "Il racconto più umano sul dramma d'un popolo." *Il Giorno,* August 7, 1990, p. 3.

CHAPTER

21

Sharon Spencer

(1933–2002)

Travel fuels my imagination.
(Sharon Spencer's favorite phrase)

S haron Spencer was born in middle America—in Omaha, Nebraska—but spent almost half a century in New York and New Jersey where she lived, studied, and taught. Although she was of Irish descent and hailed from the heartland, she had a yen for everything foreign and culturally different. The cosmopolitan atmosphere of the New York metropolitan area allowed her to pursue her literary interests in European and, later, multiethnic literature. She earned her master's and Ph.D. degrees in English from New York University during the 1960s before beginning her teaching at several colleges in the area. Upon publication of her Ph.D. dissertation *Space, Time and Structure in the Modern Novel* in 1971, she became professor of comparative literature at Montclair State College (now University) in Upper Montclair, New Jersey.

It was "on a Yugoslav freighter in the middle of the Atlantic Ocean," bound for a Slavic vacation with her then husband Srdjan Maljkovic, that she began her "personal relationship with Anaïs [Nin]" (Sharon Spencer, quoted in Benjamin Franklin V, *Recollections of Anaïs Nin by Her Contemporaries*, 77). She was reading Nin's fiction at the time in order to include the writer in her critical study of European and Latin American literatures. Subsequently, she met Nin and was invited to appear with her in a program at the University of California in Berkeley.

Spencer always had a great love for travel, especially to exotic countries such as Greece, Italy, Mexico, and Yugoslavia. Travel fueled her teaching and writing as well as her adventurous and curious spirit. She spoke and read several languages including French, Italian, and Spanish. Her travels began in the late 1960s and continued on a regular basis right up until her stroke in Mérida in the Yucatan. Having purchased a small home in the historic district of Mérida in the late 1990s, she spent as much time there as she could after her retirement from teaching.

There were two women in Sharon Spencer: the one who wanted to flee her career and urban lifestyle as a metropolitan writer/teacher and a social activist in her community and country and the woman who wanted to live in another culture to help directly those who might be in need. In the mid-1980s she fell in love with Mexico, no doubt, at first, for the same reasons her friend Anaïs Nin had given: "the warm, caressing air. It dissolves you into a flower or foliage. . . . The body emerges from its swaddling of clothes. Rebirth. . . . I love this earth, the earth of Mexico, the sun" (*Diary of Anaïs Nin, 1966–1974*, 271).

As a scholar, Spencer believed in the late 1960s that the best contemporary literature prevailed outside the United States. As a writer, she evolved to create "novels of the future," those advocated by Anaïs Nin in her major critical book, the prophetic *The Novel of the Future* (1968). Therein, Nin expressed her hope "that natural truths (realism) will cease to be spat at us like insults, that aesthetics will once more be linked with ethics, and that people will become aware that in casting out aesthetics they also cast out a respect for spiritual values" (197).

Spencer's life and work were as much influenced by her literal journeys, similar to Nin's, as by her emotional quests, invariably bound together. In her *Collage of Dreams: The Writings of Anaïs Nin* (1977), she synthesizes Henri Bergson's *Creative Evolution*, noting that Nin "would no doubt share [André] Breton's enthusiasm for escaping from the old-fashioned idea of identity as something fixed and given for all time. . . . The self is always engaged in the process of change, always modifying itself, altering, adapting, searching, expanding, growing ever closer to its most complete expression" (17–18).

Ironically, what Spencer said of Nin's use of prose collages as "the people, the relationships, the situations, and settings she actually knows" (*Collage of Dreams*, 11) could be said of *Voices from the Earth* (2002), Spencer's last published novel, which reflects the author's love of Mexico, and especially the Yucatan. The last part of her poem at the end of *Voices from the Earth* summarizes succinctly Spencer's love of travel and new experiences as representative of a deeper social responsibility.

> *And now before you leave this place*
> *Bend your knees*
> *Kneel*
> *on the brown earth with*
> *your hands flat upon the dirt. . . .*
>
> *Lie in the dirt.*
> *Taste it.*
> *Know you are*
> *part of this dirt.*
>
> *Know this, friends,*
> *you and I, we, and, yes,*
> *they, too,*
> *and even the OTHERS*
> *are ALL there is*
>
> *and ALL there can be*
> *in this world.*
>
> *Know, friends,*
> *that if*
> *you respect*
> *if you honor*
> *if you protect*
> *and*
> *Love*
> *the earth you are lying on*
> *you*
> *and*
> *I*
> *and*
> *all there is will*
> *LIVE*
>
> *forever.*

Robert Zaller calls *Voices from the Earth* "a fascinating and innovative work, combining poetry, fiction, drama, and anthropology in a single, seamless text. It takes as its point of departure the *Book of Ix Chel*, a recently unearthed Mayan codex. From this, Sharon Spencer weaves a brilliant tapestry of scenes in which ancient myth and modern experience fuse in a revelatory whole" (quoted in Rochelle Lynn Holt, ed., *Sharon Spencer, A Memorial*, 15).

Lola, the protagonist, is literally and symbolically sacrificed to appease CHAC, the rain god who has punished the land with drought. "The well becomes a Jungian site of renewal, however, from which 'Lola' emerges refreshed and enlightened, bearing the gift of rain. The wisdom she brings is that godhood is within us, and that this internal source is the inexhaustible fountain of life itself: 'Know this, friends, / there is only one god divided / into many. Look at one another. / You are looking at / the only god / there is'" (ibid., 16).

Spencer not only looked at or viewed a multitude of people of varied races, but she truly saw into the souls of so many, aiding those who were in need. She offered space in her apartments and homes. She befriended many students. She belonged to numerous human rights organizations, including Madre, which sponsored a weeklong trip to Cuba for a delegation of professors, lecturers, nurses, and students in January 2002. She was part of the delegation. She wrote "A Cuban Diary Jan. 5–Jan 12 '02" a few weeks before she had the stroke that ultimately led to her death at her only sister's home in southern New Jersey.

"If possible Sharon sought freedom more ardently than I," said Tristine Rainer, a peer. "One summer day we paged through a scrapbook Sharon cherished. The album had been assembled by an aunt—news clippings, photos, all of American women pilots, women, who like Anaïs and Sharon, loved to soar, free of the shackles that constrain most women" (Tristine Rainer, quoted in ibid., 12).

In her introduction to *Dance of the Ariadnes* (1998), Spencer identifies her story as a modern interpretation of a Cretan myth, writing that her major characters are "re-imaginings of the ancient vegetation goddess Ariadne . . . priestess . . . and a real woman." Divna is a Greek actress, technically still the husband of Dionysus. She traverses Serbia and goes back to

Greece. Divna and Miranda, the American painter, meet on a deserted road before unraveling the myth with Divna's foreshadowing dream of her descent into murky water (Rochelle Lynn Holt, in *Chiron Review*).

In Spencer's *Wire Rims* (1995), again two women (Irish-American) represent a dichotomy. In Mexico, Macha, half Mohawk, meets and learns to love a Mayan, Canche Balam. Bridget in New York is a singer and writer of political songs. She goes to the Yucatan in search of her on-the-front activist friend. In a sequel to *Wire Rims*, Bridget, the songwriter, returns to New York with the new knowledge that her way of social activism within the community is right for her. (Macha had been swallowed like a political pawn/sacrifice in the Yucatan.) Spencer also wrote a novella entitled "Gentle Revolutionaries" about four generations of Serbian women whom she had actually met. "All of them died of AIDS &/or had long-term relationships with men of different cultures" (Letter to Lili Bita, February 8, 2002).

The present writer received from Mérida, from Spencer's good friend Gabriel Álcocer Sanchez, the manuscript of her "Cuban Diary." What follows is an excerpted and edited version of the diary, quoted with permission from Patricia Barrie.

Saturday, January 5, 2002

I arrived in Habana at 2:00, at the hotel at 3:00. . . .

My first impression of Blacks in Cuba. Very poised, confident, self-assured. As courteous and helpful as Italians with their code of "bellafigura." At the airport a woman, Black, waited with me for a long time until my African bag appeared with the other checked bags on my flight from Cancún to Habana. Black cab driver. Super polite. A Black doorman helped me check in and showed me how everything worked in the room, including a private safe. . . .

My room was unexpectedly luxurious. Two big beds, ceramic tiles like the ones in my Mexican house. Matched wooden furniture. A table with an enormous mirror. Side chair. Two bedside tables, a bar refrigerator. Exquisite bathroom with a huge deep tub, a large mirror; the bathroom was completely tiled. . . . The room had heating which nobody in Mérida does.

Sunday, January 6

After breakfast we took a city tour. The breakfast brunch elimi-
nates the need for a third daily mail. Lavish. Two types of sardines,
sliced cheese, all kinds of cold cuts. Two kinds of eggs, poached and
scrambled, various breakfast meats, vegetables like steamed cabbage,
rice and beans, hash browns. A table of sweet breads, another table
for "normal" breads. A table of fruit, four kinds of juices, beverages,
including expresso and the everpresent *cafe con leche*.

We left the bus to walk, crossing a huge plaza with an uneven
surface of very old bricks. Sitting on a wall was a very old woman
cradling a tiny dog. The dog was wearing a white baby dress and a
straw hat. . . .

A pregnant woman approached me as if she knew me and wanted
to renew our acquaintance. Rubbing her belly, she asked me for 10
dollars for her baby. I gave her 5 dollars and asked where I could find
a taxi. Not in the direction in which we were walking.

At the hotel on the corner called Hotel "Ambos Mundos," I had
a good view of the street from the two large windows. I sat at the
bar and wrote for a while as I watched people.

There was a group of Santeras wearing white dresses and head
wraps. Tennis shoes! They were accompanied by male drummers.
The strangest-dressed woman was wearing a wide white headwrap
with several large bunches of artificial red flowers sticking out of the
top. The finishing touch, a bushy blonde ponytail. She wore a long
white shirt that looked like a hospital coat, blue jeans and sneakers.
Lots of women of color with dyed blonde hair.

I was surprised not to see many children promenading with their
parents. It was Sunday morning. . . .

The highlight of the day, maybe of the trip, was a visit to el Calle-
jon (alley) of Hamel, "primer mural en la via pública, dedicado a la
cultura afrocubana. Author, Salvador Gonzalez Escalona."
Amazing!

Elias, one of Escalona's assistants, briefly explained the African
religions of Cuba: Santería, another one based on the orishas—
Yemaya, Chango, etc., a third on nature gods, the fourth, a cult of
the dead. All the walls were covered with big frescos reminiscent of
Gauguin in his Tahitian period. Escalona's two-room studio was

here. There was an ingenious pool, a bathtub sunk in the ground and surrounded by big conches, also embedded in cement.

From 1:00 to 3:00 every Sunday, people rhumba to vibrant music with lots of percussion. The alley is packed with people of all ages, including many children. . . . In spite of the racket, which was tremendous, a dog was sleeping peacefully. A very beautiful woman was selling postcards and videos. She was dressed completely in creamy white—loose top over lovely flared pants. A matching head wrap. No jewelry, no make up.

We had dinner together in a private home turned restaurant. Three choices: crab, pork, grilled fish as well as chicken soup—not clear like ours but thickened slightly with yogurt or cream, lemon, fresh mint and a scattering of sugar, a mohito. Apparently, fresh lemons are scarce. If you ask for lemon in a drink, you're offered a splash of bottled lemon juice or a dash of lemon flavored soda. (Alcoholic drinks were available, i.e. white rum with agua mineral.)

Monday, January 7

A delightful visit to a child care center. Thirty children, three teachers, all women. Non-sexist tasks and games. Boys are taught to play at cooking. . . .

Education is compulsory from one to fifteen. If parents don't comply, they're called to account. Two types of higher education: preparatory for the university and technical path, the latter chosen by a third of the students; the government pays for all education. This raises a question—where does the government get the money?

All the children were clean and well-dressed. None were scene-makers or noticeably withdrawn. They sang for us. Toys and games were contributed by Madre. . . .

We then went to a family practice clinic. The focus, preventative. The doctor didn't want us to come in—too many waiting patients. There are three levels of medical care: family clinics; diagnostic services; surgery. . . .

Tuesday, January 8

Up at 5:00 to pack for the trip to Santiago 800 miles from Habana. . . . In the afternoon we visited the parents of Norma, one of the four women professionals, all Black, who addressed the group the evening before.

Norma's parents, in their mid-80s, told us what their lives were like before and after the revolution. . . . Blacks weren't allowed to receive any education. If somehow they did, they couldn't find jobs.

All twenty of us squeezed into their small house. It had a tv. Then we went to the recreation center for people in what are referred to as "the third age," 60 or more.

At the senior center, the residents were exercising. We were graciously invited to join them. . . . They sang many songs for us, including the inevitable "Guantanamera." All the predominanting women were a wide variety of shades of Black.

Wednesday, January 9

We visited the "House of Religions," dedicated to various Cuban religions of African origin. This was a museum but also a sacred space. No photos allowed. The various shrines were gorgeous! The most important is dedicated to Oshun. Entirely gold with gold draperies in different fabrics, even gold lace.

The representation of the gods and goddesses is always abstract, about five feet tall, with oval forms indicating the heads. They have shoulders but no arms. There are several of these altars. . . .

The Hotel Melia in Santiago de Cuba gave guests something akin to a bookmark with the inscription, "The Hotel's management and staff wish you sweet dreams," followed by a short poem by Federico Garcia Lorca:

> Oh Cuba, oh rhythm of dry seeds!
> I'll go to Santiago.
> Oh hot waist and drop of wood!
> I'll go to Santiago.
> Harp of living logs, alligator, flower
>   of tobacco!
> I'll go to Santiago.
> I always said I'd go to Santiago.

Next we went to the Cathedral of Cobre isolated in some small mountains where there was a virgin famed for her healing power. Little chips of unpolished copper were handed out. Many people brought flowers to offer this virgin. . . .

Thursday, January 9

We visited a home ... for mentally deficient people. First we went into a classroom where the woman doctor, the head of the hospital, greeted us and gave an introductory talk. She was trained in Hungary, obviously when Cuba enjoyed good relations with the Soviet Union.

She's been the director for more than thirty years. What amazed me was the amount of autonomy enjoyed by the residents. . . . They're encouraged to be as independent as possible and trained to perform work to the maximum of their abilities. . . .

We went to the workshops where residents make many things which they then sell in their gift shop: small dolls, everything sewn, greeting cards, bracelets, tooled leather change purses. . . .

There was a dance with Tania, winner in the "special" Olympics, as featured performer. . . . The finale was an ensemble dance. . . . For a quick change girls covered their leotards with big white t-shirts, fringed on sleeves and at bottom. Printed on the shirts were two blue palm trees.

I think this was the most impressive of our group's many visits.

We also visited a home for "at risk" pregnant women and a center for women's rights. At the latter, issue of domestic violence was prominent in our discussion. . . . The women we met said there is very little family violence. That anyone guilty of interfering with the normal development of a child is punished. Since any woman who wants to work can work, we learned that financial dependence on an abuser is eliminated. When family violence does occur, a counselor intervenes. I wondered if domestic violence was exclusively an economic problem!

Friday, January 11

On the last day of our visit, we went to a world-famous psychiatric hospital. Mazorra is directed by Dr. Educardo Bernabe Ordaz Odunge, who was a comandante in in the revolution. That this hospital is world-famous is not an inflated claim. There were many letters of praise from various U.S. institutions. They were recent. There was a small museum with photos of what it was like before the revolution. A prison, a horrible one.

The patients, all adults, performed a show for their guests. From the operatic voice of a woman to the excellent dancing, not in couples but in lines facing the audience, the program was superbly professional. A suitable conclusion to a very satisfying visit.

Our farewell dinner was at a restaurant called "El Ajibe." This was the best meal I had in Cuba. Well-cooked and not choked with condiments. Roast chicken, rice and beans (wonderfully seasoned), plátanos, flan and café. Fantastic although simple. The best style of cooking.

For the first time I understand at least a little why Cuban exiles in the U.S. are so furious at being forced to leave Cuba. To them, this must feel like the mythic expulsion from the Garden of Eden. Cuba is truly the Queen of the Caribbean. Enchanting!

But, because it's so diverse, Mexico is more interesting. I've long thought the Spanish were foolish not to have moved—lock, stock and barrel—whatever that old saying means—their country to Mexico, which they called "New Spain." No wonder the capital of their empire was Habana!

Mexico and Cuba together are the essence of Latino culture. Politics aside, Cuba is absolutely ravishing!

Rochelle Lynn Holt

BIBLIOGRAPHY

Franklin V, Benjamin. *Recollections of Anaïs Nin by Her Contemporaries*. Athens, Ohio: Ohio University Press, 1996.

Holt, Rochelle Lynn. "Dance of the Ariadnes." In *Chiron Review*, ed. Michael Hathaway. St. Johns, Kansas: Chiron Review Press, 1998.

———, ed. *Sharon Spencer, A Memorial*. Fort Myers, Fla.: Rose Shell Press, 2002.

Jason, Philip K., ed. *The Critical Response to Anaïs Nin*. Westport, Conn.: Greenwood Press, 1996.

Nin, Anaïs. *The Novel of the Future*. New York: Macmillan, 1968.

———. *Diary of Anaïs Nin, 1966–1974*. New York: Harcourt Brace Jovanovich, 1980.

Spencer, Sharon. *Space, Time and Structure in the Modern Novel*. New York: New York University Press, 1971.

————. *Collage of Dreams: The Writings of Anaïs Nin*. Chicago, Ill.: The Swallow Press, 1977.

————. *Wire Rims*. Ibadan, Nigeria, and Detroit, Mich.: Heinemann Educational Books/Africana Legacy Press, 1995.

————. *Dance of the Ariadnes*. Huntington Woods, Mich.: Sky Blue Press, 1998.

————. *Voices from the Earth*. Fort Myers, Fla.: Rose Shell Press, 2002.

22

Valentina Vladimirovna Tereshkova

(1937–)

> I see earth. . . . I feel excellent. . . .
> The machine is working well.
>
> (Valentina Vladimirovna Tereshkova,
> quoted in London *Times*, June 17, 1963)

It is certain that of the women whose exploits are detailed in this book, the most traveled of all, in terms of distance alone—one and one-quarter million miles, or roughly five times the distance to the moon—is the first who traveled in space, Valentina Vladimirovna Tereshkova. Tereshkova—known as Valya to almost everyone—was not the daughter of a Soviet Air Force general or an eminence in the Communist Party. Part of the excitement of her achievement and of her personal appeal was the obscurity from which she emerged to become the recipient of her country's most important honor, awarded her by the Soviet premier on Red Square in Moscow, witnessed by a crowd numbering in the hundreds of thousands.

She was born on March 6, 1937, in the small town of Maslennikovo, about 190 miles northeast of Moscow. Her mother was Yelena Federova Tereshkova; her father, Vladimir Aksenovich Tereshkova, was a mechanic and tractor driver who was drafted into the Soviet Army in mid-September 1939 and trained as a tanker. Like many of the soldiers who were sent by Joseph Stalin to fight in the Russo-Finnish War, he was ill equipped for the extreme weather conditions. He was killed on January 25, 1940. Since she was less than three years old when Vladimir left home, Tereshkova never knew her father, although she would come to develop an image of him from a few photographs and from stories and reminiscences of her mother and other relatives.

Her mother was left to raise three children, the youngest of whom was born after his father's death. Life in wartime was difficult, especially in a primitive small town without electricity. Water was still drawn from a communal well and carried home in buckets with a yoke over the shoulders. Tereshkova and her sister milked cows and carried the noonday meal to their mother, who, like many Soviet women, did field labor. At the end of the war, the family moved to Yaroslavl, an old Russian city about forty miles away, where Tereshkova's maternal grandmother had a large house.

Tereshkova began primary school in the fall of 1945. There was some money at home as well as enough food and several modern conveniences, including electric lights for doing homework. Besides some horses and sheep, the family owned a sewing machine, which allowed for a few silk dresses, and grandmother's house had nice furniture, carpets, and lace curtains. Her mother knew several of Pushkin's poems by heart, and there was a good collection of books, including works of Lermontov and Tolstoy. Her grandmother, though of peasant background, had friends among the local intelligentsia. A big city such as Yaroslavl also provided attractions not to be found in remote villages, in particular cinema and radio broadcasts. It was through the latter that Tereshkova would cultivate a love for opera and for the music of Tchaikovsky and Glinka.

In Yaroslavl she began to develop a reputation as a tomboy, even terrifying her mother with her habit of climbing the trees next to a local pond and then dropping from the high branches into the water. Later she would "improve" on this stunt by dropping from a bridge to a Volga tributary. At the same time, she seemed to feel no particular fascination for flying or space. It was trains and railroading, still the major method of travel, and the machinery of travel with which she became enthralled.

What I liked best, once we moved to the city, was sitting near railway stations and watching the passing trains. You can't imagine what a delight it was for me. I envied the engine drivers having an opportunity to drive them. I wished I could be in their place. I wished I could drive locomotives throughout the world. . . . Later when I started parachute jumping and flying planes I realized that nothing could be better than to be a pilot. (Tereshkova, *Valentina: First Woman in Space*, 209)

Her mother, a traditionalist, strongly discouraged her daughter's ambition of becoming a railroad engineer, despite the high salary of such a job. Thus, she was not allowed to travel to Leningrad for railroad-engineer training after graduating from high school in 1953, at the age of sixteen. While looking for a job, she registered for an evening course at the Young Workers School #10. Upon completion of the course, she enrolled in the secondary technical program in the evening school associated with the Red Perekop textile mill, at which her mother and sister worked and at which she had also found employment after a stint in a tire factory. The program was arduous, consisting of basic engineering classes as well as classes specific to the textile industry. She graduated at the age of twenty-three, in 1960, with a certificate as a textile-engineering technician.

While at Red Perekop, Tereshkova was also an active Communist, joining the Young Communist League (the Komsomol) in 1957. As her academic credentials grew, she began to move up in the factory and was elected secretary of Red Perekop Komsomol, a full-time job that required organizing and managing the activities of as many as twenty separate factory programs.

Her interest in parachuting began in the fall of 1958, when a friend from school urged her to join the Yaroslavl Air Sports Club. On the outskirts of Yaroslavl was a smooth field that served as an airport. It was particularly suited to the low-tech propeller-driven aircraft favored by amateur parachutists. At her first encounter with the air club, Tereshkova was hooked, though, unlike in certain Western skydiving operations, Russian parachutists undergo thorough training before making their first jump. She entered the training program and assiduously studied the technical details of parachuting. In about six months she would be ready for her first jump.

My passion for flying began with my first parachute jump on 21 May 1959. I was in a small green aeroplane driving along the airstrip, bouncing over the bumps, and suddenly it hung in the air. The ground below me grew distant. . . . I strained to hear the command "Go!" Jumping into nothingness

my heart turned over, and I was very happy. . . . Several seconds passed, but
then with a jolt, a white dome opened up above me. The ground came
towards me. I began to work the ropes which guided me down to the wet
grass below. . . . I felt I wanted to do it every day. (ibid., 224)

Tereshkova has said that she was not particularly interested in space as
a young person. It was not the *Sputnik* flight of 1957 that stirred her curiosity but the Luna series of unmanned satellites sent to the moon in 1959.
Her interest was aroused by Yuri Gagarin's *Vostok 1* flight of April 12, 1961,
in which Gagarin remained in orbit about 108 minutes. She read his book,
Road to the Stars, and, in a chat with her mother about the flight, the elder
woman responded, "Now a man has flown in space, it is a woman's turn
next" (ibid., 225). Tereshkova was taken by this reaction of a simple village
woman with traditional values, yet so forward-thinking concerning
women cosmonauts. The Soviet documentary film *First Flight to the Stars*
also provided much information about the preparation and training for
space travel. Although awed by the extraordinary amount of work
involved, she was undaunted:

I was sure a woman could endure the forces of the centrifuge, the silence
of the isolation chamber and the roar of the rocket launch. I wrote a letter
to the Central Committee of DOSAAF [a group promoting military/civilian
cooperation] in which I requested to be considered for the training course
in the new technology. (ibid.)

Some time later an official from DOSAAF arrived in Yaroslavl, claiming
interest in the local air club. He was in fact evaluating women who held
first-class parachutist rating, and he spent an hour speaking with Tereshkova.

In December 1961 Tereshkova left for Moscow under the cover story of
being medically evaluated to join the Soviet National Parachute team, but,
in reality, to undergo a monthlong series of tests, including medical and
psychological evaluations. She was tested on technical skills, since, as with
all potential cosmonauts, she would have to rapidly learn a large body of
difficult technical material, such as electronics, space physics, and rocket
technology. It is also quite likely that Tereshkova's social and communication skills were being evaluated. A woman cosmonaut who successfully

returned from space would become an immediate icon for the Soviet system. There would be international tours, many speaking engagements, and interviews. Just the right person was needed. After passing the tests in Moscow, she had only a few days at home with her family before heading off as a cosmonaut trainee.

A team of five women joined the men already in Star Town, the Soviet space establishment centered in a distant suburb of Moscow. Although the mixed-sex training program would aim for equal outcomes, there were some significant differences in the training: the men were all experienced pilots; the women were all expert parachutists, but none had flight training. Over the course of training, the women would learn to fly and would accumulate considerable experience as pilots.

Cosmonaut training consisted of extensive physical conditioning, along with classroom studies in astronomy, physics, navigation, and spacecraft engineering. There was also considerable training specific to space travel. An enormous centrifuge, resembling a popular amusement park ride, would spin the cosmonaut at high speeds to simulate the enormous G forces of blastoff and landing during which the cosmonaut would be pinned in her seat with a force of nine times her weight. Another testing device was known as the "Iron Maiden," a heavily padded metal box resembling a coffin in which the cosmonaut was sealed, while the box was violently shaken and spun. In this simulation of an out-of-control spacecraft, the trainee was peppered with questions to test if she could maintain a clear head in such panic-inducing conditions. This was a required exercise because the Soviet space program had chosen to go with a spherically shaped passenger capsule (*sharik* in Russian). A sphere tends to roll around easily, even in space, and on reentry it can become unstable. The Soviets, despite their general and substantial lead in space travel at the time, were well behind the United States in the electronic computing systems that would allow the more desirable cone-shaped capsules. Another simulation—large airplanes executing huge arcs at high altitudes—induced about forty-five seconds of weightlessness. Besides isolation training, cosmonauts were instructed in basic survival skills since a spacecraft might return thousands of miles from a recovery team, in jungle or midocean. Tereshkova reports that in the training program, except for the extensive flight instruction provided to the women (and a few minor chivalrous niceties), men and women were treated equally. Part of the Soviet effort in this regard was to determine specific male–female differences.

After more than a year of this extensive training, the women candi-
dates—one of whom would be the first woman in space—were given a
brief vacation at home, after which four flew, in late May 1963, to the
Baikonur Cosmodrome in Kazakhstan, then the main base for launch-
ings. Valery Bykovsky, a man, was selected to pilot *Vostok 5*, and Tereshkova *Vostok 6*. The two weeks between their arrival at Baikonur and their
flights were taken up with many final preparations. Medical personnel
were constant companions, with the cosmonauts assigned medical minders to report any changes in medical condition.

Bykovsky was launched on June 14 without incident. About thirty
hours into his mission, Tereshkova began the final routine of preparation.
There was a ceremony during which the cosmonaut inspected the spacecraft and judged it acceptable. This was followed by brief statements of
thanks and some traditional ceremonial music. Tereshkova then spent the
evening with her backup pilot, who, ready to step in, would be with her
until takeoff. They slept in a small cottage not far from the rocket-launch
site, their only company the medical minders. They were visited by the
Vostok's chief designer, Sergei Korolev, with whom they chatted about the
flight and some of the work to be carried out during the mission. They
drank tea.

On the morning of June 16 the female cosmonauts were awakened
quite early. Tereshkova reported having slept well, without dreams. There
were thirty minutes of exercises. A cleansing enema had been given the
evening before, and another would follow the exercise period. Breakfast
was space food, composed in part of veal cutlets, lemon slices, caviar, and
coffee, served up as a gel in a toothpaste-type squeeze tube. This was followed by the complex and time-consuming operation of donning the
space suit. It was triple-layered, with many body sensors that had to be
attached, with their associated wires being guided through the interior of
the suit, while avoiding disconnects and tangles in the process.

The launch conditions were generally good. The skies were clear, the
air was still, but the air temperature was an unusually searing 95°F. A
committee of important officials was on hand when Tereshkova took an
elevator to the top of the launch vehicle to the *Vostok 6* spacecraft. She
was helped into the spherically shaped *sharik*, and radio communication
was verified, after which she was alone in the space capsule. She would be

there for about two hours as the huge rocket below her was being fueled and otherwise prepared for launch.

Blastoff occurred at 12:30 P.M. local time. The experience of a rocket launch is like no other human experience. First is heard the overwhelming roar of rocket engines, and in short order the entire space capsule undergoes violent vibrations. The effect can be compared to riding a bicycle down a long stairway. As the rocket accelerates upward, G forces press occupants into their seats with a force many times body weight. Breathing in this condition is described as trying to breathe with a quite overweight person sitting squarely on one's chest. This first part of the liftoff lasts one to two minutes, while the first-stage rocket engine is firing. When the second stage takes over, acceleration is reduced as well as the physical stress on the pilot. The third stage, which acts when the spacecraft is above the atmosphere (approximately 100 miles above the earth), will push the craft into an elliptical orbit about the earth at a speed of 18,000 miles per hour, or roughly 5 miles per second. Of this experience, Tereshkova has said:

I experienced the anticipated reactions at lift-off, which was seen from the ground in white hot flames. The launch vehicle took me further away from Earth into space. Through the porthole I was able to see my Vostok capsule separated from the last stage of the rocket as we reached the programmed orbit which brought me 183 km [114 miles] from the Earth at its closest, 231 km [144 miles] at the furthest point. . . . From space the beauty of the Earth was overwhelming. . . . The blackness of the sky scattered with stars was impressive. From Earth we see the blackness at night, but from space the Earth was lit by the Sun, and the sky, although dark, was bright with stars. Instinctively the cosmonaut thinks that the dear, native home is not so far away.

It took me just 89 minutes to orbit the Earth and as I saw the planet from space I realised how small Earth is. (ibid., 231)

Tereshkova has reported on the many duties on board the *Vostok*:

[There was] the extensive set of tests that I had to carry out as part of my contribution to the space programme. . . . I had to supervise biological experiments with seeds and insects on board the spaceship. I also had to take a series of films and photographs . . . to study the Earth and its atmosphere. (ibid., 232)

Some of these images would provide vital information on the circulation of the upper atmosphere. She also maintained a log book in which are summarized her psychological and physiological reactions to the experience in space. There were constant onboard medical evaluations. Tereshkova had been advised on coping with weightlessness by veteran cosmonauts, for example, Gherman Titov, pilot of *Vostok 2*, who cautioned her to tuck her hands into her seat belt when she slept, since a loose, weightless arm waving about would disturb her sleep.

> One adapts oneself to weightlessness quite quickly and easily. . . . That is to say, everything floats in the air inside the cabin—even water. It doesn't flow or disintegrate into drops, but forms a kind of blob as if in a plastic bag. . . . [Or] one tends to forget about it. For example, one may place the flight log book on one's lap as one would do in an airplane. A small movement of the body will send the book drifting away. (Tereshkova, quoted in Edmund Stevens, "Comely Cosmonaut," 62)

In her second day in orbit, Tereshkova had the task of operating the *sharik* manually as well as conducting several experiments that would be important for future space travel. Among these was to gather data on the interaction of weightlessness on the human vestibular apparatus. For instance, at various times she would draw simple geometric figures; changes in the quality of these drawings could be correlated to changes in vestibular function.

There was much of interest outside the portholes of the *Vostok 6*, including features of the Earth's surface:

> Looking out I could distinguish many geographical features: all the continents, the oceans, seas, rivers, fjords. The Suez Canal, Egypt and the yellow desert crossed by the dark blue ribbon of the Nile. The rivers were as easy to pick out as the oceans. I could see large cities and mountain ranges. I saw the blue ice caps of Antarctica and the icebergs of Greenland. (Tereshkova, *Valentina: First Woman in Space*, 234)

Speaking of the night view of the United States of America, she has said: "The large cities with their rays of streetlights looked like diamonds on the Earth" (quoted in Mitchell R. Sharpe, "It Is I, Sea Gull," 114). And she reported that each continent had its own color: Africa was yellow, except for the blue Nile; South America was green; Asia dark brown except for the green Indian Subcontinent.

Toward the end of nearly three days of space travel, Tereshkova began to prepare for reentry. The reentry protocol for the *Vostok*, which began with a final inspection and testing of the spacecraft, was largely under the control of the pilot. With about one hour to go, actual reentry procedures began. The entire spacecraft had to be rotated, placing its rocket engine in the front, hence allowing it to be used as a retro-rocket to slow the craft. At this time, Tereshkova and Bykovsky exchanged final greetings. She would be landing first, he shortly thereafter.

At the precise moment, as determined by a signal from ground control, the rocket engine was fired, which caused the spacecraft to slow rapidly, and, as it did so, the weightlessness Tereshkova had experienced the past several days gradually diminished. Not only did her weight return, it did so in extremis: before long, the great G forces, this time of deceleration, would have her pinned again to the pilot's chair. This is a crucial time in the control of the spacecraft. Minor instabilities in the atmosphere—the kind that produce turbulence on an airliner—can cause the spacecraft to rock back and forth (as when an automobile fishtails on an icy road). Such movements can lead easily to a loss of control and a catastrophic outcome. As the atmosphere became more dense, the deceleration of the craft increased, with G forces again reaching nine times the pilot's body weight. Tereshkova was able to turn her head to the right. She saw the meteor that her *Vostok 6* craft had become, an enormous fireball spiraling toward the ground. The critical and nerve-wracking reentry procedure would last about sixteen minutes.

At an altitude of about four miles, after much of the ceramic ablative coating of the *sharik* had been burned away and the sphere had been slowed to a fraction of its former speed, the bolts holding the hatch exploded, sending the hatch hurtling toward the ground. After a two-second delay, allowing the debris from the hatch to clear the craft, rockets under the pilot's ejection seat fired, sending the pilot out of the hatch. A few seconds later an automatic parachute opened, allowing Tereshkova to descend at speeds more familiar to her. Although she was prepared to descend to either land or water, she was unhappy that she seemed headed for water. Using her considerable skill as a parachutist, she was able to aim for open land by selectively tugging on the ropes of her parachute.

By the time of her landing—380 miles northeast of Karaganda, in Kazakhstan—radio and television coverage in the Soviet Union had relentlessly broadcast news of the world's first female cosmonaut. Tereshkova's distinctive parachute was spotted by some workers, who quickly spread word of the landing. Shortly thereafter, a medical team arrived, who found the pilot in excellent condition, her only injury being a minor abrasion on her nose. A little short of three hours later, as she was being examined by medics, Bykovsky was landing about fifty miles away. The two would meet at a town on the Volga, where they would be joined by other members of the cosmonaut team. Three days later, on June 22, the two hero cosmonauts arrived in Moscow, a city transformed for massive festivities. While the celebrations were similar to others for which Red Square is famous, this one was marked by an ebullience not always present on those other occasions.

By mid–August 1963, Tereshkova and her cohorts Bykovsky and Gagarin would embark on another kind of traveling career, a thirty-country goodwill tour. (That the Soviets would use the achievements of their cosmonauts for maximum propaganda value should be obvious.) An amusing finale to Tereshkova's space saga is the many thousands of offers of marriage. She later married fellow cosmonaut Andrian Nikolayev, with whom she had a daughter, who is now a surgeon.

Richard Sussman

BIBLIOGRAPHY

Sharpe, Mitchell R. *"It Is I, Sea Gull": Valentina Tereshkova, First Woman in Space.* New York: Thomas Crowell Company, 1975.

Stevens, Edmund. "Comely Cosmonaut." *Ladies Home Journal* 80, no. 7 (September 1963): 60–62.

Tereshkova, Valentina Vladimirovna. *Valentina: First Woman in Space.* Edinburgh: The Pentland Press, 1993. (Interviews with Antonella Lothian.)

Times (London). June 17, 1963, to June 23, 1963, et seq. (Coverage of Tereshkova's flight and of events immediately following.)

Select General Bibliography

Adler, Michelle. *Skirting the Edges of Civilisation: British Women Travellers and Travel Writers in South Africa, 1797–1899.* Unpublished doctoral dissertation, University of London, 1996.

Agorni, Mirella. *Translating Italy for the Eighteenth Century: British Women Novelists, Translators and Travel Writers, 1739–1797.* Unpublished doctoral dissertation, University of Warwick, 1998.

Anema, Durlynn. *Harriet Chalmers Adams: Explorer and Adventurer.* Greensboro, N.C.: Morgan Reynolds, 1997.

Attali, Jacques. *L'homme nomade.* Paris: Fayard, 2004.

Bohls, Elizabeth A. *Women Travel Writers and the Language of Aesthetics.* Cambridge: Cambridge University Press, 1995.

Clark, Eleanor. *Rome and a Villa.* Garden City, N.Y.: Doubleday, 1950.

Cushman, Charlotte Saunders. *Her Letters and Memoirs of Her Life*, edited by Her Friend Emma Stebbins. Boston: Houghton, Osgood & Co., 1878.

Dalrymple, William, ed. *Begums, Thugs and White Mughals: The Journals of Fanny Parkes.* London: Sickle Moon Books, 2002.

Didier, Béatrice, ed. *Dictionnaire universel des littératures.* 3 vols. Paris: Presses Universitaires de France, 1994.

Fonseca, Isabel. *Bury Me Standing: The Gypsies and Their Journey.* London: Chatto and Windus, and New York: Knopf, 1995.

Fussell, Paul, ed. *The Norton Book of Travel.* New York: Norton, 1987.

Hawthorne, Susan, and Renate Klein. *Australia for Women: Travel and Culture.* New York: Feminist Press at the City University of New York, 1994.

Hoyle, Gwyneth. *Flowers in the Snow: The Life of Isobel Wylie Hutchison.* Lincoln and London: University of Nebraska Press, 2001.

Jameson, Anna. *The Diary of an Ennuyée.* London: H. Colburn, 1826.

———. *The Diary of a Désennuyée.* London: H. Colburn, 1836.

Kemble, Fanny. *Records of Later Life.* New York: H. Holt and Company, 1882.

———. *Journal of a Residence on a Georgian Plantation in 1838–1839.* Chicago: Afro-Am Press, 1969.

Kevles, Bettyann Haltzmann. *The Story of Women in Space.* New York: Basic Books, 2003.

Kingsley, Mary. *Travels in West Africa: Congo Français, Corisco and Cameroons.* London: Macmillan, 1897.

———. *West African Studies.* London: Macmillan, 1899.

Lombardi-Diop. *Writing the Female Frontier: Italian Women in Colonial Africa, 1890–1942.* Doctoral dissertation. Ann Arbor, Mich. (DAJA) 60:9, 1999.

Lovell, Mary S. *Rebel Heart: The Scandalous Life of Jane Digby.* New York: W. W. Norton, 1995.

McEwan, Cheryl. *Gender, Geography and Empire: Victorian Women Travellers in West Africa.* Ashgate: Aldershot, 2000.

Montagu, Lady Mary Wortley. *Letters* (1740). Everyman's Library. London: Campbell, 1992.

Netzley, Patricia D. *Encyclopedia of Women's Travel and Exploration.* Westport, Conn.: Oryx Press, 2001.

Panizza, Letizia, and Sharon Wood, eds. *A History of Women's Writing in Italy.* Cambridge and New York: Cambridge University Press, 2000.

Pick, Christopher, ed. *Embassy to Constantinople: The Travels of Lady Mary Wortley Montagu.* London: Century, 1988.

Piozzi, Hester Lynch. *Observations and Reflections Made in the Course of a Journey through France, Italy, and Germany.* Dublin: H. Chamberlaine, 1789.

Polk, Milbry, and Mary Tiegreen. *Women of Discovery: A Celebration of Intrepid Women Who Explored the World.* New York: C. Potter, 2001.

Pratt, Mary Louise. *Imperial Eyes: Travel Writing and Transculturation.* London and New York: Routledge, 1992.

Robinson, Jane. *Wayward Women: A Guide to Women Travellers.* Oxford and New York: Oxford University Press, 1990, 2001.

Schmidt, Margaret Fox. *Passion's Child: The Extraordinary Life of Jane Digby.* New York: Harper & Row, 1976.

Schwarzenbach, Annemarie. *Auf der Schattenseite: Ausgewählte Reportagen, Feuilletons und Fotografien, 1933–1942.* Basel: Lenos, 1995.

———. *Tod in Persien.* Basel: Lenos, 1998.

Staël, Mme de. *Corinne, ou l'Italie* (1807). *Corinne, or, Italy.* Trans. and ed. Sylvia Raphael. Oxford and New York: Oxford University Press, 1998.

Stevenson, Catherine Barnes. *Victorian Women Travelers in Africa.* Boston: Twayne Publishers, 1982.

Tinling, Marion. *Women into the Unknown: A Sourcebook on Women Explorers and Travelers.* Westport, Conn.: Greenwood Press, 1989.

Ure, John. *In Search of Nomads.* London: Constable, 2003.

Westropp, Mrs. J. E. *Summer Experiences of Rome, Perugia, Sienna in 1854; and Sketches of the Islands in the Bay of Naples.* London, 1856.

Wollstonecraft, Mary. *Letters Written during a Short Residence in Sweden, Norway and Denmark* (1796). Ed. and intro. Carol H. Poston. Lincoln: University of Nebraska Press, 1976.

Index